THE COUNTRYSIDE BOOK OF
FARMING LORE

No. 1952
$22.95

THE COUNTRYSIDE BOOK OF FARMING LORE

THE EDITORS OF COUNTRYSIDE MAGAZINE

TAB TAB BOOKS Inc.
Blue Ridge Summit, PA 17214

FIRST EDITION

FIRST PRINTING

Copyright © 1985 by TAB BOOKS Inc.

Printed in the United States of America

Reproduction or publication of the content in any manner, without express permission of the publisher, is prohibited. No liability is assumed with respect to the use of the information herein.

Library of Congress Cataloging in Publication Data

Main entry under title:

The Countryside book of farming lore.

    Includes index.
    1. Agriculture—Handbooks, manuals, etc. 2. Organic farming—Handbooks, manuals, etc. I. Countryside (Waterloo, Wis.)
S501.2.C67   1985   630   85-2712
ISBN 0-8306-0952-0
ISBN 0-8306-1952-6 (pbk.)

Contents

Introduction   vii

1 Soil   1

Cultivation of the Land—Fertile Soil Is "Used Up" by Cropping, Erosion—How to Improve Your Soil—Rotation and Tillage—Nitrogen Use and the Environment—Basic Chemistry for Farmers—Crop Fertilizing Bacteria—Soil Bacteria—Soil Fertility—Farming Acid Soils—Manganese, Iron, and Cobalt—Selenium and the Toxic Heavy Metals—The "Secondary" Nutrients—Mighty Microorganisms

2 Organic Farming   91

The Soil—Fertilization—The Nitrogen Fixation—P & K—Life Beneath Your Feet—Chemical Farming: Fad that Can't Last—The Real Difference Between Chemical and Organic Farming—Practical Organic Gardening—Organic Farming Really Works—Healthy, Wealthy & Wise—Growing Corn Organically—"Devil's Advocate"—It's a Tradition—Why Do Organic Foods Cost More?

3 Grain   205

Plant Reproduction and Control—Breeding Plants for Disease Resistance—Storing Seeds—Improving Wheat Varieties—The Acre of Flax—Dry Farming Works—Comfrey: the Plant that Builds Protein—Corn Yields Higher with Crop Rotations—Tailor the Crop to the Soil—Gleaning the Cornfields—Why Not Grow a Broom?

4 Livestock 252

A Dairy with a Difference—The Dairy that Didn't—He Raises Eyebrows . . . and Milk Production!—IMPRO: A Revolution in Livestock Health

Index 277

Introduction

The know-how and wisdom found in this book is based on the practical experiences of small farmers and homesteaders who have learned to cope with common farming problems. The information found here will also be of special value to anyone interested in organic farming methods.

Among the topics covered, there is advice on how to deal with poor soil or low rainfall, how to get the best milk production from your cows or goats, and how to make life on the farm easier and more efficient.

All of the material in this book has been made available by the editors of *Countryside* magazine. Without their efforts and cooperation, this book would not be possible.

Chapter 1

Soil

The honest effort of the majority of farmers is to produce profitable crops every year. Very few of them are so situated financially that they could till the soil as a pastime. Confronted by an increase in the value of farm land and in the cost of the necessary operating equipment, they have been forced to see that, if their handling of the soil is to yield a fair return upon the value represented, they cannot ignore the need of increased production, they have been forced to recognize the value of proper crop rotation and the intelligent application of labor to the soil. Some have sought to increase the returns from their farms by increasing the size of the farm, forgetting that better and deeper tillage would probably have increased the taxable acres, and without greatly increasing the cost of production.

CULTIVATION OF THE LAND

The common objection to intensified tillage of the soil is the cost of labor. This has found expression in the effort to multiply the implements of tillage, and the effort has been to secure economy of production by increasing the amount of ground cultivated rather than by meeting the direct needs of the soil. The error of this course is manifest from the fact that, up to a certain point, it is more economical to lessen the number of acres tilled and to intensify the tillage. Every community furnishes many illustrations of farms which, with practically identical soil conditions, show a wide difference in profits. To be sure, there may be several causes for such a difference, but the most important of these is generally found in the comparative intelligence used in the cultivation of the land.

Dry Farming

In regions where the amount of rainfall is quite limited, though the soil is of a desirable character for agricultural purposes, a system of tillage known as "dry farming" has been put into practice. Such a system is not entirely applicable to regions of heavier rainfall, but the principles upon which it is based are of prime consideration in any region where occasional periods of drought are known. The practice of disking immediately after harvest, to fit the soil to absorb possible rainfall and to check evaporation, is a desirable one in any locality; and the principles that underlie subsurface packing and surface cultivation are applicable, in a measure, everywhere.

The dry-land farmer must keep in mind that his gravest danger lies in an insufficient amount of moisture to mature his crops. He must save and store in the soil as much as possible of the moisture that falls, and carefully conserve it until it is needed by the growing crop. Wherever a season's rainfall is not sufficient to mature a crop, or the amount is very uncertain, it is desirable, with proper tillage, to carry over a greater portion of one season's rainfall to the following season, and thus strengthen the assurance of a profitable crop.

Alternate Cropping

Under such a system of tillage, crops are not grown every year, and in extreme cases the plan contemplates a crop only every alternate year. The important consideration in all dry farming, no matter how frequently the land is cropped, is a careful conservation of all moisture, and the system of alternate cropping will serve to illustrate the general principle. After a crop has been harvested, the land is either plowed or disked. This puts the surface in a loosened condition, in which it readily absorbs any rainfall that may come, instead of allowing it to waste by running off. With the disking method, a portion of the grain stubble is chopped up and mixed with the surface soil, which establishes a better connection between the furrow slice and the subsoil below, whenever the land is plowed. If the land is disked in the fall, it is usually disked again in the spring, and then plowed in the early summer. Subsurface packing usually follows spring plowing, and is used for the purpose of firming the lower part of the furrow slice and uniting it with the subsoil below.

Conserving Moisture

The land is given frequent surface cultivation during the summer. There are two effective modes of conserving soil moisture: (1) the keeping down of all weed growth and (2) the preservation of an earth-mulch to check loss by evaporation.

Objects of Soil Tillage

Speaking in a broad way, drainage or any similar operation might be included under soil tillage; but, in the usual acceptance of the term, soil tillage refers only to the operations necessary to the preparation of cultivable soil for the planting of crops, and the subsequent processes necessary to bring these crops to maturity. The principal reasons for all care and tillage of the soil are: (1) to provide a good seedbed, (2) to liberate plant food, (3) to conserve soil moisture, and (4) to destroy weeds. With proper tillage we are able to overcome or modify adverse conditions, and improve conditions already favorable.

The Seedbed

The soil is the home of all crop growth, and much depends upon the preparation of that home for the crop that is to be grown. The preparation of the seedbed will vary somewhat with the character of the crop and the quality of the soil in which it is to be grown; but in all cases it must be remembered that if a seed is to germinate readily, it needs air, warmth, and moisture, and that if a plant is to thrive and have a vigorous root development, it needs a mellow, yet compact, seedbed, in which the particles of soil are neither baked together nor in an open or lumpy condition, but are sufficiently packed together to allow a free movement of moisture in the soil, and still be able to supply the needed amount of air. When prepared in this way and thoroughly united with the subsoil below, such a seedbed offers, under favorable conditions, a most excellent opportunity for root development and continued growth.

Liberation of Plant Food

In order that a crop may be brought to complete maturity, there must be, in addition to a proper seedbed and favorable climatic conditions, an ample supply of available plant food and moisture, at all times.

Most of us are aware that good earth, brought to the surface from a considerable depth, is not productive until it has been exposed for a season to the action of air and sunlight. To some extent the same is true of the upper soil in our fields. It is benefited by aeration, and modern tillage is instrumental in bringing this about. Many of the changes that take place in the liberation of plant food are due to the action of micro-organisms in the soil; and these, like higher forms of plant life, need both air and moisture in their growth and development. Nitrates and similar products, favorable to plant growth, cannot be produced except through the agency of soil organisms, and only in the presence of air and moisture. However, this air in the soil should not be in large open spaces, but should be evenly diffused throughout the portion where the root-development of the crop is to take place. Neither should aeration be construed to mean that spring plowing should remain unharrowed for several days. Such a treatment allows too great a circulation of air, and robs the soil of its moisture.

Conserving Moisture

Tillage increases the moisture absorbing power of the soil. A stubble field will naturally be compacted to a considerable degree, after having remained undisturbed throughout the entire growing season. Much of the late fall and winter precipitation will be lost as "run-off" from such a field, particularly on rolling areas. In a fall plowed field, the loss will be greatly reduced owing to the fact that moisture will percolate into the soil readily. It has been amply demonstrated by experiment that fall plowed land, whose surface is allowed to remain rough throughout the winter, contains considerably more moisture in the following spring than land not plowed.

Excessive loss of moisture by evaporation can also be very materially checked by appropriate tillage. This will be more thoroughly understood after the nature and movements of soil moisture have been explained.

Hygroscopic Moisture. Moisture exists in the soil in three distinct forms. An air-dry soil contains a small amount of moisture. The moisture has been condensed from the atmosphere, in much the same manner as moisture is condensed upon salt, a phenomenon which everyone has noted during damp weather. This moisture is known as "hygroscopic moisture." It is held very tenaciously by the soil, and is not available for the use of plants.

Capillary Moisture. If a quantity of soil is placed in a dish containing a small amount of water, this water will begin to pass upward in the soil mass. This moisture is known as "capillary moisture." It is held by surface tension in the form of films about each soil particle and stretched across small "gaps" or spaces between the soil particles. This is the moisture which is directly available for the use of plants. It is capable of moving upward in the soil in the same manner as oil moves upward in a lamp wick, or as water moves upward in a lump of sugar.

Gravitational or Free Moisture. Soils are capable of holding a large amount of moisture in the capillary form, the amount differing with different types of soils. Soils of very fine texture, and those rich in organic matter are capable of holding the largest amounts, while coarse soils have the smallest capacity for this form of moisture.

A soil is not saturated with moisture, however, when it contains as much capillary moisture as is possible for it to hold. The spaces between the particles are as yet not filled. The remaining amount of moisture necessary to saturate it after its capillary capacity has been satisfied, is known as "gravitational" or "free" moisture. The relation between "capillary" and "free" moisture will be better understood from the following example. Suppose that several marbles or a quantity of shot are placed in a cup. Water is poured into the cup until it stands at the level of the shot. Holding the shot or marbles in place the cup is inverted and the water allowed to drain away. When drainage is complete, there still remains considerable moisture. Free moisture moves downward in the soil under the influence of gravity,until it reaches the "water table," which is the natural level at which free moisture stands in the soil. Where free moisture exists it is evident that air is excluded. Therefore free moisture in the root zone is a detriment. When it exists a few feet below the surface, however, it acts as a reservoir, from which the capillary moisture is replenished as it is used up by the growing plants or is lost by evaporation, in the same manner as the oil is raised up by the wick from the supply in the lamp.

Preventing Evaporation. The parallel just drawn introduces again the question left at the point where the digression was made, namely that of preventing excessive evaporation. Minnesota can usually depend upon some moisture in the form of rain during the growing season. The distribution of this moisture, however, is not always such as to meet the needs of our crops. It should be the object, therefore, to so till the soil as to make the most out of the moisture which already exists, and is continuously moving upward from the "water table." The upward movement of moisture by capillary attraction has been illustrated by the lamp wick.

The greater the evaporation at the surface the more rapid the upward movement of capillary moisture and hence the more rapid the depletion of the moisture supply. Obviously then, any method of checking this evaporation is of great importance. For this purpose a soil mulch, maintained by frequent tillage, is very effective. At the bottom of this mulch, a gap is formed, across which the capillary moisture cannot readily pass. This moisture moves freely up through the root zone, but cannot get to the surface where it would be lost by evaporation. As the mulch settles down upon the soil beneath, the gap is bridged, capillary connection is reestablished, and evaporation goes on again, so frequent renewal of the mulch is necessary in order that evaporation may be effectively checked. King, who has made a great many soil investigations of inestimable value, found, on comparing two fields lying side by side, one of which was cultivated to a depth of 3 inches, and the other left undisturbed, that the cultivation saved an amount of moisture equal to 1.7 inches in rainfall during a period of 49 days. This difference was a difference in evaporation solely, for both fields were kept free from weeds and other vegetation.

Destroying Weeds

A weed has frequently been defined as "any plant out of place," or as "one that is growing where it is not wanted." It is well known that weeds use moisture and plant food that would otherwise probably be used by the growing crops. They frequently crowd a growing crop, and in many ways materially add to the cost of production. The weed question is important on every farm, and no good farmer will willingly permit weeds to grow and produce seed upon his farm.

A good system of rotation that includes cultivated crops, offers the best means of combating the common weeds; but success is almost entirely dependent upon the method of persistence of cultivation. To ensure reasonable success, the disk and the harrow should be used frequently while the weeds are still small, and the crops should be given frequent cultivation while growing.

Fortunately, the same operations that are used in putting the soil in a condition to receive and conserve rainfall, to prepare the seedbed, and to liberate plant food, are likewise useful in combating weeds.

Humus and Tillage

Decaying animal and vegetable matter in the soil is known as humus; and it plays an important part in the tillage and productivity of any soil. The loss of this humus by a system of continuous cropping or through any unwise practice, is bound to make tillage more difficult and less effective.

The presence of humus in a soil tends to make it open and porous and of a better physical condition. Soils that have a tendency to become too compact, and to puddle, are helped by the addition of vegetable matter to the furrow slice. Humus also helps to prevent heavy soils from baking, and to bind soils that are inclined to wash and blow. It is of material assistance in helping to control the moisture supply in the soil; for it will help a light or sandy soil to hold moisture, and it will assist the moisture in a heavy soil to move more freely.

Its greatest importance, however, is due to the assistance it gives to the active liberation of plant food while the plants are growing. All crops need to be fed while growing, and vegetable matter offers the best means of supplying this need. Not only does its decay liberate plant food contained in itself, but the acids produced by the decay are also active agents in breaking down the inert plant food of the particles of soil. Aside from moisture, no other thing has such a direct bearing upon the producing power of a soil, and the aim should be to return all vegetable refuse to the soil, and by means of good tillage to incorporate it thoroughly with the soil.

Forms of Tillage

In a general way, tillage might be divided into plowing, subsoil tillage, broad tillage, and intertillage. Plowing would include the use of the breaking and stubble plow. Subsoil tillage would include the use of the subsoil plow and the subsurface packer. Broad tillage would include the use of the harrow, disk, and similar implements, while intertillage would include the use of practically every form of hoe and cultivator that is used between the plants of a growing crop.

There has been no marked change in the general principles of tillage, but there has been a constant change in the form, size, and number of implements. However, where the farmer has the more important implements, such as the plow, disk, harrow, and cultivator, and uses them intelligently, they can be made to serve the purpose of many of the lesser implements.

Plowing

Plowing, though seemingly a simple process, is easily the most important operation in the tillage of the soil. Upon it depend to a great degree the nature of later operations and the frequency with which they will be required. In fact, unless land is plowed in the best manner possible, and at the right time, the preparation of the land for growing a crop will require additional labor and cost. It may even be impossible to prepare a good seedbed when plowed under certain conditions.

How to Plow

The pride of every good plowman is a straight, well-turned furrow, and yet its straightness is but a small part of its merit. Its true merit is measured by its depth, the manner in which it is turned, and the way in which it lies. When properly turned, it will present a loosely pulverized and completely inverted furrow slice that leaves behind a furrow of sufficient depth, even in the bottom, and clean-cut in every part.

With land that is to be put into crop soon after plowing, as in the case of spring plowing, or of fall plowing for fall-sown crops, it is very important that the ground, if possible, be sufficiently moist to pulverize nicely, and that each day's plowing shall be harrowed at once. Working the furrow slice immediately after plowing pulverizes it more completely, and checks the loss of moisture by evaporation. With the fall plowing of land that is not going to be put into crop until the following spring, it is not so important that the furrow slice pulverize completely, for lumps and clods that are turned up with the furrow slice will crumble under the action of rain, air, sunshine, and frost.

Plowed land readily absorbs rainfall, and the loosely turned furrows increase the storage capacity of the soil. The inverted soil of the furrow slice exposes another series of soil particles to the action of the air, rain, freezing, and thawing, all of which will tend to aerate the soil and liberate plant food.

Plowing is also the principal method by which grain stubble and all other forms of organic matter are introduced into the soil. Hence it is important that the plow be properly equipped, and the furrow slice so turned that all organic matter will be completely turned under, at such a depth that the harrow and the cultivator will scarcely be troubled with it afterward.

When to Plow

Whenever land has become hard or compact, as is the case with sod and stubble, plowing is the only means by which it can again be made mellow and put into a desirable condition for grain or cultivated crops. The time at which it shall be plowed depends very much upon the crop to be grown, the climatic conditions, the type of soil and its physical condition, and the amount of manual and horse labor at hand.

Having in view the saving of soil moisture, the aeration of the soil, the destruction of weeds, and the general distribution of farm labor, we face a series of conditions that make it advisable to start fall plowing as soon after harvest as possible. This early fall plowing gives plenty of time for the furrow slice to become sufficiently compact, and encourages the sprouting of weed seeds, which will largely be killed by the first hard frost. It is also true that most of our grain crops do better on fallplowed land, except when they follow corn or potatoes on well-tilled fields.

Land that is infested with certain noxious weeds and insect pests may receive great benefit from late fall plowing. A heavy clay soil is sometimes benefited by late fall plowing, but it should never be plowed when the soil is so wet that the upturned furrow slice presents a slick, plastic, mortar-like appearance. When plowed in such a condition and exposed to the sun and a drying atmosphere, it is bound to bake and become lumpy.

No definite statement can be made as to when we should plow land that is to be planted to cultivated crops the following season. The varying success that different farmers have had with spring or fall plowing for such crops can often be traced to the different modes of handling the soil just before it was planted. The methods used in the final preparation of a seedbed will often count for more than the comparative gain from fall or spring plowing.

It is, however, desirable to plow in the fall for cultivated crops whenever they are put upon tame grass sod, or when stubble land has received an application of barnyard manure. This gives a greater opportunity for the sod to become broken down and mellow, and in case of the stubble land it gives ample opportunity for the furrow slice to become united with the subsoil below. Where stubble land must be plowed in the spring, it is well to disk the land early, and in this way chop up much of the stubble and manure and mix it with the surface soil. This gives much better union of the furrow slice with the subsoil below and greatly improves the subsoil portion of the seedbed.

Depth to Plow

The depth to which land should be plowed depends much upon the season of the year, the kind of soil, and the physical condition of the subsoil. Fall plowing, except for fall-sown grain, should invariably be deeper than spring plowing, as there is more time for the soil to become sufficiently settled and compacted. Whenever land is plowed quite deeply, and the climatic conditions do not thoroughly settle the furrows, it should be thoroughly worked before it is planted.

Heavy soils need to be plowed deeper than light ones. They usually have quite compact subsoils, which are benefited by being brought to the surface. It is also a benefit to heavy soils to bury the vegetable matter at a good depth, as this will assist in keeping the subsoil from becoming too compact.

Light soils are very different. Their subsoils are usually not too compact, and it is better to have the vegetable matter mixed with the surface soil. Deep plowing of such soils has a tendency to make them too loose, and care should be taken to see that they are thoroughly compacted before they are planted.

Plowing land at the same depth every time has a tendency to form a hard, compact layer in the subsoil at that depth. This is an undesirable condition, and can usually be avoided by varying the depth slightly from year to year. New land, when first brought under plow, should not be plowed too deeply. While it may be desirable ultimately to have a furrow six or seven inches in depth it should be brought about gradually by plowing about half an inch deeper every year.

Subsoil Plowing

A subsoil plow is an implement designed to follow in the furrow of the stubble plow and loosen the compacted bottom of the furrow to a depth of several inches. This loosened subsoil is not brought to the surface, but is covered by the furrow slice of the next round of the stubble plow. This loosening of the subsoil helps the under-drainage of the soil, and puts it in a better physical condition.

Subsoil plowing is usually practiced on heavy clay lands, where the subsoils have a tendency to become very compact. It should not be done when the subsoil is wet enough to be plastic and mortar-like when worked, as the subsoil will become puddled and no good will be accomplished.

Light sandy soils are not benefited by subsoil plowing. For most soil conditions it is far better practice to adopt a practical rotation of crops, and to provide for building up the vegetable matter in the soil. This, with an occasional deep plowing, will accomplish practically the same results as subsoil plowing.

Subsurface Packing

Subsurface packing consists in the use of some implement to compact the lower part of the inverted furrow slice, and to bring it firmly in contact with the bottom of the furrow. It is especially adapted to soils that have a tendency to become loose and open after plowing or cultivation; and its principal purpose is to establish a condition that provides a free movement of capillary moisture in the soil, and a ready development of root growth in crops. This compacted condition of the subsurface soil also hastens the decay of buried vegetable matter.

Subsurface packing is especially beneficial in semi-arid regions, but could be practiced with profit on light loam soils in other regions. If a subsurface packer is not at hand, a disk, slightly weighted and set to run nearly straight, makes a fairly good substitute for subsurface packing, as its work is entirely on the surface.

Broad Tillage

The disk and the harrow are typical implements of broad tillage. They are designed to get over the land quite rapidly, and to meet several requirements in the handling of the soil. Such implements are helpful in putting the soil in proper physical condition for seedbed purposes, and in preparing an earthy-mulch for the conservation of moisture. They are also the most practical implements we have for destroying weeds while they are still small.

Disking

There are two types of disking implements: (1) the circular or revolving disk, and (2) the curved blade, or Acme. Both are designed for practically the same purpose. They are excellent for destroying small weeds, and are especially useful in pulverizing the plowing of sod land. They are also helpful in opening up and loosening any crusted condition of a plowed surface that has laid for some time. This loosening of the surface gives air and sunlight a better chance to warm and aerate the surface soil. It promotes the development of beneficial organisms, and hastens the decay of vegetable matter.

Disking is also helpful in chopping up vegetable refuse on the surface, such as cornstalks, that might hinder seeding. Where grain crops follow corn or potatoes on well-tilled fields, it is generally better not to plow at all, but to prepare the seedbed by thorough disking. Wherever it seems advantageous to use the disk, if time will permit, it is advisable to double disk, that is, lap half that width each round. By this plan one avoids leaving the soil in a somewhat ridged condition, and the work is much better.

Harrowing

The harrow is the most universally used surface-tillage implement. It is used to follow the plow, when it is desired to pulverize the soil immediately, and scarcely a crop is grown where the harrow is not used in preparing its seedbed. The use of the harrow levels and pulverizes the topmost soil, and creates an excellent earth-mulch for preventing the loss of soil moisture.

With timely use, it destroys a countless number of very small weeds. It is not a cultivator, however, and when used for destroying weeds, it should be used while the weeds are very small, and at a time when the strong sunlight will quickly destroy the small, upturned roots. When preparing the seedbed for cultivated crops, it is wise to use the disk and the harrow alternately several times before the crop is planted. This helps very much in warming the soil, and a great many weeds are destroyed that would have grown with the cultivated crop.

Fields of grain and cultivated crops are sometimes harrowed to loosen a crusted condition of the surface soil, and to destroy small weeds. However, the value of such tillage is questionable; and whenever it seems necessary, it should be lightly done, and at a time when the growing crop will be damaged the least.

Rolling and Planking

A roller may crush or break earth clods on the surface; but it cannot be of much further service as it does not reach the portion of the seedbed that should be packed. Heavy clay lands are not materially benefited by rolling, and if heavy rains should follow the rolling of such soils, a baking of the surface soil would likely take place and result in serious damage. On light soils, that have a tendency to remain too loose and open, the use of the roller may prove a decided benefit, although rolling such a soil is quite likely to cause it to blow badly during windy weather.

Doubtless a roller can be used with profit at certain times, but its range of usefulness is very limited. A planker, made of several planks spiked together and drawn sidewise over the surface, will pack the soil nearly as well. It will destroy more small weeds than the roller, and will leave the surface soil in a far better physical condition.

Intertillage

Man owes much of the improvement he has made in the plants given him by Nature to the fact that plants are more easily improved under the changed environment of intensified cultivation. The plants of our various grain and grass crops, when grown individually, are responsive to additional cultivation during the growing period; and, were it not for the fact that it is impractical to give them intertillage, they, too, would be grown as cultivated crops. Some crops are very responsive to intertillage; and because such tillage is both practical and profitable, these crops are classed as cultivated crops, and the system of tillage is known as cultivation.

Purpose of Cultivation

All cultivation that is given during the growing season should be for one or more of the following purposes: (1) to loosen and aerate the surface soil, (2) to promote the liberation of plant food, (3) to save soil moisture, or (4) to destroy weeds. In giving this cultivation it is important to keep in mind that it is carried on among growing plants; and while it is given for their improvement, it must not interfere with their growth. Very often a wrong use of the cultivator has been the cause of serious damage to a growing crop, when a proper cultivation would have been of great benefit.

Cultivation varies slightly with the kind of crop, but more particularly with the conditions of the soil and the time of which it is given. To understand the purpose and proper form of cultivation more fully it may be helpful to classify it as early and late cultivation.

Early Cultivation

Early cultivation may be said to commence with the first intertillage operation after the crop is planted. It may even take place while the plants are still below ground. Such a cultivation may be given while the marks of the planter are still visible, and is known as blind cultivation; but, whenever given, care should be taken that only a light amount of earth be thrown over the planter mark.

Early cultivation can be used to improve a poorly prepared seedbed, but it cannot supply what a proper preparation of the seedbed would have supplied. Intertillage is not a seedbed preparation. If the seedbed is too compact, and was not sufficiently loosened before the crop was planted, an early, deep cultivation will be beneficial.

This early cultivation should be slow and careful, getting in close to the little plants, but avoiding any injury to them. It may be several inches in depth, but the tool used should not leave the soil ridged. On land free from straw and other refuse vegetable matter on the surface, it may frequently be beneficial to follow this first cultivation with a cross-cultivation, using a light weeder or hayrake as a means of leveling any ridges that may have been formed.

Whenever practical, the crop should be planted in check rows, in order that cross-cultivation may be given. This gives better opportunity for maintaining a level surface in the field, and for destroying weeds in the row.

After the plants gain in size and strength, the cultivator may be allowed to throw a slight amount of earth around the plant. This will serve as an earth-mulch, and may smother many small weeds. Hilling the plant is objectionable. It gives no direct benefit, but possibly inflicts an injury. Indeed, when accomplished late in the season, by deep cultivation, it is a possitive damage to the crop.

Cultivation should be frequent in the early part of the growing season. Weeds should be destroyed while they are still small, and any crusted condition of the surface soil should be broken immediately. Rains should be followed by cultivation as soon as the soil will permit, but it should be remembered that some soils should not be cultivated too soon after a rain; also that every cultivation should be given, if possible, at a time when the physical condition of the soil is right.

Late Cultivation

As the growing season progresses, succeeding cultivations should gradually become more shallow, until the last cultivation of any crop should stir no more than an inch or two of the surface soil, leaving it as level as possible. Late cultivation is largely for the purpose of conserving soil moisture, that will be needed to bring the crop to a full state of maturity; and the important considerations are a light, loose earth-mulch, and the complete absence of weeds.

Whenever late rains come, the soil should be cultivated lightly to conserve the moisture that has fallen and to break any crust formation. A crusting of the surface may take place merely by the rise of moisture from below, and even though the crop is well advanced, this crust formation should be broken by a light cultivation. Many farmers have found that this extra cultivation has materially added to the profit of the crop.

It may be said, and it is possible, that farmers occasionally become extremists and carry their tillage operations too far. It must also be said that every well-directed tillage operation tends to produce a balanced growing condition, stimulates the forces of nature, and brings an increase in productivity.

FERTILE SOIL IS "USED UP" BY CROPPING, EROSION

American farmers and ranches are using up the land at a rate unsurpassed in the history of mankind, a professor of plant science told a group of conservationists recently.

Dr. Lawrence O. Find, professor of plant science at South Dakota State University, was addressing about 80 of the state's top conservationists, the winners of county soil and moisture achievement contests attending a soil and moisture clinic at SDSU.

Water erosion caused by intense farming practices is taking away the nation's topsoil and nutrients, Find pointed out.

"The real capital of South Dakota agriculture, the soil, is depreciating at an alarming rate. This has been demonstrated by yield reductions of up to 60 percent on seriously eroded slopes in eastern South Dakota," said Dr. Fine.

Farmers need to increase the use of crop residues on the surface. They plow land that is not suitable for plowing, washing great quantities of soil into valleys and sloughs, said Fine.

"Erosion losses are costing us two to four times as much as what we take out in crops."

South Dakota studies near Madison in the 1960s found that clean tillage fallow loses 8.6 tons of soil per acre per year, while corn planted with a till planter on the contour only loses .39 tons per acre per year to erosion, Fine said.

The wind isn't doing much damage any more. Water erosion is removing four times as much soil as wind erosion in South Dakota, he said.

"Nitrogen content of run-off soil which leaves the land is 2.7 times as high in that soil as in the soil from which the sediment came. So we can see severe nitrogen deficiences on side-hills where this sorting process is most easily seen."

Fine showed slides of erosion at work and pointed to fields of corn with the rows running down the hills instead of on the contour. Man used to burn crop residue, a practice which contributed to massive erosion in the past and still is a factor today.

Now he takes silage off. On areas of thin topsoil continued silage removal is destructive to the soil because of rapid decline or organic matter in the soil.

Farmers also have gone to wide machinery which makes it impractical to maintain grassed waterways. "Super-large machinery caused conservation to take it on the jaw."

He showed winter wheat on summer fallow with once-effective terraces broken, allowing the field to erode with the rain.

"In winter wheat areas some gullies are so big you can't cross them with a tractor."

"We overgraze some of the land" causing erosion.

Soil stands alone as the major deletable resource used in agriculture, said Dr. Fine.

"In South Dakota, the State in which the economy is the most exclusively agriculture-based, we have been blessed with soils basically and originally very productive, although quite shallow in some areas.

"Our supplies of total soil nitrogen and phosphorus were excellent. Out soil reserves of many of the other mineral nutrients required by plants are still among the best in the world," said Fine.

"Agricultural practices, however, have been largely exploitative, with little thought to maintaining the productive potentials of the soils. From our 17 million acres of croplands alone we are removing each year about 750 million pounds of nitrogen, or an average of about 39 pounds per acre in crops taken off the land." Farmers are returning about 182 million pounds or about 24 percent of that removed. No estimate is made of removal by haying or grazing the 27 million acres of grasslands in the state.

Cropping and grazing removal, however, "are dwarfed in many years by erosion losses of topsoil and precious nutrients from most of the gently sloping and sloping lands of the state."

Measurements have been made indicating topsoil losses can be as much as one-half inch in only one storm on slopes as slight as two percent.

"We can afford to buy back in commercial fertilizer the plant nutrients contained in the crops and livestock we sell, but South Dakota agriculture can never afford, under the present economic standards, to buy back the plant nutrients being lost in erosion," said Fine.

"Neither can society afford the loss of these elements to the ocean, or the destruction of lakes and watercourses by the sediment deposited. The federal nonpoint pollution legislation now being implemented is evidence of that fact.

"Our purpose in this 28the annual Conservation Clinic is to so motivate the farm and ranch leaders here assembled that they will return home and do an ever-improved job of conservation farming and ranching and be ever more zealous in their efforts to convince their neighbors of the wisdom of such procedures.

"If we fail in this educational effort at attaining proper use and conservation of our soil and water, society will not long forbear and will eventually legislate land use zoning practices that will attempt to ensure sustained productivity of our lands and the value of our lakes and rivers for posterity.

"We may have as little as five to 10 years in which to do this by voluntary methods," said Dr. Fine.

HOW TO IMPROVE YOUR SOIL

No farmer would turn down an opportunity to improve his soil ... not, at least, unless he were very lazy or very stupid. But notice that "improve" means to enhance in value or quality, to make better.

Do conventional agricultural methods improve your soil? Hardly. They are designed to feed the plant. It doesn't take much experience to recognize that our soil itself is definitely not improved by "improved" methods of agriculture. Soil is only improved by making it better, which includes not only the mineral elements in chemical fertilizers, but properties that our continued applications of chemicals are destroying.

It's impossible to say that for good results you should add so much of this or that, or you must do one thing or another. Your soil and your conditions are unlike anyone else's, and there is no reason to believe that what works for them will work for you. In many areas, in fact, you will find varying conditions requiring varying treatments right on your own farm, or even in different areas of the same field.

The best farmers are and always have been good students. What's more, they are students who are eager to learn, not ones who sit in class for four years and expect to pick up a degree for attendance or good behavior. They are eager to question, to experiment, to work. They are willing to make mistakes.

No farm, or even a garden, should be without experimental plots, constantly checking varieties, methods of fertilization and other soil treatments. Taking the nearest agricultural experiment station's word that a given plant variety or cultural method is "best," when your conditions might be quite different, makes about as much sense as saying International tractors are better than John Deere's. Farming is not a profession for dullards: you need knowledge and experience, for you have to make your own decisions.

You wouldn't expect to set out on a journey without knowing where you are now. If your destination is Chicago, it makes a great deal of difference which direction you strike out in, depending upon if you are in New York, Denver, Atlanta or Sault Ste. Marie.

If your goal is a healthy, fertile soil, you must know what its condition is now. This involves a soil test, and an on-the-scene analysis.

For the analysis, ask yourself what your land is really like: is it sandy, loam or clay? How much does it slope? Are there wet spots, is it rocky or are there other tillage problems? What is your climate, what is the normal precipitation and its distribution throughout the year? What is the nature of the bedrock from which your soil was formed? What have your weed and insect problems been? What crops have been grown recently and in the more remote past, and what have the yields been?

No magazine article, no book . . . and in reality not even a visiting expert who spends a few minutes or an hour on your place . . . can provide the answers to all of those questions. Make use of such sources whenever you can, of course, but recognize that the final analysis is up to you.

Then comes the soil analysis, the audit of your present balance in the savings account of the soil. The soil test should not include only N, P and K, but organic matter (because of its action as a buffer, a catalyst, its mechanical properties and its contribution of minor and unknown elements of fertility that cannot, or cannot economically, be tested for). The test should show soil pH, calcium, and ideally some of the other major trace elements such as magnesium, sulphates and sodium.

The reason for the importance of the comprehensive test was stressed throughout this series with the time-honored illustration of the stave barrel. Each stave represents a different soil element. (When this analogy was first used it included such things as air, water, and temperature, but for purposes of dramatizing the importance of the elements covered by testing, these are usually omitted today.) If the stave that represents calcium, for example, is broken halfway down the barrel, you will never be able to fill the barrel. You can add all the nitrogen, all the phosphorus or potassium you want to or can afford, but you can never fill the barrel so long as that stave is broken. The obvious remedy is to repair the broken stave, to add calcium. A soil test is the only reliable method of determining what factors are limiting your production.

If soil improvement (as opposed to short-term growth) is your goal, the manner in which those broken staves . . . for you will likely have several . . . are repaired becomes a matter of importance. The most important reasons revolve around humus and the soil life that depends on humus. You will want to avoid, for example, those forms of chemicals that inhibit rather than enhance the production of humus from organic matter by destroying soil life: anhydrous ammonia for nitrogen; triplesuperphosphate; and in general most of the usual chemicals used to feed plants instead of soil. The gardener might decide to use such materials as blood meal or leather dust for nitrogen and bone meal for phosphorus, but as these are generally too expensive to be used on large acreages, the commercial farmer usually has to find substitutes, often from suppliers of "organic fertilizers."

A word about these fertilizers, or soil amendments as some of them are called, is in order. County agents have been issuing stock news releases (probably written in some federal office) warning farmers about these products and their salesmen. Unfortunately, they are often valid warnings.

Worthless fertilizers have been sold ever since the beginning of industrial agriculture: in fact, fertilizer analysis was the primary job of the U.S. Dept. of Agriculture experiment stations when they were first organized. There are always farmers who are willing to try something new and different, and there are always hucksters willing to take a man's money for a valueless product.

The situation is compounded today by the burgeoning interest in organic fertilizers and the lack of knowledge about them, not only among farmers but among county agents and other advisors. And it's worse because most of these advisers are still thinking in terms of feeding the plant, not the soil, and they are confused by the concept of someone wanting to apply "fertilizer" that doesn't fertilize, that is, that contains little or no N, P or K. Asking someone like that about organic fertilizers is like asking a mackerel how to fly:

they can't even understand the concept.

Does this mean the hapless farmer is a sitting duck for con artists? Not necessarily. But the farmer who is thinking of going organic requires much more knowledge than the one who is only educated enough to be able to read soil test results and analysis labels on fertilizer bags. He must have a much greater appreciation for the symphony of the soil, the harmony between humus, mineral elements, soil like and all the other factors that determine a soil's health and fertility.

Even then, not being a chemist, a bacteriologist or a specialist in all or any of the many disciplines involved, the choice is not easy and there is no assurance that it will be the right one.

We obviously aren't in a position to recommend specific companies or sources, for a variety of reasons, topped by the fact that we don't have personal experience with all of them. But we can offer some guidelines based on experience.

As with any other commercial product, name and reputation counts. Producers and sellers of good products don't stay in business long making wild promises they can't back up. This is not to say that some fledgling ma and pa operation down the road from you isn't capable of putting out a good product: it merely suggests that, unless there is something to back up their claims for their product, it should be approached much more cautiously than the established brand.

Even at the turn of the century, farm writer C. Harlan claimed that 20 percent of the nation's farm manure was wasted by poor management. Manure is the farmer's capital, he admonished. "What business can be carried on with profit if you are obliged to borrow money at an interest rate of 20 percent? And if you lose 20 percent on your capital every year, what is the difference between you and the reckless borrower?"

Ask for the names of farmers in your area who are using the product, and talk to them. Ask specific questions about applications, yields, and their opinions of the product. Don't be surprised if you find that many of these farmers—and even the salesmen themselves—don't know as much about the principles of organic farming as you do after reading this series! Many of them have only a superficial idea of what they're doing or why, which may or may not affect their results. Organic fertilization is not just a substitute for chemical fertilization; it's only one cog in the works.

Don't be misled by enthusiasm for results of one or two years' application . . . or discouraged by results that may not be as dramatic as you would like. Getting back to some semblance of normalcy, surviving the withdrawal symptoms as chemical drugs are eliminated, is not an overnight or get-rich-quick proposition.

And finally, experiment. You are your own best agricultural experiment station, and certainly in this area where the tax-supported stations aren't doing you any good at all. If a manufacturer recommends that you use 400 pounds of his product, use it, even if only on selected fields. If you have access to or are interested in several products, used them on similar plots and tally the results. In a few years you can be much more confident when placing your order for the winner.

The basis for organic farming is humus and soil life. Reestablishing and building up these factors involves more than eliminating chemicals and adding organic fertilizers. The entire management of the farm should be devoted to the task.

Tillage is paramount, and all of the major producers of organic fertilizers that we are familiar with unstintingly recommend parking or selling your moldboard plow. Use a chisel, they say, under most soil conditions. Avoid plow sole layer, pulverization of the soil, and burial of trash. Keep crop residues near the surface where they can help control erosion, improve tilth, and be worked on by soil micro-organisms and larger life forms.

Proper handling of manure is of obvious importance, but since this is being preached by conventional agriculture as well, it's hardly necessary to dwell on it here. It's even more important to organic farmers, though . . . and they also get more value from it, too, as in the case of nitrogen: adding artificial nitrogen makes soil organisms lazy, and they live off what you provide rather than producing their own, which is nitrification.

Crop rotation is important for a number of reasons including weed and insect control. Setting up a rotation can be a problem, however, particularly without livestock and in situations where farms are devoted to cash crops. Because of the economic considerations inherent here, rotations often present a major dilemma. However, it should also be pointed out that there isn't complete agreement even among organic farmers on this point and that many of them do in fact operate on much the same basis as their conventional neighbors.

Adding humus by green manuring has always been held in high esteem . . . at least until all-out production became the goal and the practice was dropped as uneconomical. Many who are serious about organic farming, especially when they stop to consider the tremendous importance of this element of soil fertility, will surely find a way to make use of it. It can often be accomplished at little or no expense, and certainly without withdrawing land from production for an entire year as was formerly the practice. In certain situations, however, as when organic matter is treacherously low, a concentrated effort at building up humus might well be the wisest and most profitable course. Even without diverting acreage to green manure production, many other options are available: clovers should always be planted with small grains; catch crops can follow early harvests; rye can be sown broadcast in corn at the last cultivation.

And in any case, the preservation of organic matter of crop residues is a must. Chopping corn stalks for feed or bedding and similar practices demand that the farmer return that organic matter to the soil in one way or another. The farmer who consistently exports hay and straw off his property is living off capital as surely as if he sold his topsoil. The only possible reasoning behind such action has to be the intention to make an extra buck today, and to sell out to some sucker or real estate developer tomorrow.

Organic farming is not merely turning away from chemical fertilizers and other agricultural chemicals; it is a whole series of management practices, all aimed at one specific goal: healthy, fertile, living soil.

When that goal is reached, according to present theory, fertility can be maintained with a minimum of additional input. Many organic farmers have already proven to their own satisfaction that a healthy, fertile soil presents fewer weed, insect and disease problems than they encountered when they used chemicals. Natural fertility can be maintained by natural means, primarily by enhancing the humus in the soil and by implication the soil life that goes with it. While certain elements may have to be replenished from time to time (according to soil tests) due to the nutrients which are removed in the form of crops, sent to the cities, and according to current practice flushed out to sea or buried in sanitary landfills, this is far different from the tons of products used today on conventional farms, in quantity, cost and effect.

One of the most unmistakable signs of a new organic gardener is one who gives you a description of growing potatoes by merely pressing them into the ground, and covering them with at least a foot of mulch, with a "what will they think of next?" expression.

This was a common method of culture in the United States until 1983, when potato bugs appeared and necessitated walking between the rows for debugging. The walking damaged the unburied tubers. Yields in excess of a thousand pounds per acre were claimed in some farm journals of the day.

Trace elements are like a key to door weighing many pounds, on a house weighing tons. Their ability to unlock soil fertility is all out of proportion to their weight.

ROTATION AND TILLAGE

Probably there is no other region in the United States where crop rotations and tillage methods are of greater importance than in the Great Plains. The fact that the number of staple crops that can be profitably grown in any section of the Great Plains is somewhat restricted, by climatic and marketing conditions, increases rather than decreases the necessity for a proper rotation of crops, and the annual distribution of the limited rainfall necessitates careful consideration of tillage methods calculated to conserve moisture by reducing weed growth as far as possible.

The selection of the crops to be grown in any given locality, the sequence in which they are to be grown, and the relative quantities of each crop grown must be carefully planned in advance for a long series of years. Tillage methods, on the other hand, must be planned from day to day to meet the ever-changing combinations of soil and climatic conditions, the reduction and the distribution of labor, the arresting of soil blowing and weed growth, and the conservation of precipitation.

Field investigations conducted by the Office of Dry Land Agriculture in the Bureau of Plant Industry at 10 field stations located in the western portions of North Dakota, South Dakota, and Nebraska, and in the eastern portions of Montana and Wyoming during the last 20 years have demonstrated that corn, spring wheat, and oats are the crops best adapted to the northern Great Plains, and that the wheat should be sown on the unplowed disked stubble of the corn crop which precedes it in the rotation.

Root Zones Go Deep

As the above states, the problems involved in tillage methods, or, in other words, the preparation of the seedbed, can not be treated in any such general way as can the selection and the sequence of the crops to be grown in rotation. But as it is known that the root zones of nearly all agricultural plants grown in the Great Plains extend far deeper than the deepest plowing, and that a good seedbed from 4 to 6 inches in depth will produce crops just as good as one twice that depth, we need no longer waste time, energy and money in subsoiling or in deep plowing. It is also known that a dust mulch serves no useful purpose, but is to be avoided, as it blows when dry and puddles when wet, and thereby retards penetration and increases runoff of surface water. It has also been demonstrated that, in the preparation of the seedbed, the time and the method of tillage and the choice of the implements used are both dependent almost entirely upon the physical condition of the soil, the suppression of weed growth, and the economical distribution of labor. The substitution of the duck-foot cultivator and other implements of similar type, or of the disk type, for the plow will often be found advantageous, by reducing cost and improving seedbed conditions.

In view of these facts, each individual farmer should feel free to prepare his seedbed by such means as are warranted by the combination of circumstances and conditions at that particular time and place. There is no necessity for deep plowing or intensive surface tillage. The time of plowing, whether in early or late fall or in spring, should be determined by conditions of weed growth, the physical condition of the soil, and the economical distribution of labor, rather than by some predetermined schedule.

Experience the Ultimate Guide

Every good farmer knows, or he must learn from experience and observation, what constitutes a good seedbed for each crop and each soil with which he has to deal. He can not be taught by precept. Knowing the soil condition required for a good seedbed, he should spare no effort in bringing about that condition, by using such implements, in such ways and at such time, as seems necessary. Good farming is as essential to success in the Great Plains as elsewhere. Good farming means practicing the best methods of producing the largest crops at the lowest cost and leaving the soil in the best condition for the crop that is to follow.

Probably the greatest advantage to be gained by the adoption of the general type of crop rotation briefly outlined above is that it necessitates for growing the sufficient livestock to consume the corn crop, both grain and fodder. It also requires a systematic organization of the farm enterprise and provides for a fairly even distribution of the labor of the farmer, his family, and his hired help throughout the year. It also encourages the preservation of the American farm home, which has been such an important factor in American civilization.

E.C. Chilcott (1927)

NITROGEN USE AND THE ENVIRONMENT

A recently concluded study has found no evidence to support fears of some scientists that increasing use of nitrogen fertilizers poses an immediate threat to the environment.

"We could not identify any mass buildup of nitrates," says study panel member Dennis Keeney, a University of Wisconsin-Madison soils scientist.

Keeney did say, however, that further research is needed to answer questions on the role of nitrogen and its compounds in environmentally troubled areas. At present too many unknowns exist to establish that role and to warrant controls.

Keeney and seven others were members of the National Research Council panel that studied the effects of man's activities on the "nitrogen cycle," a complex of pathways in which nitrogen occurs in a variety of forms.

The study, funded by the Environmental Protection Agency, concentrated primarily on nitrates, one of several nitrogen compounds, and their effect on the environment.

Fertilizer use is expected to double by the turn of the century to meet the food needs of the world's rapidly growing population. If researchers can demonstrate that nitrogen fertilizers endanger the environment, changes in agriculture and in society on the whole may be necessary, Keeney says.

The panel did project that the trend of increasing fertilizer use in the world probably will deplete the ozone layer by 1.5 to 3.5 percent by the year 2100.

The threat to the ozone layer, which shields the earth from the sun's harmful ultraviolet rays, is considerably less than that posed by aerosol sprays that use clorofloromethane propellants, or a large fleet of supersonic transports.

The panel concluded that the benefits of nitrogen fertilizer for increasing crop yields to feed the world's hungry far outweigh the distant effect on the ozone layer and that no corrective action is required.

Serious concerns have also been expressed over the effect of fertilizers on ground water and the deterioration of water quality in lakes and streams.

In areas of heavy fertilization and sites of accumulated barnyard waste, nitrates can percolate through the soil and become concentrated in the ground water. When this water is used for drinking, a potential health hazard is created, to which infants are particularly susceptible.

In their bodies, nitrates may be transformed into nitrite and can result in methem globinemia. Infants with this condition are commonly referred to as "blue babies."

Studies in the Corn Belt have shown that areas with clay-pan soils and shallow water have had problems with nitrate pollution of well waters.

Nitrogen in large amounts in lakes and streams has been associated with excessive weed and algae growth, but its exact role and the contribution of other factors remains elusive.

Studies cited by the panel estimate that "90 percent of the nitrogen entering surface water comes from nonpoint sources and that 80 percent of that portion is from agricultural lands (including livestock feedlots)."

Another study of 473 stream sites found that streams draining agricultural lands had nitrogen concentrations that were five times higher than those draining forested watersheds.

Because of the diversity of the factors in the nitrogen cycle and in agriculture, including climate, soil type and farming practices, determining the cause and effect relationship between nitrogen and water quality is an extremely complex and costly undertaking, the study found.

Although Wisconsin brings in twice as much nitrogen in the form of fertilizer than it exports in food and feed each year, Keeney says the state has no serious problems with the over application of fertilizers.

He adds that simple economics may be the most effective means of altering the trends of fertilizer use. As fertilizer prices increase, farmers will be forced to use less or find alternative sources.

This was also a conclusion reached by the Illinois Pollution Control Board, which studied the possibility of placing limits on fertilizer application rates. It noted that during the period between 1971 and 1975 corn prices rose only 2.2 times while fertilizer prices increased 3.4 times. This, the board said, will lead to more careful monitoring of fertilizer application by farmers.

It also determined that the efficiency of fertilizer used for corn depended more heavily of crop management than on the application rates themselves.

Although a clear case cannot be presented for instituting fertilizer restrictions, the study does suggest ways to use nitrogen more efficiently.

Among these are matching fertilizer to crop needs, using nitrification inhibitors or slowly available forms of nitrogen fertilizer, and measures such as planting cover crops. As fertilizer costs increase, crop rotations including legumes, such as beans and alfalfa, which are able to supply much of their nitrogen needs with the help of bacteria, will become more popular. Other alternatives, such as adding organic carbon supplements to the soil, are too expensive.

One the distant horizon of science lies the possibility that corn and other nonleguminous plants will be developed into forms that can use microorganisms to help them meet their nitrogen needs.

While this might not alleviate pollution, it will help extend our dwindling supply of fossil fuels.

What this article does not cover are the more serious concerns of organic farmers, to whom pollution is only one relatively minor factor. Excessive use of artificial nitrogen—especially anhydrous ammonia—has detrimental effects on life in the soil and therefore on the ecological balance in the soil system, with far-reaching consequences for soil fertility. Applications of artificial nitrogen inhibit natural nitrification. Nitrogen fertilizers are manufactured from natural gas, with consequences on energy. There is also evidence that use of artificial nitrogen fertilizers lower crop quality in a number of ways.

BASIC CHEMISTRY FOR FARMERS

No doubt about it, chemistry has its jargon. But then, so does farming, or driving a car, or making love. Jargon can be an essential means of communication amongst people of a group. But, it can also get out of hand and isolate that group from society as a whole. Certainly this has been the case with science in general, and with chemistry particularly.

Science is a wonderful, awe-inspiring, and even funny branch of knowledge. But scientists have been talking to themselves for far too long, and have been talking quite a bit of drivel at that.

Somewhere between the mutual absurdities of "Any chemical is bad" and "Any chemical is good," those of us who are concerned with the overall welfare of our planet must strike a compromise. In doing this, we must realize that understanding modern agriculture requires a knowledge of chemistry. However, for most of us, our knowledge isn't suited to the task at hand. It's rather like trying to plough a 10 hectacre field with a garden tractor. Some of us have never studied chemistry, and those of us who have, have probably forgotten whatever we did learn.

Before getting into the heavy going, let's go back to ancient scientific thought—back to that branch of knowledge which the

Greeks called "natural philosophy." Their world was made up of four elements: earth, water, air and fire. Substitute the words solids, liquids, gases, and energy, and we find that the ancients weren't so dumb after all.

Over the centuries, it became apparent that the system as they had described it was too simple. During the 18th and 19th centuries the alchemists and their successors added a new dimension to man's design of the universe. They developed the idea that gold was made up of tiny particles of gold and that lead was made up of tiny particles of lead. They called these particles atoms, from the Greek word meaning, "can't be divided."

In practice, of course, atoms can be divided. For our purposes though, let's define an atom as a chemically unique combination of a core of positively charged particles surrounded by a cloud of negative charges. What makes an atom of one element, say oxygen, different from that of another element, say nitrogen, is that oxygen has eight positive charges (protons) in its nucleus (core) and nitrogen has seven.

When two or more atoms combine, they are called a molecule. A molecule that contains more than one kind of atom is called a compound. Carbon is an atom. Oxygen (O_2) is a molecule composed of two oxygen atoms joined one to the other. Salt, too, is a molecule. But since it is made up of two different atoms (sodium and chlorine), it is also a compound. There are 90 elements and millions of compounds in nature. Of those 90 elements, all but 10 are rare near the earth's surface. All but two dozen are extremely rare.

The 17th, 18th, and 19th centuries saw the discovery of certain patterns in the chemical behavior of these elements and compounds emerged. Some would react with water; some would dissolve in acid; some were poisonous. By the end of the 19th century, most of the naturally occurring elements had been discovered. Only since the 20th century has chemistry as a science come to dominate our lives. We may be frustrated by the existence of chemical-industrial pollution, but the explosion of knowledge in the past 50 years regarding chemistry has also brought us sulfa drugs, the discovery of vitamins, and a better understanding of how our soil works.

The following four topics are the foundation of soil chemistry. If they serve as a prod to get a proper text and investigate more fully, fantastic. At the very least, they should make chemical jargon easier to understand and maybe a bit less threatening.

Ions

In many ways chemistry may be described in electrical terms. An atom normally has no electrical charge. If there are 15 protons (positive charges) in the nucleus of phosphorus, one expects that there will be 15 electrons (negative charges) around it in a cloud. This is true in many cases. However, there is another force which often turns out to be more powerful.

An electron is associated with a particular "district," depending on how energetic it is. The farther away from the nucleus an electron is, the higher its energy level. Electrons tend to be grouped into different energy levels (districts) which can contain up to a certain number of electrons and no more. For example, in the case of sodium, which should have 11 electrons, the lower energy levels can only hold 10 electrons. In most cases, the 11th electron will leave the sodium atom because it is easier to have an unbalanced electrical charge than to try to keep a high-energy electron around. If your haymow is full, you don't store the extra hay on the barn roof.

Because an electron cloud of 10 is very stable, it overrules the normal tendency of a sodium atom to contain 11 electrons. Consequently, sodium spends most of its time having one more proton than electron. Any atom which carries a charge, plus or minus, is called an ion. The sodium ion has a charge of plus one, written Na^+.

Magnesium has 12 protons and forms an ion with a charge of plus two—Mg^{+2}. Two of its electrons have been advised to get out of town. It spends a good deal of time in the Mg^{+2} state. Aluminum, another common soil element, has 13 protons. While it spends much of its time as a neutral atom, under only slightly favorable circumstances, it, too, will form an ion Al^{+3}. Oxygen has eight protons and one would expect to find eight electrons. But, it is more stable when the electron cloud is filled to 10 rather than to the eight needed to balance the charges of the protons. The forces which form ions by driving the electron cloud to the 10 electron structure are powerful indeed.

Groups of atoms can also act as an ion. Carbon and oxygen form the carbonate ion:

$$C^{+4} + 3\ O^{-2} \rightarrow CO_3^{-2}$$

Looking at common ions in the soil we find two groups. The cations (pronounced cat-ions) carry positive charges. The anions (pronounced ann-ions) carry negative charges. Chemical processes in the soil involve at least some of these ions.

To form compounds from these ions, it is necessary that the number of positive and negative charges be the same. For example, common salt is sodium chloride, NaCl. Saltpeter is potassium nitrate, KNO_3 Limestone is calcium carbonate, $CaCO_3$. Phosphate rock is calcium phosphate $Ca_3(PO_4)_2$ [note that there are three calcium ions (total charge +6) and two phosphate ions (total charge −6)]. You can play an endless number of mix 'n match games with ions, as long as the charges balance.

Acids and Bases

If a compound readily gives up a hydrogen ion, it is called an acid. If it accepts a hydrogen ion, it is called a base (or an alkali). When acid is mixed with water, it splits into a hydrogen and whatever anion made up the other part of the acid. If the acid dissociates (splits apart) almost completely as in the reaction between hydrochloric acid and water

$$HCl + H_2O \rightarrow H_2O + H^+ + Cl^-$$

then it is said to be a strong acid. If the acid dissociates only slightly as in the reaction between carbonic acid and water

$$2\ H_2CO_3 + H_2O \rightleftharpoons H_2CO_3 + H^+ + HCO_3^- + H_2O$$

it is said to be a weak acid. The strength of bases can be measured in the same way. Note that one of the carbonic acid molecules loses only one hydrogen and that the other remains intact.

In practice, acidity and alkalinity are measured according to pH. The pH system assigns a value of 7.0 to a neutral substance, one that is neither an acid nor a base. For each full point the pH drops, there are 10 times as many hydrogen ions present as at the previous reading. Thus pH 6.0 is 10 times more acid than pH 7.0; pH 5.0 is 100 times (10 × 10) more acid than pH 7.0; pH 4.0 is 1000 times (10 × 10 × 10) as acid as pH 7.0; etc. Similarly, a pH of 8.0 is 10 times as basic as pH 7.0 (and one-tenth as acid); pH 9.0 is 100 times as basic (and one-hundredth as acid) as pH 7.0; etc. Viewed from a slightly different angle, any acid is twice as strong as one 0.3 pH points higher. A soil of pH 6.1 is twice as acid as a soil of pH 6.4.

The acidity of a soil is one of the major factors controlling the behavior and availability of other chemicals in the soil. It is important to remember that the pH scale changes by multiplication and not addition. A soil with a pH of 6.0 is slightly acid; one with a pH of 4.0 is extremely acid.

"Organic" Chemistry

Any compound containing the element carbon is considered to be an "organic" compound. This is a fact which has fueled many needless arguments, no doubt. With the exception of a few bizarre minerals (inorganic) and some very simple organic compounds, organic chemistry is much more complex than inorganic chemistry. This complexity results almost entirely from the nature of the carbon atom. It can bond to other atoms in any or all of four directions at once. Its four chemical bonding sites take the shape of a tetrahedron. When two carbon atoms form a bond it can be like those shown in Fig. 1-1.

This bonding style allows carbon to form chains, rings and networks with plenty of bonding sites left over for elements such as nitrogen, hydrogen and oxygen. Lest the importance of the ability to form different sorts of bonds be overlooked, consider the difference between a phenol (poison) and blood sugar (a necessity). In large measure it is a difference between double-bonded carbon atoms and single-bonded carbon atoms arranged in the same basic ring structure.

Carbon is the currency of our ecosystem. There is no simple way to describe its chemistry. The tetrahedral bonding of silicon gives us thousands of minerals. The tetrahedral bonding of carbon gives us life itself.

Chemical Reactions

If sodium metal is placed in water, the following reaction occurs:

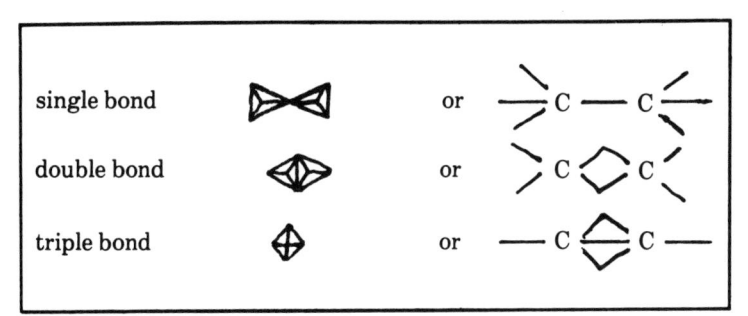

Fig. 1-1. Organic chemistry.

$$Na + HOH \rightarrow NaOH + H$$
$$(H_2O)$$

This reaction produces enough heat to ignite the hydrogen, which explodes when oxygen is present, forming water.

$$2H + O \rightarrow H_2O$$

In both these reactions, there is a great release of energy. Why? The pure sodium, which is very unstable, literally forces the hydrogen out of the water, rather like starlings at a bird feeder. Sodium in its pure state has a high energy level, but in compounds of sodium that energy level is much lower. The difference is released as heat. The same thing happens with put hydrogen and oxygen, except that the hydrogen is just stable enough in its pure state to need a bit of a nudge to start it combining with oxygen. Once that reaction is started, lots of energy is released. The hydrogen is much more stable as part of water than it was in its pure form.

Chemicals are constantly rearranging themselves according to conditions (pH, temperature, etc.), to gain the greatest energy advantage in the circumstances. See Table 1-1. The change may be great, as above, or it may be subtle. Chemical reactions proceed in the direction of the greatest stability (lowest energy), releasing energy in the process. The only reason our system doesn't always run down as each reaction releases its energy is that some reactions are forced to run backwards, either by living organisms (which use the heat of one reaction to make another run backwards) or by the sun, which adds energy to the system.

Table 1-1. Chemical Reactions.

Cations		Anions	
Hydrogen	H^+	Chloride	Cl^-
Sodium	Na^+	Hydroxide	OH^-
Potassium	K^+	Nitrate	NO_3^-
Ammonium	NH_4^+	Carbonate	CO_3^{-2}
Magnesium	Mg^{+2}	Sulphate	SO_4^{-2}
Calcium	Ca^{+2}	Phosphate	PO_4^{-3}
Zinc	Zn^{+2}	Borate	BO_3^{-3}
Copper	Cu^{+1} or $^{+2}$		
Iron	Fe^{+2} or $^{+3}$		
Manganese	Mn^{+4}		

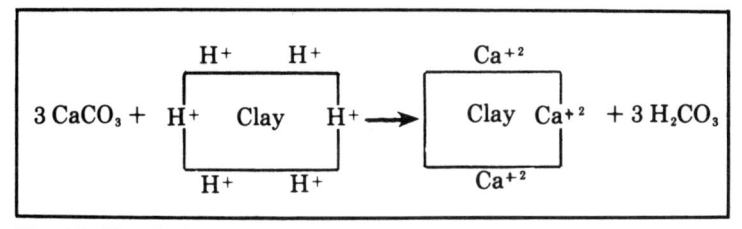

$$3\,CaCO_3 + \begin{array}{|c|} \hline H^+ \quad H^+ \\ H^+ \quad Clay \quad H^+ \\ H^+ \quad H^+ \\ \hline \end{array} \longrightarrow \begin{array}{|c|} \hline Ca^{+2} \\ Clay \quad Ca^{+2} \\ Ca^{+2} \\ \hline \end{array} + 3\,H_2CO_3$$

Fig. 1-2. Chemical reaction.

CATION EXCHANGE

In soils, a good example of this chemical movement in the direction of greater stability is the exchange of cations between one substance and another. Clays are weak anions, but they have a very large surface area where chemical reactions can occur. Since clays are anions, most reactions involve attaching a cation to the clay. If most of these cations are H^+, then the soil will be acid. When limestone is added, the following reaction occurs over the period of a year or more. See Fig. 1-2.

Since carbonic acid (H_2CO_3) dissociates to water and carbon dioxide, what remains is a basic (non-acid) clay. If this reaction occurs often enough, the soil becomes less acid. This is why people in the humid temperate regions lime their soil.

So there it is, chemistry in the proverbial nutshell. If it's completely new to you, run it by again tomorrow or next week. Once these basics are understood, you will have most of the principles of chemistry in your toolbox. From this point you should be able to use scientific research to the benefit of your pocketbook and your planet. And if you're talking to a scientist who's too tied to jargon, ask to have the goods in plain English. It will do us scientists a bit of good!

CROP-FERTILIZING BACTERIA

Some farmers' best friends are bacteria—a type called rhizobia. Agricultural researchers (Fig. 1-3) want to get better acquainted with the one-celled microbes, and introduce them to more farmers.

In fact, a current surge of interest in rhizobia by scientists around the world has prompted officials of the USDA to establish a special rhizobia project at the Beltsville Agricultural Research Center in Maryland. Scientists there will collect and study strains of rhizobia and similar "friends," and distribute them to other USDA and non-USDA labs where rhizobia investigations are underway.

Just what is so friendly about these bacteria?

"Rhizobia have the natural ability to provide crops with nitrogen,

Fig. 1-3. Fertilizing with bacteria.

an element that plants need for growth and to make proteins," explains USDA microbiologist Deane F. Weber who will supervise the new USDA Rhizobium Collection and Study Project at Beltsville. "In their own way, rhizobia fertilize certain crops. This happens without applications of commercial nitrogen fertilizers, which require enormous amounts of natural gas to manufacture. Farmers simply coat seeds with rhizobia before planting to increase harvests."

According to Weber, scientists in many labs now may be within reach of greatly increasing rhizobia's fertilizing abilities. If only a few of the current research projects on rhizobia are successful, agriculture could benefit greatly.

But rhizobia research may be up against a tough deadline. Since 1972, the cost of chemical fertilizers has skyrocketed. If prices remain high, as experts predict, commercial nitrogen fertilizers could soon be out of reach for farmers in lesser developed countries and hopes of meeting food demands of growing populations will diminish.

The burden seems to be on research to "exploit" natural systems of fertilizing crops, USDA says. Rhizobia, by far and away, provide the most prolific natural system. Worldwide, rhizobia provide crops with nearly twice the nitrogen as does bagged fertilizer.

Rhizobia's fertilizing system evolved millions of years ago when the bacteria learned to share the roots of plants that later became some of our major food and forage crops. Rhizobia found protection and nourishment in the roots, while the plants selected those bacteria which could best help them grow and form seed.

For scientists, the USDA Rhizobium Project will be a dependable source of a wide variety of rhizobia strains, which Weber hopes will keep research moving at near optimum levels. Also, for areas of the world where farmers are not familiar with rhizobia, the project will help spread the word on how to use current rhizobia technology. Each growing season, farmers in many less developed countries plant crops that could be improved by "inoculating" seed with rhizobia. But inoculating products, such as a rhizobia-peat mixture commonly used by farmers in advanced countries, are often not available.

Scientists discovered the plant-rhizobia association some 90 years ago. Since then, they have found that soybeans, alfalfa, clover and other members of the protein-rich legume family of plants could each be inoculated with a specific strain of rhizobia to increase yields. The bacteria work in small root nodules, combining nitrogen atoms from air in the soil and hydrogen atoms from sugars in plant tissues to make ammonia, the basic ingredient of nitrogen fertilizer, whether natural or manufactured by industrial means.

The natural process is called "biological nitrogen fixation." It often leaves fields more fertile after harvest than before the legume crop was planted. Before widespread use of artificial nitrogen fertilizer in developed countries, the traditional way of adding nitrogen to the soil for succeeding crops was to use legume crops, such as soybeans or clover, in crop rotations.

Since 1912, scientists at USDA's Beltsville Agricultural Research Center have been studying nitrogen fixation and adding superior nitrogen-fixing bacteria to what is now this country's largest public collection of rhizobia and other (less significant) nitrogen-fixing microorganisms. Each year, Weber sends hundreds of rhizobia cultures to scientists around the world. Laboratories in 53 foreign countries have so far received rhizobia from the Beltsville collection.

With financial support for the Rhizobium Project for USDA and the State Department's Agency for International Development. Weber and a group of Beltsville colleagues trained in related fields of "rhizo-biology" will expand their efforts to collect, characterize, test and distribute strains of rhizobia that are effective on different types of legume plants. Of an estimated 13,000 species of legumes, only 50 are domesticated. Of the possible legume-rhizobia associations, Weber estimates that scientists have identified only 10 percent that form nodules and benefit the plant.

The expanded collecting and testing, however, "will not be a numbers game," says Weber. "Nor are we interested in keeping this valuable resource as a museum piece. It is a working collection. The future will likely bring a high demand for bacterial fixation of nitrogen for crops, and there is great need for scientists to know what Rhizobium genes or characteristics are available."

Current-research being conducted in many of the world's agricultural research labs includes identifying genes in rhizobia that control nitrogen fixation in order to develop bacteria that work harder and more efficiently. Scientists are also trying to extend nitrogen-fixing associations to non-legume crops, such as corn, wheat and other cereals and grasses.

While such "pioneering" research continues, applied research devoted in improving rhizobia inoculation techniques has been largely ignored, according to Weber. "When commercial fertilizer became cheap in the late 1950's," he says, "research on rhizobia inoculation and the training of rhizobia technicians sharply declined, and have never recovered. Now, just when the need is perhaps greatest, there is a troubling shortage of qualified scientists and technicians. The USDA Rhizobium Project should help to fill this void."

But we also know that mulch has complex effects on nitrate concentrations in the soil (E. Walter Russell); that mulch increases the amount of exchangeable potassium and phosphorus in the soil (I.W. Wander and J.H. Gourley), and that it has other beneficial effects, but there is much research to be done in these areas.

Putting it all together, the value of mulch cannot be determined merely by its weight and chemical composition. Nor is it a simple matter to weight the cost of mulch versus the value of harvesting a crop or crop residues. While some research has been done, it's not enough, and not all of the answers are in.

However, for anyone who takes the view that the soil is a living biosystem that must be cultured and fed, there is no need to wait for scientific evidence before deciding whether to scrape the soil bare or to culture it with mulches and green manures. The answer is clear.

SOIL BACTERIA

The organisms (Fig. 1-4) that inhabit our soil range in size from less than one-millionth of a meter to that fat old woodchuck in the back pasture; the soil supports only a few large organisms and myriad small ones—it is the web of life on which we all depend. In all soil, there are five basic groups of microscopic life: fungi, algae, actinomycetes, protozoa, and bacteria.

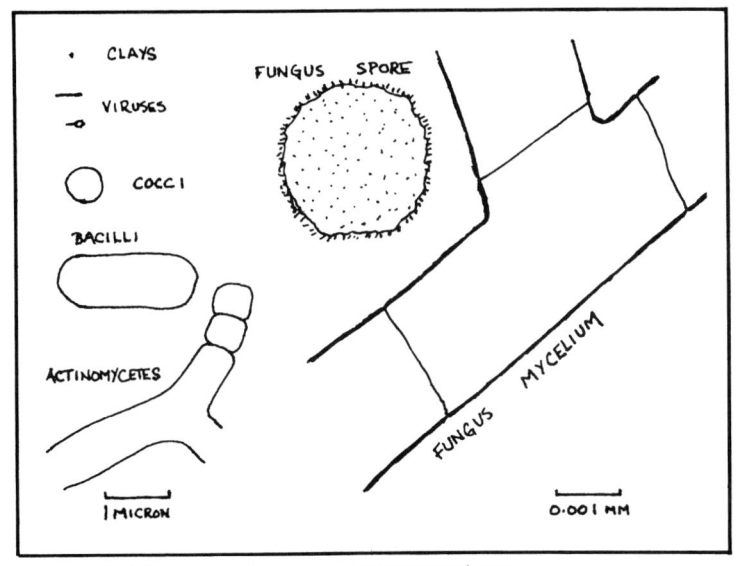

Fig. 1-4. Relative sizes of some soil microorganisms.

Bacteria are the most numerous creatures in the soil, and they are very important in any number of soil processes. Some are necessary for the growth of plants, while others compete with crops for nutrients or cause diseases. A gram of good healthy soil is home to about 1,000 million bacteria, and when conditions are favorable they can double their population in half an hour. This population explosion can't be maintained for very long (several hours—up to maybe 100,000 million per gram!) but it allows bacteria to take advantage of a "windfall" source of food, such as a carcass or an overripe apple, and compete successfully with other soil beasties. These trillions upon trillions (1,500 kg of them per hectare) are literally beyond numbering, and their true importance may be measured by the fact that they account for better than 0.1 percent of the soil mass in the first quarter-meter of soil.

There are a number of ways of dividing bacteria into different groups, but two of the most common methods are by response to oxygen and by shape. The oxygen division gives three distinct categories: the aerobes which must have oxygen to life: the obligate anaerobes to which oxygen is fatal, and the facultative anaerobes which can cope with either the presence or the absence of oxygen in their environment.

Cell structures are also a useful way of characterizing bacteria; the bacilli are shaped rather like cold capsules; the cocci are spherical; and the spirella are spiral shaped. The bacilli are the most common and are generally less than a micron (1/1,000,000 of a meter) wide and up to a few microns long. Many are coated with a gum which may protect the bacterium from predators like amoebae. The presence of large numbers of these gummed bacteria will greatly improve the crumb structure of the soil by cementing humus and mineral particles together. One of the causes of poor soil structure on land that has been abused with manufactured chemical fertilizers is a great reduction in the population of bacteria, with the result that this cementing doesn't occur.

The Soil as a World for Bacteria

Nonbiological factors can and do alter greatly the type of bacterial population, and thus its biological potential in the soil. These factors are water, oxygen, temperature, organic matter, pH, and mineral supply. Cultivation practices will change many of these factors considerably, having a profound influence on the quality of the soil.

Water, being the major component of protoplasm (the guk inside a bacterium other than its "organs"), is essential for plump, happy bacteria. When there isn't enough of it, many bacteria die, while others form spores and go dormant. This tactic of forming spores seems to work well for the bacteria, as the Soviets recently had a batch of 200 million-year-old spores, extracted from a rock, spring to life in a culture dish. The ideal amount of water is around two-thirds field capacity, and much more than that causes a decrease in the population of aerobes (aerobic bacteria) and an increase in the population of anaerobes.

Temperature influences all life greatly, and each group of bacteria has a temperature range in which it most readily thrives. Most prefer temperatures between 25° C. and 35° C., but will function between 15° C and 45° C. Other species do well only at temperatures below 20° C., but these aren't soil bacteria. Some require very warm temperatures (45 to 65° C.) to grow, but their significance is limited. Beyond its direct effect on bacterial microbiology, temperature controls the rate of biological processes carried out by bacteria; in general, warmer temperatures stimulate biochemical reactions.

The bacterial population in most soils is more greatly influenced by the organic matter content than anything else. Soils rich in humus support immense numbers of microbes, and thus plowing down green manures or crop residues initiates a rapid microbial response which lasts for several months. We'll discuss the dining habits of microbes in some detail a bit later.

Extremes of pH are rough on most bacteria, as their optimum is near pH 7.0. In general, the more acid a soil, the lower the microbial population, but evenly a terribly acid soil (pH 3.0) will still contain many bacteria. Among its other effects, liming an acid soil will greatly increase the population of bacteria.

With bacteria, as for all life, inorganic (non-carbon) nutrients are required, and bacteria are affected by both natural and added levels of inorganic elements. Chemical fertilizers rarely exert a beneficial influence on soil bacteria, and often depress the population. These harmful results come not from the elements themselves (bacteria need sodium, magnesium, phosphorus, sulphur, chlorine, potassium, calcium, etc. just as we do) but from the fact that most commercial fertilizers create an acid environment.

The ammonium-containing fertilizers are the worst of the lot because the microbes oxidize the ammonium to nitric acid and proceed to put themselves out of business.

Anhydrous ammonia, on the other hand, simply kills the bacteria (and a few farmers besides) outright. Ammonium and ammonia may be good for the crop, but they're really rough on soil life.

Organic versus Chemical Debate

All these influences, of course, act in combination rather than alone. Plowing and tillage are drastic environmental alterations which often cause major rearrangements in the bacterial population. These changes can be either good or bad, and are, in my opinion, at the heart of the "organic" versus "chemical" or "conventional" farming debate.

On one extreme we have the farmer who double-discs the soil until it is as find as talcum powder, running heavy machinery over the soil again and again, and then, having planted his maize crop, proceeds to knife in anhydrous ammonia. The net result is low oxygen (compacted subsoil); topsoil with plenty of oxygen but not water, and an extremely hostile pH environment. Were I a bacterium, I'd consider moving to Mars.

On the other extreme is the farmer who tills down a lush legume green manure crop in the fall, spreads a good load of manure and rock powder in the spring, and goes over it all lightly with a cultivator before drilling in the seed. The net result here is a moist but well oxygenated soil with lots of organic matter and enough minerals to keep a microbe happy all summer.

Now it's silly to pretend that one set of cultural practices is all good or all bad, but you should realize that your cultural practices make quite a difference to the soil bacteria.

Weather and season are variables over which you have no control but which have a great influence on the bacterial population nonetheless. In general, in the temperate part of the world, a bacterial population burst occurs every spring as the soil warms. There is plenty of water and lots of organic matter from the previous fall.

A decline occurs during the hot, dry summer months, and it is during the summer that "organic" farming methods are most beneficial to bacteria by providing a relatively cool, moist world for them.

In winter, depending on where you live, bacterial activity is put on "hold" for a greater or lesser period of time. This period of inactivity is so long in Alaska and the Canadian north that the bacteria cannot break down organic matter as fast as it accumulates and thick, black, acid soils build up, often to a meter deep. In California, as a contrast, moisture is the controlling factor and the addition of organic matter is essential to a healthy population of soil bacteria.

To be a proper steward of the bacteria in your soil, you have to understand their needs and try your best to meet them.

The Dining Habits of Bacteria

Bacteria, indeed all organisms, can be divided into two classes based on their energy and carbon sources heterotrophic organisms require pre-existent carbon compounds to serve as sources of energy and carbon; autotrophic organisms obtain their energy from the sun or by the oxidation of inorganic compounds, and obtain their carbon from carbon dioxide.

Fungi, actinomycetes, protozoa, all animals, and most bacteria are heterotrophs and must eat to survive. Autotrophs are of two types: photoautotrophs whose energy is derived from the sun, and chemoautotrophs which derive energy by "burning" inorganic substances. Algae, green plants, and some bacteria are photoautotrophic. Only a handful of bacterial species are chemoautotrophs but their means of obtaining energy is crucial to all agriculture.

The chemoautotrophs may, like anaerobes (anaerobic bacteria), be separated into obligate chemoautotrophs, which are limited to inorganic oxidation exclusively, and facultative autotrophs which obtain energy either from the oxidation of organic or inorganic compounds. The obligate chemoautotrophs usually eat only a small group of related compounds, such as ammonia; most are strickly aerobic, while those which can survive in the absence of free oxygen required an environment rich in oxygen-bearing compounds.

These bacteria are extremely primitive from the point of view of their nutrition—they are alive, yet meet all their needs from an inorganic environment, To do this, their biochemistry must be incredibly complex, because they have all the enzymes, vitamins, and

Chemoautotrophic Bacteria

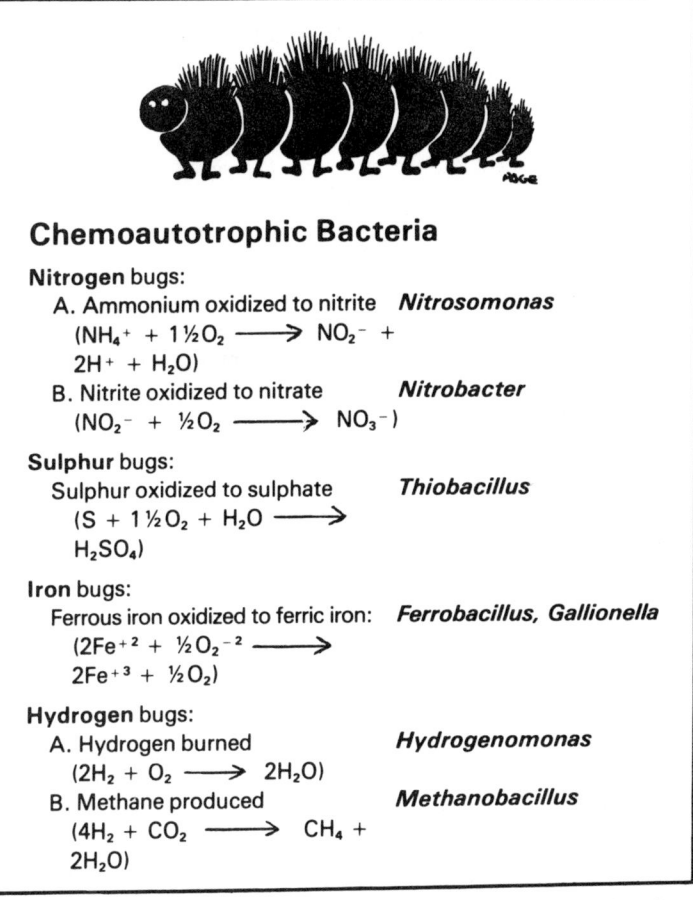

Nitrogen bugs:
  A. Ammonium oxidized to nitrite   ***Nitrosomonas***
  ($NH_4^+ + 1\frac{1}{2}O_2 \longrightarrow NO_2^- + 2H^+ + H_2O$)
  B. Nitrite oxidized to nitrate   ***Nitrobacter***
  ($NO_2^- + \frac{1}{2}O_2 \longrightarrow NO_3^-$)

Sulphur bugs:
  Sulphur oxidized to sulphate   ***Thiobacillus***
  ($S + 1\frac{1}{2}O_2 + H_2O \longrightarrow H_2SO_4$)

Iron bugs:
  Ferrous iron oxidized to ferric iron: ***Ferrobacillus, Gallionella***
  ($2Fe^{+2} + \frac{1}{2}O_2^{-2} \longrightarrow 2Fe^{+3} + \frac{1}{2}O_2$)

Hydrogen bugs:
  A. Hydrogen burned   ***Hydrogenomonas***
  ($2H_2 + O_2 \longrightarrow 2H_2O$)
  B. Methane produced   ***Methanobacillus***
  ($4H_2 + CO_2 \longrightarrow CH_4 + 2H_2O$)

Fig. 1-5. Bacteria that obtain their energy from inorganic sources and their carbon from carbon dioxide.

such that "normal" bacteria have, but they create them from the most primitive raw materials they can find. It's rather like building a working car entirely from knives, forks and spoons.

The heterotrophs can digest many different compounds, including cellulose, chitin, sugars, alcohols, hydrocarbons, and some acids; it is these bacteria which are responsible for the breakdown of organic matter in the soil, including some of the pesticides.

Probably the most important role of soil bacteria in general is as the prime movers in the nitrogen cycle. Soil organisms almost always live in an environment much richer in nitrogen than carbon, but that nitrogen is unavailable to all but a few (autotrophic) bacteria. The autotrophs are responsible for changing ammonium to nitrate, and the heterotrophs convert complex nitrogen compounds like protein to forms which the autotrophs can use. The bacteria which convert complex nitrogen to ammonia are called the ammonifiers and in large masses of nitrogen-rich matter (such as manure) or under alkaline conditions, they perform their biochemical manipulations much faster than the autotrophs, with the result that ammonia is frequently lost to the atmosphere.

Nitrogen is taken up by plants mostly as nitrate, and the process of forming nitrates in the soil is therefore extremely important. The key bacteria in the process are the chemoautotrophs, getting all their energy by oxidizing ammonium to nitrite and nitrite to nitrate. The first stage is the conversion of ammonium to nitrite, accomplished by *Nitrosomonas* bacteria, but this is not directly beneficial to plants as nitrites are poisonous.

Nitrification and Denitrification

Nitrite is usually prevented from reaching toxic levels in the soil by *Nitrobacter* bacteria which convert it to nitrate. Because of their relative populations and some biochemical considerations, nitrite is usually oxidized by *Nitrobacter* faster than *Nitroscomonas* can make it, but when large amounts of ammonium are present in an alkaline soil and the soil temperature is low, nitrite will accumulate. Thus if *Nitrobacter* activity is low (due to cold soil, soil sterilants, anhydrous ammonia, etc.) and the farmer has added lime and either ammonium nitrate or anhydrous to the soil, toxic nitrite accumulation is a real possibility.

Unfortunately, a number of other bacteria (e.g. *Pseudomonas*) and fungi use nitrate as a source of oxygen. This occurs particularly in wet soils rich in organic matter and can cause a major loss of nitrogen. Plowing and draining can improve the aeration sufficiently to halt the denitrification. Nitrates are also highly soluable and will rapidly leach through the soil profile.

The soil would be in grave trouble indeed were it not for another group of bacteria, members of the genus *Rhizobium*. The *Rhizobia* can fix nitrogen from the atmosphere when living on the roots of the legume family, and although when living on the roots of the legume family, and although they can live away from the roots of their host plants, they will gradually die off. A future article in the series will discuss nitrogen fixation in detail, but you should be aware that the relation between the *Rhizobium* and the host legume is a specific one. The strains that inhabit alfalfa could care less if there's red clover about, and vice-versa. Thus legume seed is usually mixed with the appropriate strain of bacteria before planting, and when the resulting nitrogen fixation in progressing well, a crop like red clover can add 500 kg of N per hectare annually.

There are also a number a free-living bacteria which fix nitrogen, the best known of which are the aerobic *Azobacter*. These relatively rare bacteria occur primarily in fertile, neutral to slightly acid soils and are about half as effective as *Rhizobium*. Equally good at fixing nitrogen is the anaerobic, spore-forming *Clostridium,* which even in well-aerated soils may be more abundant than *Azobacter.* The *Clostridia* are on the whole a bunch of nasty creatures, causing botulism, tetanus, overeating disease in sheep, and other fun diseases. That is another story, but it does underline that while many bacteria are beneficial, many are decidedly harmful.

Bacteria frequently live on dead material (the fancy name is saprophytes) but many live on organisms that are alive. These are called parasites. Most of the bacteria which cause plant diseases can live as parasites or saprophytes, maintaining themselves between susceptible crops by feeding on dead tissue. All the bacteria which cause plant diseases are of the cold-capsule form, and none are spherical as is the case with some animal or human diseases. The bacterial diseases of plants are legion. They cause wilts and galls; retard growth; stunt plants; deform fruits, ears or leaves; cause numerous rots and cankers; and if they don't kill the plant outright, can totally destroy its economic usefulness.

The number and variety of soil bacteria is immense, being of great benefit to the soil, and often of great harm to the plants that grow in the soil. We have in the past damaged our soil ecology in an attempt to preserve our crops, but in making a new effort to correct our past mistakes, we should remember that soil bacteria are often in direct competition with us for the crops we grow.

Many books have been written about soil microbiology. As complicated and as full of five dollar words (like chemoautotroph!) as this article has been, it only skims the highlights. It's a beautifully interwoven world beneath our feet, and the bacteria are only one of the many types of life which inhabit the soil.

SOIL FERTILITY

Once a soil test of series of soil tests has been evaluated, the real nuts and bolts of farming and soil stewardship lie ahead. The weaknesses and strengths having been recognized, it is now up to us to do something about them in a manner which is consistent both with the limits of our purse and such ecological considerations as we choose to bring into our decision. The planning of a soil fertility program can be as expensive as it is complicated, and gardeners who attempt to apply their methods to whole fields are in for several surprises.

There are nearly as many soil fertility programs as there are fields and for the sake of brevity as well as accuracy I intend to limit my discussion to soils in the humid, cool part of North America; in general central and eastern Canada and the U.S. Midwest, Northeast, and Middle Atlantic regions. Readers elsewhere are cautioned-that their situations may be different enough that specific suggestions might not be entirely accurate for them. Nonetheless, it is hoped that where the suggestions are of limited utility the model of how to go about planning a fertility program may still be a help.

How then, in general terms, does one approach the question of a soil fertility program? Depending on how you look at things there are about eight steps which can be applied to soils in almost any area.

1. Determine the major problems: If you live in the Northeast these are likely to be acidity and leaching of nutrients, but other regions are dominated by problems of drought, salinity, excess magnesium, and the like.

2. Evaluate the effect of these problems on specific nutrients: Leaching will result in chronic shortages of N, K, S and Mg; other soils have low P availability, etc.

3. Decide how to correct any nutrient deficiencies in crops: This often means fertilizer-in-a-bag for a least a few years, but it might also mean a change in the crop grown, or massive additions of a material like phosphate rock.

4. Decide how to build the soil in order to cure or lessen the major problems: In areas where drought is a problem this would include raising the organic matter level in the soil to retain more water; in areas of leaching it might mean a commitment to yearly additions of potassium and greater reliance on long-term rotations.

5. Determine the cost: Building the best soil in the world does you no good if you've gone broke doing it too quickly.

6. Decide on the compromises which must be made for financial reasons: There are few farmers who can afford to apply phosphate rock at 5 t/ha all in one go, and some high analysis fertilizer might help cushion the blow.

7. Implement the program: Don't be too hasty, and you should consult an expert or two along the way.

8. Evaluate the success of the program at regular intervals: Using soil tests is the most obvious method here, but it usually pays to have the advice of a consultant firm for fine tuning.

In this article I intend to concentrate on steps 3, 4, and 5, since they are often the most tricky, and the area in which a response of "Oh, just sock the fertilizer to it and you'll be all right" is all too common.

Assuming then that you already know the major nutrient problems on your land, or will be determining them (Fig. 1-6), let us examine a number of sources of nutrients ignoring those such as anhydrous ammonia which are devastatingly harsh or blood meal which is devastatingly expensive.

Fig. 1-6. Determine nutrient problems on your land.

Nitrogen

By far the most stable (ecologically) method of ensuring a good supply of nitrogen to crops is with the use of legumes (see *Countryside*, March 1978, p. 22). Alfalfa will add between 125 and 300 kg of N per hectare to the soil every year; the clovers between 80 and 200 kg per hectare; and vetches and peas about 80 to 150 kg per hectare per year. A number of legume crops will fix nitrogen at a profitable rate, but the one serious problem with legumes is that they are picky about the soil in which they grow. The best person to see about growing legumes in your area is your government agronomist or a private consultant.

Legumes all gain their value when grown as a green manure crop or when grazed. If the crop is cut for hay the manure must be returned in order to realize any net gains in the soil nitrogen levels. If you sell the hay off the farm the value of these crops in building the nitrogen fertility of your soil is greatly reduced.

If you live in an area where animals must be stabled for a significant portion of the year, then barnyard manure will be an important element of any nitrogen fertility program. The major choice most farmers have to make is whether to spread manure on corn or on hayland. It is certainly tempting to pile on the manure when a grain crop like corn is involved but in doing this it is easy to forget that you are stealing nitrogen from the land where the hay that produced the manure was grown. Very few mixed farms ever have enough green manure.

One tonne of fresh manure without any bedding will provide between five and 15 kg of N depending on the type of animal, cattle and swine being on the lower end of the scale. Hence we might assume that a heavy-yielding crop of grain corn (6 t/ha) would have its 100 kg/ha N requirement met by spreading 20 t/ha of cattle manure.

Not so. At least not so in most cases. Before very long most manure, given average storage treatment, has lost about half of its nitrogen. What's more, not only is storage a factor, but time and method of spreading also exert an influence on the amount of nitrogen that gets to the crop (see Table 1-2).

Be sure, before spreading manure on a particular crop, that it is needed. Once you know the rough nitrogen needs of the crop (150 kg/ha for grass; 100 kg/ha for corn; 50 kg/ha for grain) deduct first for any legume crops plowed down: 150 kg/ha for a lush stand of alfalfa, 110 kg/ha for a stand of at least 50 percent legumes, 55 kg/ha

Table 1-2. Nutrients Supplied by Manure.

Solid Manure		Liquid Manure		Nitrogen	Nutrients Supplied (kg/ha)			
tonnes/ hectare	tons/ acre	m³/ha	Imp. gal/ acre	Spr. Cov.*	Spr.	Phosphate Fall/Win.		Potash

Beef and Dairy Manure

20	9	50	4400	60	50	25	20	90
30	13	75	6700	90	75	40	30	135
40	18	100	8900	125	100	50	40	180

Pig Manure

20	9	30	2700	60	50	25	25	35
30	13	45	4000	90	75	40	35	50
40	18	60	5300	125	100	50	50	70

Poultry Manure

| 4 | 2 | 10 | 900 | 60 | 45 | 20 | 25 | 22 |
| 10 | 4 | 25 | 2200 | 140 | 110 | 50 | 60 | 44 |

*Manure applied in spring and covered immediately after application (Spr. Cov.)
Manure applied in spring and not covered immediately (Spr.)
Manure applied in fall or winter (Fall/Win.)

for a stand of 30 to 50 percent legumes, and nothing for a sparse stand of legumes.

That done, deduct the nitrogen obtained from any manure spread according to Table 1-2, or plan to spread manure to meet any deficit. If for example, on one field you plowed down a crop of red clover/timothy (50 percent legume) and intend to grown grain corn which usually yields about 6 t/ha (100 bu/acre), the corn will require 100 kg/ha N of which 55 kg/ha is provided by the red clover/timothy which was plowed down. The deficit of 45 kg/ha can be met by spreading 15 t/ha cattle manure and covering immediately. If no legume had been plowed down, 35 t/ha should have been spread to meet the nitrogen requirements of the corn. Even a lousy stand of legumes will make your manure go twice as far, and the combination of green manuring and spreading barnyard manure will have saved you $60 on just one hectare.

Still, circumstances arise when we just can't have enough manure to go around or disease has reduced a legume stand to the point where it contributes very little to the succeeding crop. The financially sensible thing to do is to purchase commercial nitrogen and add it, as a last resort, to make up the difference. Least toxic of all the sources of comemercial nitrogen are ammonium sulphate (AS) and monoammonium phosphate (MAP). Ammonium nitrate (AN) is a pretty strong oxidant and should be avoided unless you can't get anything else. If you have an acid soil MAP is preferred over AS because AS will require 110 kg of limestone to neutralize the acid formed by every 100 kg of AS. By comparison MAP requires only 65 kg of limestone. By all means, use commercial fertilizer when forced to do so by economic or other circumstances, but realize that you are paying both an economic and an ecological cost. In most instances if your crop rotations and manure use have been well planned you won't need to buy much commercial nitrogen.

Phosphate

Phosphate fertility is a growing problem. Phosphate is now at least as expensive as nitrogen, and unlike nitrogen there is no way it can be "grown." Much of the world's reserves of phosphate are in unstable parts of the world, and American reserves are the object of growing environmental controversy. To make matters worse most soils actually contain very little phosphate; what there is often being preserved by the low solubility of most phosphates.

Manure is one means of recycling phosphorus on the farm but when crop requirement of 80 kg/ha P_2O_5 easily reached the amount of manure required (upwards of 50 t/ha) isn't possible or practical. Manure should be considered primarily as a source of nitrogen, and spread as such, but the phosphate it contributes (see Table 1-2) should be taken into account. If your overall phosphorus fertility is good, then the 15 kg/ha or so obtained from manure might be adequate.

Most of us will have to face the fact, right from Day One, that we are going to have to bring phosphorus onto our farms and the planning of a fertility program hinges on the form of P to be purchased. In general, all phosphate fertilizers come from phosphate rock in one form or another; hence my concern for assured supply at a reasonable price. Straight phosphate rock is the "organic" farmer's major source of phosphate. Certainly it is useful stuff, but suffers from very low availability in any given year in spite of its 30 to 33 percent P_2O_5 content. Colloidal phosphate has a lower overall percentage of P_2O_5 (20 to 24 percent) but usually has from two to seven percent available P_2O_5 depending on soil conditions, compared to zero to four percent for phosphate rock.

To be fair, it must be noted that all phosphate fertilizer materials suffer from problems in the soil. Geochemical conditions toss phosphate availability to and fro like nobody's business, and it is conceivable that treble superphosphate may have less available P_2O_5 under certain conditions than colloidal phosphate! The chief advantage of applying high analysis phosphate fertilizer is that you pay freight on phosphate and not something else such as the clay in colloidal phosphate. Most phosphate materials, except for diammonium phosphate (DAP) have very low toxicity in the soil, so they're all more or less equal in that respect. Most phosphate materials also contain a significant amount of fluorine, and when applied to sandy, acid soils fluorine toxicity might build up with heavy applications of P. If, however, the soil pH is above 6.5 the fluorine in the soil will be mostly unavailable and present no problem.

The core of planning a phosphate fertility program lies in trying to tailor the material to your particular soil conditions. Unless you have somewhat acid soil phosphate rock is probably a waste of money if you are trying to feed plants with it. If used in conjunction with an acid forming fertilizer it becomes much more available, but most strict "organic" farmers would see no need to add ammonium sulphate to their soil! If you are going to make a compromise between "organic" and "chemical" methods I would strongly suggest monoammonium phosphate (MAP) which has more phosphorus then treble superphosphate and about 12 percent N as well; if freight costs are a consideration it can't be beaten for total nutrient content per 100 kg.

Wood ashes are a minor source of phosphate (about two percent) and because they are available only in limited quantities are usually best applied to the garden. Bone meal is another source of phosphorus (11 percent P_2O_5) but it is very expensive to purchase. If you have a large wood burning stove, bones can be burnt in it while you have a good hot fire going; not only does this get rid of your bones, but it also increases the phosphate content of the wood ash.

It is difficult to make any real recommendations regarding phosphate fertility programs other than to report my personal use of phosphate materials on a somewhat acid, sandy loam. Crops are fed phosphate with MAP, and this material at the same time creates some short term reserves which become available over a couple of years. Over the long term the soil is being built with applications of as much colloidal phosphate as I can afford. It is my intention that the "chemical" phosphate incorporated into green manures and crop residues become part of the reserves of the soil, because to a certain extent green manures allow a "chemical" plant nutrient to become an "organic" soil component.

Potash

However difficult and uncertain the whole question of phosphate fertility might be, it is offset to a large degree by the ease of supplying potassium to the soil. In the humid northeast of North American you are going to have to purchase potash regularly, probably every year. Fortunately there are immense reserves of potash in Saskatchewan and major reserves in New Brunswick and New Mexico so ample supply at a reasonable price is assured. Most of the potash that is used in "chemical" fertilizers is muriate of potash (really potassium chloride, KCl) and it is used in blends or spread alone just as it comes out of the ground. Another major source is potassium sulphate (K_2SO_4) which, while it is largely manufactured, does occur naturally. The New Mexico deposits consist of a complex potassium sulphate which also contains about 11 percent Mg; the Canadian deposits are almost entirely KCl.

As sources of potassium, both potassium sulphate and potassium chloride are about equal, contain 50 and 60 percent K_2O respectively. There is a difference, however, in that a number of people have questioned whether or not all the chlorine added to the soil with muriate of potash is really good for the soil. Since many soils in North America are deficient in sulphur it makes sense to me to use one of the sulphate sources of potassium instead of the chloride source since sulphur is a nutrient which might otherwise have to be purchased. In any case the chlorine needs of crops are easily met from rainfall and massive amounts of chlorine might even be harmful in the quantities applied. This is one area in which "natural" may not always be best, and to editorialize a bit, it demonstrates one reason why I get annoyed with people who pay too much attention to labels like "organic." We're in the business of farming, and to stay in that business not only do we have to look after our purses, but we have to look after the long-term interests of our soils. It is quite conceivable that the combination of "chemical" fertilizers MAP and potassium sulphate may be a lot better for our soils and our purses than the "organic" or "natural" combination of phosphate rock and potassium chloride as they come from the mine.

One "natural" source of potash can't be praised too highly. This is sulphate of potash magnesia, also called K-mag or Sul-Po-Mag. Soils in areas of high leaching are usually deficient in potassium, magnesium, and sulphur, all of which are provided in one convenient mineral fertilizer (22 percent K_2O, 11 percent Mg and 22 percent S). Of all the potassium salt fertilizers, sulphate of potash magnesia is the slowest to dissolve in the soil, reducing the rate of leaching considerably compared to muriate of potash. It is not an inexpensive fertilizer, but for what it provides it is not overpriced.

Another good source of potassium, provided you don't have to haul it any distances, is wood ash, containing five to nine percent K_2). It's not worth buying, but if it would otherwise go to waste, use it, by all means. A number of "organic" farmers apply granite meal as a source of potassium (one to eight percent potassium, mostly unavailable), but this source is getting to be quite expensive. Simply mining a rock like granite costs about $20/ton and to mill it to 100 mesh is not at all cheap. As a source of available potash it is a waste of money compared to the sulphates. The one major advantage of granite meal is that it is so slowly available. In areas of high leaching, it is an excellent method of building the long term potash reserves of the soil. Whether or not you choose to do that is your decision, but if you wish to purchase a granite meal, you should get "syenite" meal (like granite but with much less quartz) if you can.

Organic Matter

Much has been written about the importance of building organic matter in the soil, so I shan't repeat that information here. It should be noted, however, that many "organic" farmers, especially beginners, make the mistake of believing that all the nutrient needs of crops and soil can be met by adding organic matter alone. A sound soil fertility program includes both mineral and organic fertilizers. While there is no doubt that organic matter is crucially important it is sometimes overemphasized at the expense of mineral (and maybe even "chemical") fertilizers. If properly cared for, manures and green manures are an excellent source of nitrogen and organic matter. The other major and minor elements that they contain should be considered a bonus.

I hope that you have been able to realize that two central strains are running through this article. First, planning a soil fertility program is a very personal thing, depending on the specific needs of crops, soil and the farmer. Second, it is a very complex thing, requiring the services of laboratories and either government or private consultants in many cases.

To survive financially you must be flexible. Your farm should be fairly diverse and include a number of different animals and crops with varying nutrient needs. Above all this variety allows for a flexibility in planning soil fertility programs because it gives you a broad base from which to work when price or supply problems throw your plans out of whack. Not only does this flexibility make economic and ecological sense, it's what keeps farming interesting and fun.

FARMING ACID SOILS

By reducing crop yields in many areas of North America, soil acidity has become a relatively serious agricultural problem. While most severe in the eastern half of the continent it is also a serious problem in the colder areas such as Alaska, the Prairie Provinces, and the Rocky Mountains, which all share the problems usually associated with the East. These problems are wide-ranging and important.

   1) There is straightforward damage to delicate plant tissues by acids, resulting in an insufficient root network.
   2) There is little available phosphorus, since under acid conditions phosphorus is fixed in rather insoluble minerals.
   3) There is little available calcium or magnesium.

4) The potassium requirements of the crop are greatly increased because of the shortage of calcium and magnesium.

5) The rate of production of organic matter is low, and organic matter levels in the soil decrease, resulting in poor soil structure.

6) Organic matter present in the soil decomposes very slowly, resulting in an overly large C:N ratio, a decrease in soil life, and slow release of many tract elements.

7) Toxic levels of aluminum and manganese can build up.

8) The chemical availability of molybdenum is reduced.

9) Populations of nitrogen-fixing bacteria are low.

There's going to be a lot of variation from one acid soil to another as far as which problems are the dominant ones, but one soil from Quebec is pretty typical. With a pH of 4.8 it is strongly acid, but not unusually so. In spite of having more than seven percent organic matter the development of humus is poor. Available levels of all nutrients are very low, and the cation exchange material is a disaster. Of the cation exchange sites, 58 percent are occupied by hydrogen, 35 percent by aluminum and iron, and only seven percent are occupied by calcium and other nutrients. Normally, about 65 percent of the sites as occupied by calcium and another 20 percent by the various nutrients.

It is little wonder, then, that such soils produce very poorly, if at all. This problem is often made worse by the fact that "chemical" fertilizers will increase the activity of the soil even further. If we insist on destroying our prime agricultural land, either by paving it over or by ruining the soil, we shall have to rely on increasingly marginal soils (like the one above) to produce our mainstream food supply. Having farmed such soils myself, the prospect doesn't please me a bit. In addition, many *Countryside* readers find themselves trying to cope with an acid soil for the simple reason that marginal lands were the only ones available at an affordable price.

If money was in short supply to purchase the land in the first place, it isn't likely that there will be a lot floating around to spend at a rate of several hundred dollars a hectare for limestone. Farming with the land becomes a consummate skill in this situation, and an understanding of the acid tolerance of various crops is the most important aspect of this skill (see Fig. 1-7A).

If you want any yield at all, forget about alfalfa and sweet clover if your soil pH is under 6.0 (see Fig. 1-7B). Between pH 5.5 and pH 6.0 a number of crops such as barley, wheat, rape, clovers, trefoil, corn, beans and carrots will grown, but their yields will not be as

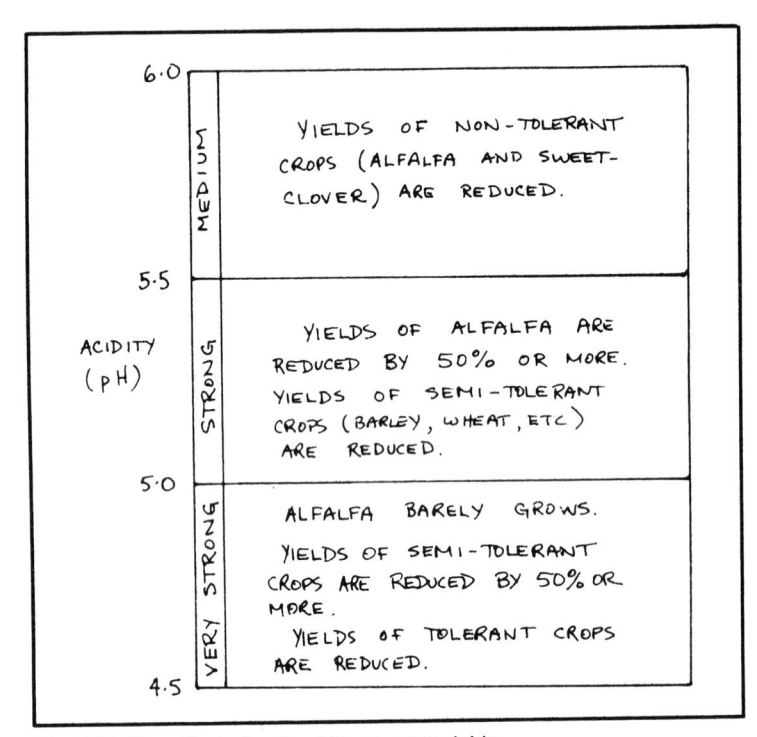

Fig. 1-7A. The effect of soil acidity on crop yields.

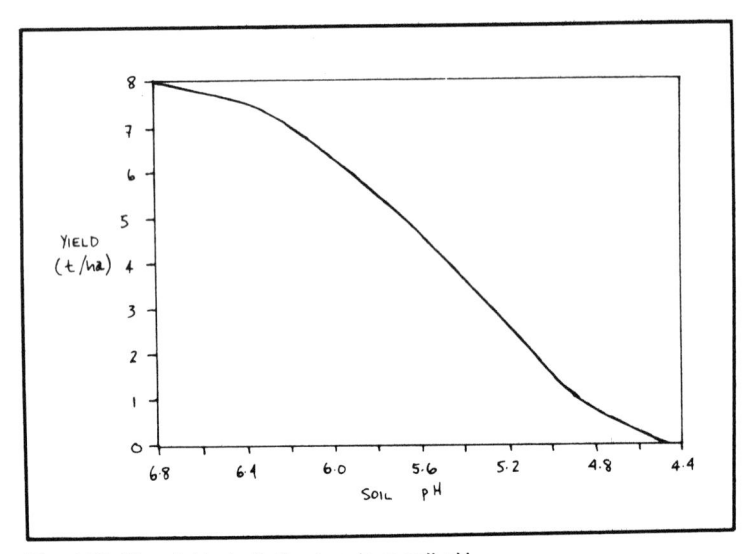

Fig. 1-7B. The yield of alfalfa at various soil pH.

high as they would have been had the crops been grown on more nearly neutral soil. There are also crops which tolerate strongly acid soils, amongst them oats, timothy, brome, lespedeza, wheatgrass, ryegrass, reed, fescue, potatoes, and blueberries. If you can afford no lime, grow these acid tolerant crops. Potatoes especially, do better below pH 5.5 because the potato scab organism is rare in such acid soils. Blueberries can be a good cash crop, but they tend to be labor intensive.

Lime is Essential

By far the most preferable method of dealing with acid soils is to lime them. Liming is a broad term for adding materials (Fig. 1-8), usually ground limestone, to the soil in order to replace some of the hydrogen on the exchange sites and to react chemically to neutralize some of the acid present. The effectiveness of a liming material depends on its neutralizing value (compared to calcium carbonate) and on the fineness of the grind. On the whole, the finer the grind of the limestone the more quickly it can be absorbed to neutralize the acid in the soil, but if limestone is too finely ground it's quite difficult to spread. As a general rule it should be between 0.1 mm and 1.0 mm with a large percentage of the material in the 0.25 mm (60 mesh) range, a size which gives both speed of neutralization and east of handling. It is important as well to mix the lime thoroughly with the top 10 to 15 cm of soil so that most of the plow layer will be involved with the neutralizing reaction.

At a given soil pH the need for lime varies, as we have seen, from crop to crop. With crops like alfalfa there is not only an intolerance of low pH conditions, but there is a great requirement for calcium in the nutrition of the crop. Below pH 5.5 the yields of crops such as the cereals are reduced, but this reduction is due not so much to deficiencies of calcium as to toxic levels of soluble aluminum which build up under acid conditions. The level of soluble aluminum will often increase as the pH decreases, but depending on a number of soil conditions a soil at pH 5.3 can have 1 ppm soluble aluminum or it can have 8.0 ppm or more. Figure 1-9 shows the effect of increasing levels of soluble aluminum on barley yields.

The need for lime also depends a great deal of the type of soil involved. The reasons for this are fairly complex, but as an approximation of what is involved we can say that as the cation exchange capacity increases the amount of lime needed to neutralize a soil at a given pH also increases. In a practical sense this means that sandy soils need a lot less lime at a given pH than clayey soils, or

Fig. 1-8. Lime is heavy stuff; this truckload weighs 20 tons.

soils with high organic matter, need at the same pH. For this reason many soils labs will determine the lime requirement directly, but it is also done by a knowledge of the type of soil involved. Figure 1-10 expresses this in the form of a graph, but please remember that soils do not falls into clear categories; the numbers on the graph are approximations.

Several substances can be used to decrease the acidity of a soil, and your choice should depend on what's available locally more than

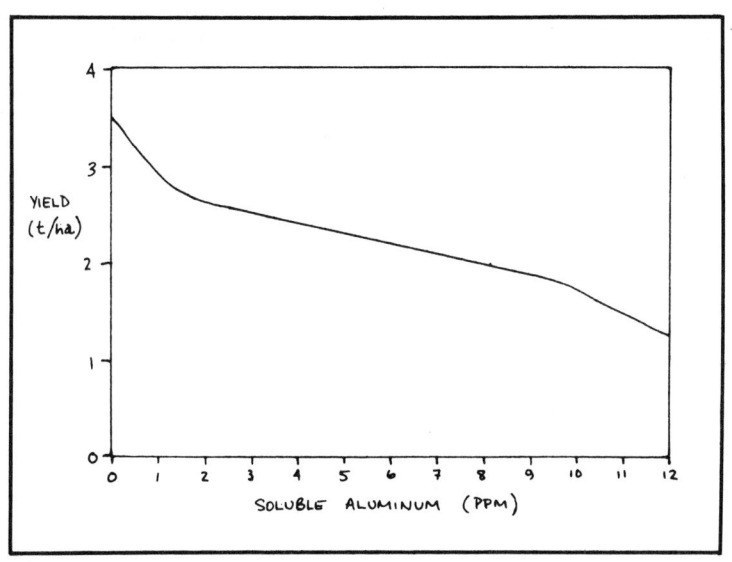

Fig. 1-9. The yield of barley at various aluminum concentrations.

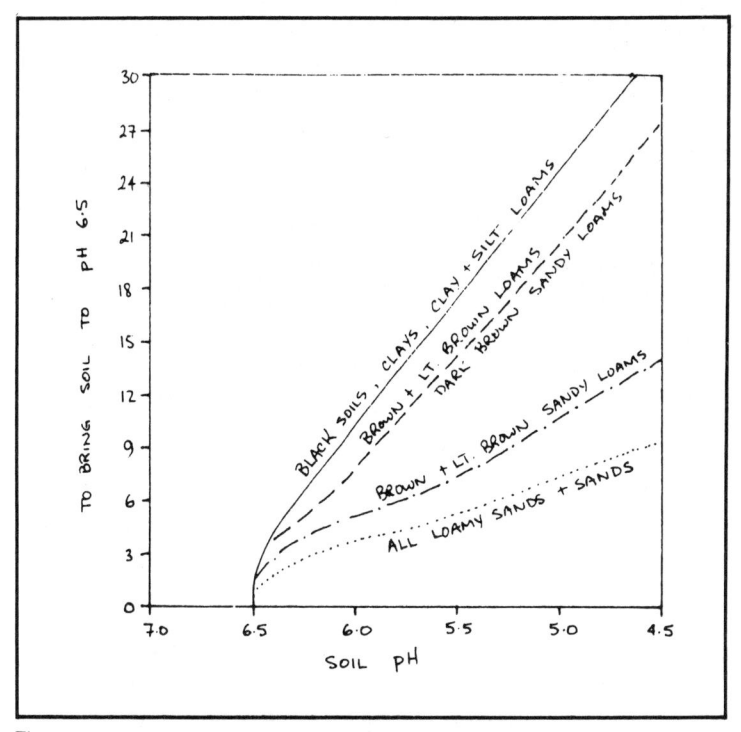

Fig. 1-10. Neutralizing soil acidity of different soil types.

anything else. Transportation will push the price of limestone ($3/tonne at the pit) up very rapidly to $40 or $50 per tonne, and unless you live in a jurisdiction which has a lime transport subsidy the cost of a "better" material from far away will almost always be a lot greater than that of a "poor" local material. One exception is in cases of magnesium deficiency, where it is advisable to buy dolomitic lime to provide magnesium. The neutralizing values of some common liming materials are listed below:

Ground limestone (reference material)	100%
Superfine limestone	125%
Hydrated lime (not recommended)	200%
Dolomitic limestone	105%
Basic slag	90%
Marl	79%
Wood ash	50%

From this we can see, for example, that it takes twice as much wood ash to neutralize a particular soil as it takes ground agricultural lime. On the other hand, wood ash contains plant nutrients to the extent that its NPK value is about 0-2-6. However, since over 90 percent of the neutralizing material used here in Canada is either calcitic or dolomitic limestone, I think that the choice of most farmers is rather clear.

Spreading Lime

The techniques for spreading lime will vary with the material being used, the amount to be spread, and the fineness of the grind. Since it is so important that lime be well mixed with the plow layer of the soil, large quantities of lime (say over about four t/ha) shoud be spread by split application. Half should be spread before plowing, then plowed and disced in, and the other half should then be spread and disced in. It is also possible, depending on the crop grown and cultural practices to split the application between two years. On extremely acid soils, requiring many tonnes of lime, this system has the decided advantage of evening out the cash flow from year to year, especially when the entire application is not needed for the crop to be grown in the first year. It is usually necessary to have a special lime spreader because the rates of application of lime are much greater than those of today's high analysis fertilizers. Modern fertilizer spreaders usually can't put out the lime at a fast enough rate to be practical. For large areas the broadcast spreaders mounted on the back of trucks or drawn behind tractors are much more practical and easily hold several tonnes.

Much Lime Is Lost

After having gone to all the expense and trouble of liming the soil it would be a shame to lose a great deal of the lime applied, yet by erosion of topsoil this occurs at an alarming rate in many parts of North America. This is inexcusable waste, and entirely preventable by soil conservation techniques well known even 30 years ago.

Nonetheless, there will be leaching losses on the order of 250 kg/ha per year in the humid Northeast, and somewhat more in the Southeast. Since the calcium is leached downward in the soil profile the leaching is not a total loss as it serves to neutralize the lower horizons and is not out of the root zones of the deeper rooting crops like alfalfa. Crops like alfalfa contain a great deal of calcium in the harvested portion, and this is also removed from the soil. Thus total losses by leaching and crop removal will be about 400 to 500 kg/ha per year in the Northeast, and you should figure on reliming about every eight to 10 years with something like two tonnes per hectare.

Areas with high rainfall, or with soil that doesn't freeze in winter, or both, will have much higher loss rates. Since you should have your soil tested every three to five years in any case you'll be able to evaluate your success in raising soil pH and get a good idea as to whether you'll have to reliming in the near future.

Lime Has Two Functions

Bear in mind that liming performs two functions in the soil, neutralizing the acid, and providing calcium (and in some cases magnesium) to the crops. Both are important but it is easy for many people, having discovered the considerable importance of calcium and magnesium as plant nutrients, to underemphasize the importance of neutralizing the acid in the soil. After the problems of erosion of topsoil and lack of organic matter (which tend to be related to each other) the problem of acid soils is the most important one facet in large areas of our continent. It is the easiest of the three problems to solve, however, and if done with action and a concern for the overall balance of the soil, liming will contribute in the well being of the soil and of all concerned.

MANGANESE, IRON, AND COBALT

Between calcium (20 protons) and zinc (30 protons), lie a group of metals called the Transition Elements. They are so called because they lie as a transition between calcium and zinc which form similar ions and which are chemically very much alike.

You may never have heard of some of these elements, but some are household words, or nearly so, for they form the metallic basis of our industrial technology; scandium (21), titanium (22), vanadium (23), chromium (24), manganese (25), iron (26), cobalt (27), nickel (28), copper (29), zinc (30). Of all these, we know that manganese, iron, cobalt, copper and zinc are essential micronutrients. Nobody can agree on whether chromium is toxic or useful, and if scandium, titanium, vanadium and nickel are of any value in the soil, nobody has been able to figure it out yet.

Manganese (Mn)

Manganese is a fascinating element. While most of the elements will form one or two different ions, manganese forms five ($Mn^{+2, +3, +4, +6, +7}$), not counting complex ions like permanganate (MNO_4^{-1}). With this many different ions of manganese running around, the study of manganese in the soil could be quite hairy. Fortunately (for us, not the plants), Mn^{+2} is the only available form.

Overall, the amount of manganese in the soil is quite variable, between 200 ppm and 5000 ppm on the average. In extreme cases, however, it can be as low as a few ppm or as high as a few percent. In spite of the variability in ions formed or amount present in the soil, the great simplicity of manganese soil chemistry arises from some very complex chemical considerations which dictate that under acid conditions manganese is present as the available Mn^{-2} ion. In neural to alkaline conditions the various other ions will exist and are generally unavailable to plants.

It's just about like throwing a switch—above pH 7.0 manganese can easily be deficient, below pH 7.0 manganese will be adequate, all other considerations being equal. The contacts on our imaginary switch are a bit cruddy, though, so it doesn't always work at pH 7.0, and you sometimes have to jiggle it a bit to get it to turn on or off. In my own garden, for example, the pH of the topsoil is more or less neutral, and I can see where the tiller dug deep and brought up some alkaline subsoil—the lettuce and kidney beans are having a rough go of it.

The chief biochemical role of manganese is in the formation of chlorophyll, which it accomplishes in partnership with iron. Another important function, which is a direct result of all the different ions of manganese which may exist, is the control of ion formation by other elements. Because manganese can provide up to seven electrons per atom (remember, that is what Mn^{+7} means—that it has seven fewer electrons than it should) it serves as an electrical buffer (shock absorber) and prevents other ions, chiefly iron, from losing too many electrons to oxygen. Oxygen is the chemical equivalent of Sesame Street's Cookie Monster, and the tendency to grab every electron in sight must be controlled for iron to perform its function in chlorophyll formation. These chemical systems aren't particularly simple, but we can summarize what goes on by saying that manganese, vitamin C (another oxygen controlling chemical), iron, and a couple of other substances all function together to make sure that the conditions are just right for iron to form good healthy chlorophyll.

Because manganese deficiency screws up the formation of chlorophyll, the most obvious symptom is pale green to yellowish leaves. This symptom is a common one—it can result from nitrogen, sulphur, iron or molybdenum problems, or from a hot, dry spring. In the case of manganese deficiency it is noticed on the younger leaves first. It also tends to be a bit more noticeable in the parts of the leaves between the veins, and the clincher (not always present) is a series of small dark spots parallel to the veins.

While the relation of manganese availability to pH would lead us to expect manganese deficiency problems west of the Lime Line in the alkaline soils there, it's more common in the humid regions of the East. See Fig. 1-11. In fact, a deficiency is nearly always observed sooner or later on wetlands which has been drained and put into crop production. What happens is that there is a great flow of water through these soils, and manganese is readily leached in its soluble form, Mn^{+2}. East of the Lime Line, soils are generally acid (producing the highly soluble Mn^{+2}) and there is a great deal of rain, leaching the manganese.

On drained lands this can turn out to be doubly bad, as many drainage systems become quite clogged with manganese scales and nodules (the same type as are found on the ocean floor). Thus the crops don't get the manganese they want, and the manganese is down there clogging up your $4,000 tile drainage system. The people selling tile drainage don't usually tell you that. If you can't cope with wet areas on your farm, I'd suggest using a system called "le labour Richard" ("labour" is the French word for plow)—a series of parallel ditches about 20 meters apart. It makes working the fields a bit trickier, but it is inexpensive and doesn't lead to the problem of no manganese where you want it and too much where you don't.

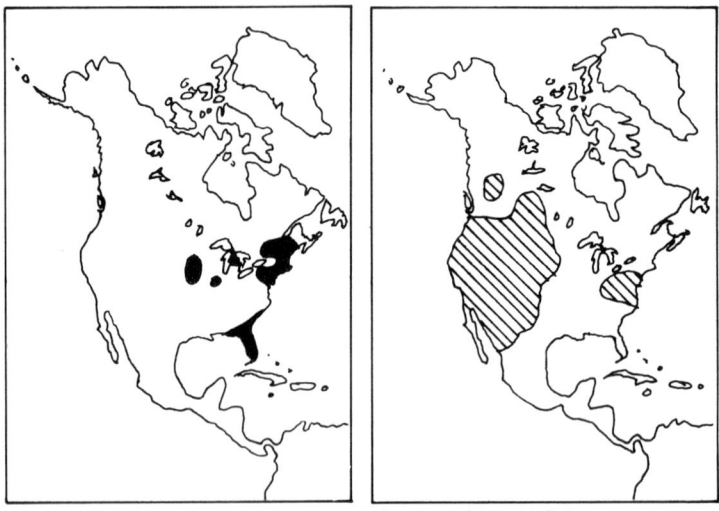

Fig. 1-11. Areas of cobalt deficiency, and areas of iron deficiency.

So to a certain extent, manganese deficiency in eastern Canada and the northeastern U.S. is a problem of cultural practices more than of simple geography. In some lands which remain undrained manganese toxicity, not deficiency, is the problem. Soils with a pH below about 5.5, especially poorly drained ones, are the most subject to this toxicity. It's humorous, in a sad sort of way, to see some of these very soils badly deficient in manganese after they have been drained (leaching), and limed (converting manganese to unavailable forms).

Nature has solved this problem more or less adequately by giving plants which prefer acid soils a fairly high manganese requirement, and by giving plants which feel more at home in neutral to alkaline soils a fairly low need for manganese. Some alkali loving plants even have a limited ability to use forms of manganese other than Mn^{+2}. These generalities don't hold true for crop plants, but for the most part, grasses, large-seeded legumes and fruits have fairly high manganese requirements. Most of the manganese problems in the West are with fruit crops. There are three notable exceptions: corn, rye and blueberries (that acid-loving crop!) have low manganese requirements.

Aside from the crop's requirements for manganese, the pH of the soil, soil drainage, and such, a few other things can induce a manganese deficiency. Because high light intensity makes chlorophyll function more efficiently, it also lowers the plant's need for manganese. One the other side, long cloudy periods can induce temporary manganese deficiency in plants, as the plants make more and more chlorophyll in a struggle to maintain their food production at adequate levels. Dry or cold weather can also induce a deficiency.

If your manganese deficiency is a result of poor soil conditions (very high or low pH, leaching, etc.) there is little that you can do about it other than feed the plant at first (four kg/ha manganese as $MnSO_4$, foliar spray) while you are moderately correcting the original soil problem. Manures tend to acidify an alkaline soil, and they contain between 10 ppm and 50 ppm Mn on an as-is basis. One hundred tonnes (100,000 kg) of pig manure per hectare will add two ppm manganese to the soil. On a garden scale this works out to ten kilos per square meter. The slow acidification of the soil, however, may be the biggest help. Unless the deficiency was induced by the weather, in which case it will go away, you will have to make the choice between feeding the plants for a while or accepting lower yields for a few years.

Iron (Fe)

Iron is the most abundant of the heavy metals in the soil. Normally it comprises between 0.02 percent to 10 percent (200 ppm to 100,000 ppm) of the soil, but in tropical areas it can be much higher since most of the other elements are leached out. It isn't known yet which forms of iron are available to plants, but most of it either isn't available or the plants don't want it. No test for available iron exists, but iron is so abundant in most soils that we're familiar with that it doesn't make a lot of difference.

Many minerals contain iron, and it is one of the seven elements present in most minerals. Iron forms only two ions, Fe^{+2} and Fe^{+3}, but then, manganese is a pretty hard act to follow. The first ion is called "ferrous" iron, and the second is called "ferric" iron. These "ous" and "ic" endings are common in chemistry and an "ous" ion always has more electrons than an "ic" ion of the same element. Cuprous copper is Cu^{+1}, and cupric copper is Cu^{+2}. Ferrous iron is common where oxygen is slightly limited, such as in the acid soils of the cool, humid regions.

Iron is absolutely critical for all green plants, since it is the key component in photosynthesis. Without iron, there would be no green plants. It is involved with a number of proteins, enzymes, and carriers, but these roles are less spectacular. Recent research also suggests that iron plays a key role in nucleic acid metabolism.

Since the biochemical role of iron is so critical to the plant it becomes very easy to detect iron deficiency in plants. The plant basically stops making chlorophyll, and without chlorophyll it isn't green. With mild deficiencies, the leaf is generally pale with no particular pattern to the paleness. A moderate deficiency will lead to a yellowing between the veins of the leaf. If the leaf turns entirely yellow, or even worse, white, the deficiency is severe. These iron problems are collectively called "chlorosis" or "iron chlorosis," and the plant is in some big trouble. It is always the young, growing parts of the plant which are affected, and in severe cases the growing point of the plant dies quite quickly.

As a general rule, where soil is alkaline or calcareous (calcareous is the two dollar word for "limey") iron deficiency can be a problem. Since roughly one-third of the earth's land is calcareous, it can be an extensive problem. It is a particular problem of arid regions, but can exist in high-lime regions of eastern North America as well. This geographic determination of iron deficiency isn't too important by itself.

Any number of conditions will induce iron deficiency. Several crops, particularly grasses (including grains), legumes, and small fruits, have high iron requirements. Where soils are locally very wet, or compacted, plants can become short of iron. Low organic matter in acid, sandy soils can create shortages of iron. Our old friend, high soil phosphorus, causes shortages of iron as well as of copper and zinc. Extremes of temperature can cause a temporary deficiency as well.

Since iron deficiency is so easy to diagnose (all plants show the same symptoms) you'll know if you have it, and then you can pinpoint the source of the trouble. Some problems, such as those of trying to grow blueberries in an alkaline soil, suggest an obvious solution: don't grow them. But with grains and legumes often requiring more iron than certain soils have to give, one must look at amendments.

Ferrous sulphate is a good inorganic source of iron for soils, containing about 20 percent iron. It can also be used as a foliar spray to feed the plant. Since organic matter holds iron in what seems to be an available form, manure is the best suited substance for the iron problems of an acid soil. Manure applied to alkaline soils will only make the problem worse. Fifty tonnes of straight manure per hectare will boost soil iron by 20 ppm, much of it available. For you gardeners, that works out to five kg/square meter.

Cobalt (Co)

Cobalt deficiency in North America has been a problem of animals rather than of plants, but legume crops in Australia and elsewhere have responded well to cobalt amendments. Ever since the seventeeth century it has been noted in eastern North America that ruminants often did very poorly on the native grass. About 40 years ago it was discovered in Australia that the same sort of "wasting" in animals was caused by a cobalt deficiency in the forages eaten. Since that time, most farm animals have received their cobalt from salt licks (the blue ones) or from rumen boluses. Very little has been done with the cobalt problem in soil since cobalt amendments have seemed to have little effect and it has been so easy to treat the animals to prevent the deficiency.

In plants, cobalt occurs almost exclusively in a coenzyme called cobamide. The legume root nodule bacteria (*Rhizobia*) require very small amounts of cobalt for the fixation of nitrogen. Except in extreme cases, such as the Australian case, these bacteria can get all the cobalt they need from the soil, even if there is as little as 0.5 ppm cobalt present.

Cobalt in soils is almost always complexed to the fulvic acid fraction of the organic matter. If there are at least five ppm cobalt in the soil, forage crops grown on that soil will contain enough cobalt for the rumen bacteria to continue making vitamin B_{12} (cobalamin). As a general rule, coarser soils have a much greater tendency to be deficient in cobalt than do silty soils, but the overriding factor is geography.

Soils of the Coastal Plain in the U.S. Southeast have considerably less than one part per million cobalt. In the U.S. Northeast and eastern Canada, cobalt is also deficient in the soil, though not as much so. In the Northeast, soils derived from the White Mountain Granite are particularly deficient in cobalt, containing less than three ppm. By comparison, soils with more than five ppm cobalt will grow plants containing enough cobalt to keep the ruminants which eat them from becoming deficient.

At present, there doesn't appear to be any relationship between cobalt-poor soils and deficiencies in monogastric farm animals (pigs and chickens, etc.) or omnivorous humans. I don't know of any research done on cobalt and vegetarian diets, but monogastrics, including us, get their cobalt from animal products or mineral supplements. It doesn't matter a bit what your soil is like—deficient in cobalt or not, the plants grown on it are not significant sources of cobalt.

Cobalt is an element you don't have to worry about. There are no plant deficiencies in North America. Cobalt-poor soils affect ruminants, but not monogastrics, and in ruminants it's easy to prevent deficiency.

The most fascinating aspect of cobalt in the soil was the rather recent discovery of its essential nature. What don't we know about titanium, vanadium, nickel, and a score of other elements? It might be 10 years, or forever, until another essential soil nutrient is discovered. There are a lot of people who still think of the soil only in terms of NPK, but it is only a small step from there to thinking of the trace elements as individual components of the soil. We must recognize that we know bloody little about how the soil works as an ecological subsystem, and dealing with its components in isolation only magnifies our ignorance in the long term. A knowledge of soil chemistry is a tool, and a very useful one, but we have to know and understand the "machine" which we are trying to keep working efficiently.

SELENIUM AND THE TOXIC HEAVY METALS

Up to this point, we have dealt with trace elements and soil chemistry from the point of view of the plant, but with this article we take a detour in which the soil is only one of many components. I've tried to point out all along that we can't deal with any element or subsystem in isolation, and this is especially true in the case of lead, cadmium and mercury. A lot of ink has been spilt on account of these toxic heavy metals, and while I can't solve the controversy, and won't add to it, I hope that by viewing the soil as one component of the total ecosystem I can clarify some things for farmers and gardeners.

There is a technical difference between pollution and contamination, but usually the words are used almost interchangeably. Contamination is a broader term than pollution, and I shall use it in the broadest sense possible.

Our real concern about heavy metal contamination of our ecosystem is focused on animals, and especially on people, since the plants don't seem to mind the heavy metals and they can be devastating in people. Thus your plants aren't going to be waving any flags to tell you something is amiss, and it falls upon you to learn to recognize potentially troublesome situations.

For a start, we can look at an element, selenium, which occurs as a natural contaminant and causes problems, either by its presence or absence over most of North America.

Selenium (Se)

Selenium is a classic example of "too much of a good thing" being deadly. It is a required micronutrient of most animals but levels only a few times higher than those required for well-being are toxic. Selenium (34 protons) is very similar in chemistry to sulphur, and the dual problems of selenium toxicity and selenium deficiency are related almost exclusively to geography. (See Fig. 1-12.)

The level of selenium in the soil depends upon the parent rock from which the soil was derived, and in central North America there are a family of shales which are noted for their high selenium values. These rocks were formed in the Cretaceous era (60 to 125 million years ago), and if your county soil report shows your soil as having been derived from the Pierre shale, the Morrison shale, or the

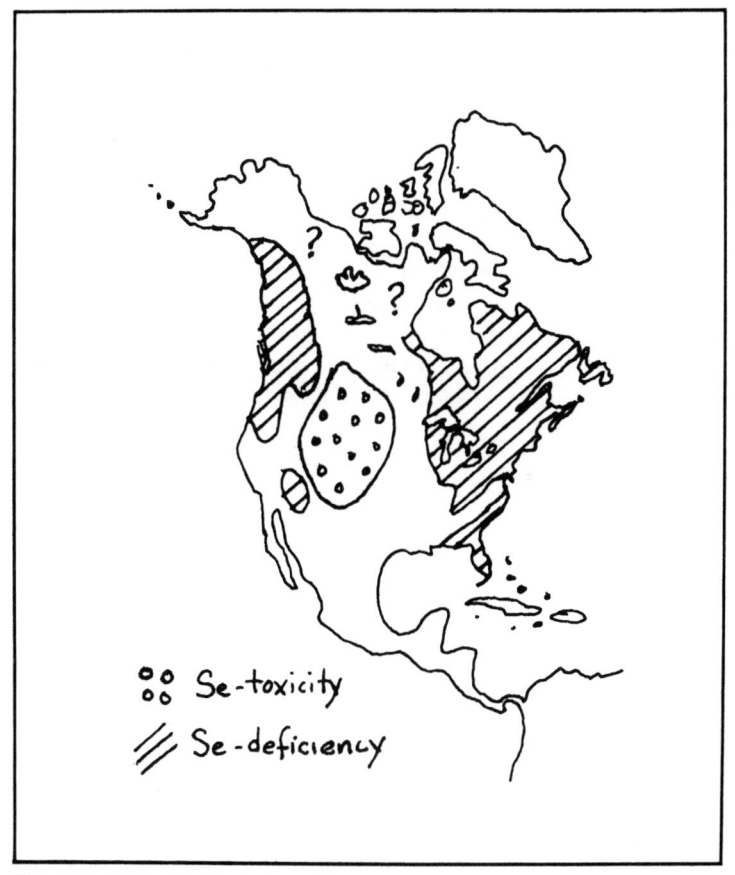

Fig. 1-12. Areas of selenium problems.

Niobrara shale, then your livestock may have trouble with selenium poisoning.

These rock formations are not uniformly rich in selenium, however, so having soil derived from them is no guarantee of selenium toxicity problems. Similarly, only certain plants, which tend to accumulate selenium up to about 60 ppm are highly toxic, but forage crops growing in the same area will contain enough selenium (five to 10 ppm) to cause some toxicity.

All the soils with selenium toxicity problems are neutral to alkaline soils, and high selenium, but acid, soils in Hawaii and Puerto Rico have not produced high levels of selenium in plants. It appears that soils containing free lime ($CaCO_3$) or gypsum ($CaSO_4$) comprise an environment which favors the selenate ion (SeO_4^{-2}), a soluble and available form. Acid soils, on the other hand, seem to favor the formation of the selenite ion (SeO_3^{-2}) which forms insoluble complexes with ferric iron.

It was just 20 years ago that it was discovered that selenium was required in animal diets at levels around 0.1 ppm to prevent a group of economically important nutritional diseases. Chief amongst these diseases was white muscle disease, common in lambs and calves, and it became clear that the crops grown across vast areas of the continent had woefully inadequate levels of selenium to meet the needs of livestock. The parent material, and hence the soil, simply didn't have enough selenium. Parts per billion, not parts per million, are the order of the day.

To correct this problem with soil amendments would require more selenium than is produced, so the deficiency in animals is corrected by a supplement given directly to livestock. Selenium is approved as a feed additive for monogastrics in Canada, and for both ruminants and monogastics in the U.S. Injections of vitamin E plus selenium are very common in both countries as a supplement for lambs and calves. It has been shown that animals can store selenium for a long time and that vitamin E can reduce an animal's need for selenium about 10 times. It is a very effective and long-lasting combination, often given at docking or dehorning time.

The question of dietary selenium for humans is really quite open. It has been suggested that unduly low levels of selenium in the diet increase the risk of certain forms of heart disease and blood cancer, but this has not been proven. To a certain extent, our varied diet, coming from all over the continent, evens things out, but the question becomes more important to people who raise most or all of their own food. What has yet to be known about selenium would fill a large book. For now, an awareness of geography and its effect on livestock is enough.

Lead (Pb)

Aside from the small amounts naturally present, lead comes to be present in the soil from the air, from precipitation, and from ground dust blown in from elsewhere. These unintentional sources of contamination are augmented by lead from pesticides and fertilizers such as superphosphate. Lead arsenate was a pesticide common in the 1950s and is seeing greater use again since the ban on DDT.

By way of comparison to some figures which I shall cite to explain the problem of lead, lead in soils should average about 20 ppm. Some rock formations produce soils with lead contents several times higher than that, so in all fairness, not all lead in the soil is a contaminant from our industrial society.

Still, in the case of soils near roadsides the evidence is pretty damning. Natural deposits of lead contain several different varieties (isotopes) of lead in a proportion which is unique to that deposit. A great many studies have shown that the lead in roadside soils has the same isotopic composition as that used in gasolines. And the quantity of lead added is tremendous.

Freeway studies have shown that 200 meters from the highway soil lead is increasing by 0.3 ppm per year in the plow layer. At 100 meters, the increase is 0.5 ppm per year, and at 15 meters the increase is 2.0 ppm per year! On a moderately busy state or provincial highway (one car each way every 25 seconds) the figures are about 10 percent of what they are for the freeway, but that is still a fair bit of lead.

Lead from freshly burned gasoline is usually associated with chlorine (or similar elements) and is highly soluble. Along a roadside this can be taken up by plants either through the roots or the leaves, and once inside the plant it tends to remain in the chlorophyll-containing sites, or in the cell walls. Studies in which airborne lead was not a factor have shown that when grown in a high-lead medium plants will increase the amount of lead stored in them only slightly. So the real problem here is airborne lead, before it even gets to the soil.

In general, the lead contents of plants decrease as distance from traffic increases. Of greater concern is the fact that plant tissues when analyzed do not give an accurate picture of the lead problem. Washing tomatoes grown in a high airborne lead environment removed 80 percent of the lead. Washing alfalfa removed better than half the lead, but I can't picture too many people washing their hay, pasture, and haylage before their stock eat it. Thus airborne lead may be of limited consequence to us if we wash vegetables grown near highways, but forage crops are another question. The price you and your stock pay for the "free" hay along the highway could be a high price indeed.

What I'm going to say about lead and humans applies, of course, to your stock, but it's better to start as close to home as possible and you can move from there to your stock. We get our lead either by breathing it of by eating it, and it readily enters the blood. The bones, liver and kidneys will concentrate lead, but we carry about 90 percent of our lead burden in our bones. This is because lead has a similar chemical behavior to calcium, both in charge and ion size, and our bones are mostly apatite (calcium phosphate).

Under conditions prevalent in the late 1960s our lead intake is divided as follows: 300 micrograms (a microgram is one one-millionth of a gram, 0.000001 g) from solid food, 20 micrograms from liquids, and 10 to 150 or more micrograms inhaled. This level of total lead intake has not changed significantly since the 1930s—a typical example of the complexity of the human ecology of environmental contamination.

The increase in airborne lead has been tremendous, but simultaneously we have done away with lead plumbing, lead pewter, leaded solder in food tins, and we have reduced the use of lead-based pesticides. Similarly, studies from 1931 to 1967 have shown no increase in blood or urine levels of lead, in spite of the great level of environmental contamination. In fact, lead levels in bones were higher at the height of the Roman Empire than they are now; mind you, the Romans managed to poison themselves by the use of lead utensils, but the point should not be overlooked.

In my opinion these data reflect more on the fact that our bodies can cope with a daily lead intake of 600 micrograms than on any improvements to our environment. Certainly we have not cause for complacency. Because of atmospheric mixing there is startling uniformity of blood levels all over the world, and from rural to moderately urban areas. As long as our bodies' excretion mechanisms can cope with the intake, the blood levels, etc. should remain fairly constant. Present overall environmental lead levels are not putting too great a strain on the excretion capacities of our bodies, but we're a bit closer than I'd like.

For the immediate future, then, the hazard from lead comes not from overall environmental levels, but from localized and specific situations. The high levels of lead inhaled by workers such as parking attendants is probably not of immediate concern to the readers of *Countryside*, but people who care about their animals and themselves should think twice about that "free" hay.

Also consider that if you eat the lettuce from one square meter of garden (not drastically much for a real salad freak) 30 meters away from that moderately busy highway we talked about earlier you could be adding an extra 100 micrograms to your body's daily lead burden. That starts to get uncomfortably close to your body's ability to dump lead via the urine.

A good deal of the airborne lead does end up in the soil. Lead levels in the soil of southern California have trebled in the last 40 years. To be optimistic, liming the soil will make a lot of lead unavailable to plants, and having the lead end up in the soil gets it out of the air where it is certainly more immediately dangerous. To be pessimistic, we are getting a lot more lead into our soil than in the past. Once it's there it's hard to get rid of, and in conditions of phosphorus shortage lead can completely discombobulate plant metabolism. Even though we can "disarm" lead to a certain extent, the stuff does get into crop plants where it screws up several enzyme systems, particularly those which involve manganese and zinc. In the presence of significant quantities of lead the nitrogen-fixing bacteria will go on strike and the plant's whole protein metabolism is screwed up. The plants don't die or anything, but their yields get knocked for six. You don't have anything to go on to figure out what's wrong, just a bunch of plants that aren't yielding well.

This question of lead in the environment is immensely complex and the soil is only one part of it. I personally believe that people should not farm land near busy highways (or for that matter build busy highways through prime farmland!). Garden crops should be well washed to get rid of the lead on (but not in) them, and you shouldn't feed your animals hay from near highways. Beyond that, I have no answers.

We leave this discussion of lead with a paradox which typifies our frustrations and confusions as we stand in the threshold between two different sorts of worlds. There has been a tendency in recent years towards the use of unleaded gasolines. Even if reduction of environmental contamination was not the intention of that move, that has been one result. But while decreasing lead contamination noticeably, such gasolines have resulted in a threefold increase in the levels of certain cancer-causing aromatic compounds, and some increase in the amount of cadmium released to the environment.

Cadmium (Cd)

Cadmium is extremely sneaky stuff. It tends to accummulate in the bodies of mammals over the years, and this long-term but low level accumulation can cause all sorts of problems. These read like a catalog of modern ills: high blood pressure, heart disease, anemia, digestive disorders, respiratory disorders, and more. I'm not implying that cadmium is the cause of all our ills—just that it can result in a serious deterioration of health without being particularly noticeable. What's worse, cadmium readily enters plants, and thus the body of anything that eats those plants, as well.

Cadmium is present as a contaminant in rock phosphate and superphosphate fertilizers. It is a component of fungicides and worming preparations, and the manure of animals on a heavy worming program can be loaded with cadmium. Along roadsides (here we go again) cadmium contamination can be heavy because the metal is common in motor oils and tires, and it is an additive in some gasolines. Zinc metal contains quite a bit of cadmium, generally around 500 ppm in "purified" zinc. The zinc used in galvanizing iron has even more. Tremendous amounts of cadmium are released into the air by lead and zinc smelters, and this eventually ends up in the soil. Even paper contains cadmium, because cadmium readily enters trees. Burning paper, or using a paper mulch is probably adding cadmium to your soil, but wood ash contains very little cadmium since it vaporized and went up the flue.

Once in the soil, cadmium is quickly taken up by plants. The cereal grains, peas, beets, and lettuce are the crops which absorb cadmium the most quickly. As with lead, there is also the problem of aerial deposits—cadmium-rich dust on lettuce leaves, for example, is in addition to what the plant has taken up so readily from the soil. Plants seem to prefer cadmium to zinc (which it closely resembles), so cadmium in plants can be present in greater amounts than in the soil in which the plant was grown.

Normally, soils contain about 0.2 ppm cadmium. Locally it can be much higher. In one western state, the population of an entire valley was told that they must not have vegetable gardens because of cadmium fallout from the local smelter. Along roadsides, both the soil and the crops grown on it can have high levels of cadmium.

Fortunately, all is not bleak. Liming the soil seems to make cadmium much less available by precipitating it as a carbonate, phosphate or sulphate. The calcium in lime seems to be favored by plants over cadmium, and will be taken up instead of cadmium.

A couple of final points about cadmium. When cows eat cadmium contaminated grass or hay (such as that from near a highway) their milk will probably contain about 30 micrograms of cadmium per liter. By comparison, the average North American daily diet contains about 60 micrograms, more in the West, less in the East. Contaminated milk could be enough to cause some real problems.

Secondly, cigarettes are a major source of cadmium intake, both for the smoker, and for those unfortunate enough to be around a smoker.

The fact that cadmium is present in rocks formed long before mankind crawled down out of the trees indicates that it has been with us for a long time. Mammals can cope with a light cadmium burden, but we must do what we can to avoid increasing that burden. Pollution control, proper care of our soil, avoiding highway-contaminated feed, and avoiding cigaret smoke will never remove cadmium from the total ecosystem, but it can make a difference for the subsystems over which we do have a certain measure of control: our bodies, our livestock, and our land.

Mercury (Hg)

Given the right conditions, mercury is more deadly than lead. Methyl mercury (CH_3Hg^+) and dimethyl mercury (($CH_3)_2Hg$) have been responsible for the poisoning of many people in places as diverse as Minamata, Japan (an industrial city), Grassy Narrows, Ontario (an Indian Reserve), and 19th century hat factories all over the world (the mercury used in making felt for hats caused severe brain damage, hence the expression "Mad as a hatter"). It is certainly stuff that we should avoid, but this is nearly impossible, and mercury pollution has been a highly controversial subject in recent years.

Annual worldwide production of mercury amounts to about 7000 tonnes (7 million kilograms), of which one-third gets into the environment by careless or intentional dumping. It is this industrial contamination, especially when concentrated, which has caused all the fuss. This is rightly so, in my opinion, because it is preventable, but to put the mercury problem in its proper perspective, 15 times as much mercury gets into the environment from natural evaporation as from human action. Another 2000 or 3000 tonnes is released by burning coal, a figure which is bound to increase as the energy-consuming economies reconvert to coal. The fact that 50-year-old laboratory specimen fishes contain more mercury than those presently being caught is attributed directly to the use of coal in the 19th century industrial economies. In short, it is impossible to avoid mercury.

Where we luck out is that it is only methyl mercury and its cousins which are extremely dangerous. This has been a particular problem where anaerobic methylating bacteria are present and act on industrial mercury contaminants. The sediments of lakes and oceans are ideal for this, but so, I imagine, would be a methane generator using manure from animals on a heavy worming program. These methylated forms are easily absorbed and concentrated upward in the food chain. By the time it gets to the top of the food chain (eagles, humans, etc.) it can do a lot of damage. Since these methylating beasties are anaerobes (oxygen kills them) they are lacking in well aerated conditions and mercury remains in a number of less dangerous forms.

With land plants there are two unusual paths for mercury to enter the food cycle. Mercury in the air or dust may be absorbed by the leaves (as with lead and cadmium), or mercury in the soil may be taken up by the root system. In past years, but fortunately not much anymore, mercury based pesticides were in common use, especially as a seed treatment. It was common a decade ago to find high levels of mercury in eggs because the mercury used in seed treatment had found its way into the grain which ripened that fall and was fed to the hens.

With the banning of mercury pesticides in many countries, the main concern of small farmers should focus on mercury in the soil. Organic farmers strive towards a well-aerated soil, exactly what is needed to terminate the methylation of any mercury which might be present. Waterlogged soils are often anaerobic, just what the methylating beasties require to get up shop, and should be avoided if possible. High levels of organic matter in the soil will tie up the mercury so that it is not available to plants. Keeping the soil pH at about 6.5 caused insoluble mercury to precipitate as a carbonate or hydroxide.

In short, maintaining, well-aerated, slightly acid soil, high in organic matter will be pretty effective in keeping the effects of both natural and industrial contamination by mercury to a minimum. It's just one more reason why the methods of organic farming make sense.

THE "SECONDARY" NUTRIENTS

Many people who have for years been caught up in the NPK mentality, that is, thinking of soil fertility only in terms of the three primary nutrients (nitrogen, phosphorus, potassium) are gradually becoming aware of a new family of soil nutrients.

Indeed, the "secondary" nutrients are every bit as important to healthy plants as the "primary" nutrients but the quantities required are low enough that magnesium, calcium, and sulphur have received secondary emphasis. Magnesium and calcium are both cations with a charge of plus two and either 12 or 20 protons, respectively, in the nucleus; they are in many ways quite similar to each other. Sulphur, on the other hand is an anion—charge minus two—with sixteen protons in the nucleus.

Magnesium (Mg)

Right smack dab in the center of the chlorophyll molecule is a magnesium atom, and that atom is therefore crucial to the ability of a plant to capture solar energy in a form that can be stored and used later. Gross levels of magnesium in soils vary from 0.05 percent to 1.4 percent, but as usual, much of that is tied up in the structure of various minerals, so available magnesium is much less, say between 5.0 ppm and 3,000 ppm (0.3 percent). Nearly all the magnesium that is not tied up in mineral structures is held as exchangeable cations on clays and organic matter.

Aside from its crucial role in photosynthesis, magnesium concentrates in the seeds of plants; in fact, as a plant matures it will snitch magnesium from its leaves so that the seeds will be well supplied. This is important, because when magnesium is deficient in the seed its germination is greatly retarded. There are also a number of amino acids which contain magnesium. As in the case with all of the common cations (Na^+, Mg^{+2}, K^+, Ca^{+2}) the plant uses magnesium to balance internal acidity which results from normal metabolic processes.

The efficiency of a plant's uptake of phosphorus is also improved when adequate amounts of magnesium are present. At that, I'd be surprised if we understood half of what magnesium does in a plant. This kind of research is extremely time consuming and often requires machinery worth hundreds of thousands of dollars, so the money and research people just aren't around to find out. I'm not so sure that's all bad, because we do have a general picture of what's going on in the plant (certainly enough for you or me) and I'd rather have research moneys going into more immediately useful and beneficial things like biological control.

At this stage we do realize that there is a problem with

magnesium in agriculture. It is a very easily leached cation, and deficiency is very widespread (see Fig. 1-13). Areas with acid soil are often deficient, sometimes very severely so. A similar problem exists for sandy and coarse soils especially those which are high in potassium or which have had heavy applications of commercial nitrogen. Thus while within the magnesium-deficient regions there may be pockets of soil with adequate levels, so may there be soils which have hardly any magnesium at all. The frequent use of commercial fertilizers hasn't helped a bit because they will acidify a soil, and the limestone used as a filler usually contains no magnesium.

Magnesium Depression

High rates of nitrogen fertilizers, especially ammonium fertilizers, will depress the magnesium level in plant tissue regardless of soil conditions. The ammonium ion is much worse than nitrate for causing this problem. In the spring magnesium depression may occur naturally, particularly in eastern North America. If the weather has been cool, the *Nitrosomonas* go on strike and stop converting the ammonium ion to other forms, with the result that enough ammonium builds up to cause magnesium depression in the plants. When your animals are on this grass for an early bite it can cause a condition called "grass tetany" (acute hypomagnesemia) in which

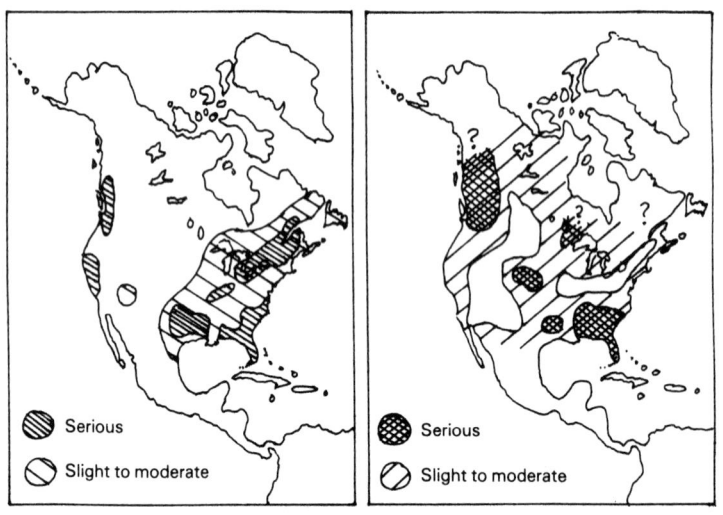

Fig. 1-13. Areas of magnesium deficiency, and areas of sulphur deficiency.

the livestock's body fluids become so poor in magnesium that the animal is paralyzed and will quickly die unless given some magnesium.

Magnesium is deficient in your soil if less than 50 ppm are present. This should be considered a minimum level, because other factors are involved. Since magnesium and calcium are very similar cations there exists between them a certain amount of competition, and if the balance between magnesium and calcium gets too far out of whack then your soil may be deficient with far more than 50 ppm. While there is no ideal Ca:Mg ratio something between 3:1 and 15:1 seems to be about right. A wide Ca:Mg ratio is asking for trouble (say over 15:1) and soils are known in the East which are over 150:1—on the calcareous soils of the West it can be even worse.

Deficiency symptoms are found on the lower leaves of the plant since the plant "borrows" magnesium for the growing portion. Lower leaves either die or turn a reddish or yellowish orange, usually around the edges and between the veins. In maize it can be confused with zinc deficiency, so the advice of your agricultural representative or county agent is a big help.

Whether or not you agree with some of the biases of most government agronomists, they're paid to help you and are often a lot more help than some general comments in a book. You don't have to follow their advice, but by all means get their opinion, especially on something like nutrient deficiency in plants.

The overall magnesium fertility of a soil is largely in the hands of the farmer. You can't do anything about geography, but once you realize that you're in a magnesium problem area it's fairly easy to stay ahead of things. First, the odds are good that you have a pH problem as well. Avoid pure calcium soil sweeteners such as marl, pure limestone, paper mill sludge, and sugar beet pulp.

Always use dolomitic limestone to correct pH (see Table 1-3) or add sulphate or potash magnesia ($K_2SO_4 2MgSO_4$)—"Sul-Po-Mag" is a common trade name for this natural mineral—as an amendment. You should increase the organic matter in the soil, as this will hold magnesium against really serious leaching. Be aware of what is removed by the crops you are growing (see Table 1-4). If you sell a load of wheat off the farm, you're selling magnesium as well even if you plow down all residue, and you had better plan to replace it. The same goes if you cut hay, feed it to cows, and ship milk. In short, a farmer following a good crop rotation probably should worry more about magnesium than nitrogen.

Table 1-3. Fertilizer Nutrient Content.

Material	Approx. NPK	Mg	Ca	S
Activated Sludge	(6-2-0)	1.8	0.9	0.4
Basic slag	(0-5-0)	3.4	32.0	0.2
Blood meal	(13-0-0)	0.4	trace	trace
Bonemeal, steamed	(2-11-0)	0.3	24.1	0.2
Gypsum	(0-0-0)	trace	22.4	18.6
Limestone, dolomitic	(0-0-0)	12.0	21.0	—
Limestone, pure	(0-0-0)	trace	40.0	trace
Manure,† beef	(0.7-0.5-0.6)	0.1	0.1	0.1
Manure, dairy	(0.5-0.3-0.5)	0.1	0.2	0.1
Manure, pig	(0.5-0.3-0.5)	0.1	0.6	0.1
Manure, poultry	(1.3-1.3-0.6)	0.3	1.8	0.2
Manure, sheep & goat	(1.4-0.5-1.2)	0.2	0.6	0.1
Monoammonium phosphate	(12-50-0)	0.3	1.4	2.6
Peat	(3-0-0)	0.3	0.7	1.0
Phosphate rock	(0-6-0)	0.1	33.1	trace
Potassium sulphate	(0-0-50)	trace	trace	18.0
Sulphate of potash magnesia	(0-0-22)	11.0	trace	22.0
Tankage	(7-10-0)	0.3	10.9	0.4
Wood ash	(0-2-5)	0.2	14.0	trace

†fresh manure, as it comes from the animal: urine, feces, but no bedding.

Table 1-4. Nutrient Removal.

Removal by harvested* portion of crop (kg/ha)

Crop	Yield (t/ha)	Mg	Ca	S
Alfalfa	9	22	130	22
Barley	3	6	11	6
Cabbage	45	9	22	35
Clover	6	19	80	12
Grasses	10	28	40	30
Maize (Corn)	6	5	47	11
Oats	2	9	7	9
Peanuts	1	22	85	22
Potatoes	9	17	55	20
Soybeans	2	10	8	8
Wheat	2	13	11	11

*This is not the requirement of the crop, but what is removed when a crop is harvested and the residue returned to the soil.

In summary, the conditions which should cause concern for soil magnesium levels are:

Acid soils (pH under 5.5)
Coarse or sandy soils
High rainfall
High natural levels of Na or K
Heavy N or K fertilization
Use of common chemical fertilizers

Calcium (Ca)

The function of calcium in plants is low key but crucial. While it may not be readily apparent whether or not the plant has enough calcium to meet its needs, a shortage will seriously hurt the overall health and productivity of the plant. For example, the accumulation of Ca^{+2} at the root surface changes the rates of precipitation and absorption of the other ions in the region; this can be a crucial important to the plant when certain nutrients are in short supply because it helps the plant to alter its surroundings in a manner that allows it to obtain the maximum amount of the deficient nutrient.

Calcium also protects plant tissues against the loss of soluble cell nutrients at low pH and against acid damage to root tips and other fine structures. The absorption of cations at low pH is stimulated by calcium, though this is not applicable to all cations; calcium will stimulate potassium uptake, but is known not to block the harmful effects of an acid environment on magnesium uptake.

There are few reported cases of calcium deficiency because most acid soils are limed adding calcium or because fertilizers such as superphosphate contain a lot of calcium. Potatoes are often deficient when grown in soils below pH 4.0, as are flax and spinach when grown on certain calcium poor soils in Australia.

In Illinois heavily nitrogen-fertilized maize on acid soil is also deficient. Crops such as alfalfa which have a heavy need for calcium (see Table 1-4) may not be deficient, but their yields and persistence are often improved by the addition of calcium. There are no particular deficiency symptoms (cell walls are weak and roots do not grow) in plants, so in a practical sense calcium deficiency in plants is no more than a curiosity item unless something is desperately out of line.

However, the importance of calcium to the health of the soil is not related so much to the plant directly as it is to the overall status of cation exchange. Relatively large amounts of calcium are present in the soil, even if it is rather acid, with the calcium being divided among the soil solution, primary minerals such as calcite, and the exchange sites on clays and organic matter.

As calcium is released from the primary minerals and goes into the soil solution it is picked up and held in exchangeable form by clay minerals and organic matter. The amount of exchangeable calcium varies from 0.03 is very acid sandy soils to about 1.0 percent in neutral, dark clay soils. Not all exchangeable calcium is available since in acid soils hydrogen may be too competitive and in alkaline soils sodium and potassium may be too competitive.

In humid regions, Al^{+3} and H^+ are the major exchangeable cations along with calcium. There exists an equilibrium of soil solution and exchangeable (on clays and organic matter) forms, and as the activity of calcium in the soil solution decreases as a resul of leaching or crop removal the exchangeable reserves of calcium are depleted. Because of this, even soils formed from a limestone parent material may be highly acid and calcium deficient in the plow layer. However, if the levels of calcium in the soil solution are greatly increased the exchangeable reserves are increased.

Know Your CEC

All of the soil solution calcium and most of the exchangeable calcium is available; with calcium there are no "fixed" or non-available forms, except in any minerals present, and these are gradually dissolved and made available. The availability of calcium to the soil solution (and thus the plant) is controlled by several factors: the amount of calcium present on exchangeable materials (clays, organic matter, etc.), the type of exchange materials, the degree of exchange complex saturation, and other ions present on the exchange material.

Thus, the total amount of calcium in the exchange complex is not as important as the amount of calcium present in relation to other cations. A soil which tests 1,000 kg/ha exchangeable calcium but with a total low cation exchange capacity (CEC) may supply more calcium to plants than one with 5,000 kg/ha and a very high CEC. A measurement of total calcium is meaningless until you know your CEC.

If you're handy and already have a small lab on your farm CEC is fairly easy to determine, but most of us will have to have a government or private soil testing service do it for us, so I'll try to explain the meaning of the data output. First, CEC is expressed in milli-equivalents per 100 g of soil. A milli-equivalent (meq) takes the charges of different cations into account and puts them all on an equal basis; an exchange site which will hold two aluminum ions (Al^{+3}) will hold three calcium ions (Ca^{+2}) or six hydrogen ions (H^+). Since the exchangeable cations are extracted from the soil and then measured you want to be able to describe the soil's potential and not its present state (although that is possible, and even useful).

The number you have for the CEC on a given sample of soil can tell you a lot about the makeup of the exchange complex, but you have to come in through the back door. In addition to organic matter there are two broad families of clays called the 1:1 clays and the 2:1 clays, referring to their structure. The 2:1 clays are a "sandwich" with one slice of a certain type of clay material bound between two slices of a different material; the 1:1 clays are similar to an open-faced sandwich. The 1:1 clays characteristically have a CEC of 10 to 20 meq/100 g. The 2:1 clays usually show a CEC of 40 to 80 meq/100 g, and organic matter often has a CEC in excess of 100 meq/100 g.

If your soil test shows a CEC of 15 meq/100 g then you are pretty safe in assuming that the soil contains mostly 1:1 clays in the exchange complex. A test of 120 meq/100 g would indicate a lot of organic matter in the exchange complex. However, a test value of 50 meq/100 g could indicate either a predominance of 2:1 clays, or a mixture of organic matter and 1:1 clays or a mixture of all three!

Common Sense and Scientists

At this point common sense has to take over or you will become a slave to numbers and technology. If you know that you've got a lot of organic matter in the soil (and you ought to) then it makes sense to figure that all the organic matter is going to distort the nice neat scientific pigeonholes a bit. It is quite possible, but expensive and time-consuming, to get a detailed breakdown of the ratio of 1:1, 2:1, and organic matter in the exchange complex, and unless you've got a serious problem it's almost certainly a waste of time and money.

The nature of the materials in the exchange complex is important, however, because (to return to our discussion of calcium) the 2:1 clays must be 70 percent saturated with calcium before they will release any calcium to plants at a rate fast enough to be of use to the plant. Organic matter and the 1:1 clays require only a 50 percent saturation to do the same thing.

This is where your government labs and all the high-powered scientists can be useful. The need for lime on a soil is not only a question of acidity, but of calcium saturation of the exchange complex. If you're willing to pay for it you can find out what the cation exchange capacity of your soil is, and how much of it is occupied by calcium. This is of greatest use to you if, for example, you are trying to meet Dr. Tiedjens' goal of 85 percent calcium saturation.

But, to return the discussion to a much more practical level, the pH of a soil will usually reflect the amount of calcium present on the exchange complex. This is entirely coincidental since pH measures the degree of hydrogen ion saturation, not calcium, but in more of North America calcium and hydrogen are the only cations on the exchange complex in any quantity. As a result, the government liming recommendations will usually correct not only an acid soil but any potential calcium shortage. Unless you have a good reason to get involved with the details of cation exchange capacity I wouldn't bother with it, but I wanted to include it not only for those readers who might need it someday, but also as an example of the complexities of our soil.

The mineral gypsum ($CaSO_4 \cdot nH_2O$) is a good source of calcium in the West, where the pH often should not be increased. On non-acid soils sodium and potassium are often on the exchange complex in some quantity. In these situations, the pH of your soil is of no value whatever in determining calcium requirements and you should find out what is the calcium saturation of the exchange complex.

Sulphur (S)

Although soil sulphur is derived from sulphides and sulphates most of it is tied up in the organic matter, or adsorbed to clays. In humid regions nearly all soil sulphur is found in the organic form (amino acids, etc.), but in arid regions the sulphate form (SO_4^{-2}) dominates either as sulphate salts or complexed onto the 1:1 clays in exchangeable form. Plant roots absorb sulphur almost exclusively as sulphate, and it is the concentration of that ion in the soil which is important to plants.

Sulphur is required for nitrogen fixation by the *Rhizobia,* but grasses are better able to absorb sulphate than legumes with the result that unless sulphur fertility is maintained the grass will crowd out the legumes in a forage mixture. In the plant, sulphur is often found in the amino acids methionine and cystine, or in compounds known as mustard oil glycosides which provide the flavor in onions and the Cruciferae (cabbage family).

There are no sharply defined symptoms of sulphur deficiency. Plants usually turn pale but do not die, developing short thin woody stems. The Cruciferae often display a reddish tinge on the leaves. A tissue analysis is the best way to discover if sulphur is deficient in the plant. In spite of the difficulty in determining sulphur deficiency, crop responses to sulphur additions were noted in Switzerland as early as the late 18th century.

Much sulphur is added to the soil by rainfall as a result of atmospheric contamination, ranging as high as 100 kg/ha annually near industrial areas and as low as 2.0 kg/ha annually in rural parts. The recent drive to clean up the air has led to a reduction in the sulphur content of fuels so I suspect that these figures (1968) are higher than at present. However, about two-thirds of all the sulphur in the air comes from hot springs and volcanoes. Since the EPA hasn't yet required stack gas scrubbers on volcanoes the rural figure of 2.0 kg/ha is probably consistent from year to year.

The close relation to sulphur to organic matter suggests that the N:S sulphur ratio holds fairly constant between 7:1 and 10:1. this N:S ratio is important since if it becomes too wide (say 15:1) most of the sulphur in the soil becomes tied up in living organisms. This is the same sort of problem as develops when you add a high-carbon substance, like sawdust, to the soil—the microbes breaking it down tie up all the available nitrogen in their bodies. Similarly, if the C:S ratio is too much wider than the usual 100:1 the sulphur will also be tied up by microorganisms. The reverse is also true; if sulphur is added to a soil with a low N:S ratio the nitrogen will be tied up in living creatures. Ideally, the C:N:S ratio of your soil should be about 100:8:1.

Distortion in Tests

In dry soils sulphur is mineralized to sulphate. When a soil is tested this becomes quite important because tested soils are air dried, often for long periods of time. Soils labs test for sulphate (the available form) and may determine that adequate sulphur is present in the dry soil. Since drying a soil increases the sulphate to about 120 percent of its "real" value the soil test results may tell you that no sulphur is needed when in fact it is.

Deficiency of sulphur is widespread (see Fig. 1-13) so most people will need to add sulphur to their soil. A number of common fertilizer materials contain some sulphur, and there's always that 2.0 kg/ha you can count on from the sky, but it will probably come down to adding gypsum, sulphate of potash magnesia, or basic slag to your soil (see Table 1-3). Any source of sulphate sulphur is equal to any other as far as both the plants and the soil are concerned, so your only consideration has to be the cost per kilogram of sulphur. Some convenient sources, such as "Sul-Po-Mag" are very expensive (over $200 tonne) but may be worth the extra cost. The best advice I can give for sulphur fertility is to assume that your soil is deficient but to remember the N:S ratio when you are correcting the deficiency.

Aside from standard "organic" farming practices you needn't worry about trace minerals unless a plant deficiency is evident. With magnesium and sulphur the opposite is true. Both elements are easily leached from the soil and seriously deficient over large portions of North America. Your soil should be tested for these low elements at least as often as every three years, and materials such as gypsum, sulphate of potash magnesia and dolomitic limestone should be regularly added in addition to manure and green manure.

MIGHTY MICROORGANISMS

Aside from bacteria, a number of other microscopic creatures inhabit the soil: fungi, actinomycetes, algae, viruses, and protozoa all form part of the delicate network of life in the soil. They are all very different sorts of organisms, so let's look at each one in its turn.

Fungi

Fungi are essential plants in the soil ecology. Although there are only about 1 million fungi per gram of soil, they constitute about 0.2 percent of the mass of the plow layer. By weight, this is about double the mass of the bacteria which are 1,000-fold more numerous.

About 700 different fungi have been isolated from soil and researchers have certainly missed some, but we can say that 10 percent account for most soil fungi: *Penicillium, Fusarium, Mucor, Aspergillus, Achyla, Mortierella, Pythium, Chaetomium, Saprolegnia,* and *Monosporium.*

Because fungi contain no chlorophyll, they must obtain their carbon for cell functions from pre-existing organic molecules. Fortunately, fungi as a group are not at all picky about what they digest, though some strains are fairly specific about what they "prefer" to digest. Of particular interest is the fact that many fungi digest lignin. Lignin is a component of wood and old grasses, etc. which is almost totally immune to bacterial digestion, and in digesting this wood fungi play a very important role, especially in forest soil ecology. Other items in the fungal diet run the gamut from simple sugars to fats, pectin, and proteins.

Fungi are often classified on the basis of their principal foods:

sugar fungi, lignin fungi, dung fungi, root fungi, and predatory fungi. See Fig. 1-14.

The idea of predatory fungi is enough to give most people the heebie-jeebies, bringing to mind some sort of super athlete's foot, or worse. Their prey, however, is limited to amoebae, nematodes, and some other small soil animals. A filament from the fungus simply skewers an amoebae or strangles a nematode, keeping the animal from escaping, and the fungus then digests the victim as needed.

Functioning in the soil as decomposers of simple and complex organic compounds, fungi accomplish biochemical transformations which are at least as important as those resulting from bacterial action. Fungi, being adapted to a wider range of soil conditions than bacteria, also become extremely important in the restoration of abused or marginal land. Many fungi can grow at pH 3.0 and pH 9.0. In particular, fungi are important decomposers in the acid soils of the northeastern U.S. and much of Canada.

Soil fungi are quite temperature dependent, thriving at generally cooler temperatures (5 to 20° C.) than bacteria (25 to 35° C.) with the result that within a given soil profile the warmth-loving fungi (*Aspergillus,* etc.) will be at a deeper level. Fungal populations will

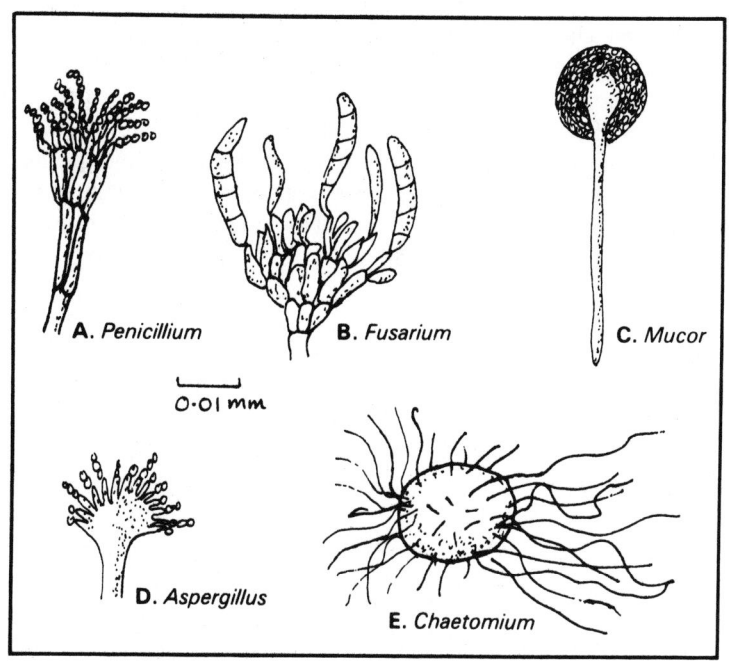

Fig. 1-14. Common fungi.

also be displaced relative to the soil profile to shallower or deeper levels as you move north or south, respectively. Similarly, the population levels at a given point in the soil profile will change with the seasons.

When fungus spores germinate, they will grow only a little unless the germ tube penetrates a source of food, be it a piece of wood or a plant root. When the food involved happens to be a living plant some interesting results ensue.

If the fungus is a pathogenic fungus (disease-causing) the host plant is in some kind of trouble if it is the right kind of plant for the fungus, and the fungus is in trouble if it is not. Root diseases are often quite costly, and damping-off is one of the most notorious, killing thousands of young seedlings.

In some cases, being invaded by a fungus turns out to be of great benefit to the plant when the fungus establishes a symbiotic relationship with the plant. The fungus uses its network of filaments to provide the plant with minerals (especially phosphorus) and the plant in return provides B vitamins and some energy to the fungus.

The growth of fungi is rather complex and varied, which is why it has been left to last. Soil fungi are of many types ranging from one-celled fungi to mushrooms with their large and complex fruiting bodies. One characteristic common to the growth of many fungi is the development of a dense network of fine filaments, or hyphae (pronounced high-fee), which is the plant's food supply network. In one gram of soil, there are about 100 meters of fungal hyphae.

Fungi also produce a wide variety of spores, and some species produce more than one type of spore. Asexual spores seem to function as one of several means of dispersal for the fungus. These spores will survive more adverse conditions than the hyphae and will germinate when conditions are once again appropriate for growth. Sexual spores are a means for creating new genetic material and this allows the fungi to adapt, to an extent, to changing conditions. These spores are borne on fruiting bodies, which are highly varied organs for the production of great quantities of spores which generate when conditions are just right. Most soil fungi produce a fruiting body of some sort (see Fig. 1-14), but usually not as prominent as those of mushrooms. Even the yeasts (which are fungi) produce spores, but they reproduce by budding and don't grow a fruiting body.

Actinomycetes

Until fairly recently, the actinomycetes were regarded as fungi because of their general appearance and the growth of a network of hyphae. About 20 years ago it was decided that these plants were closer to bacteria than to fungus. This decision was based on the similarities of internal structure and the chemistry of their cell walls (fungal cell walls contain chitin and/or cellulose; bacterial cell walls do not).

Highly variable plants, actinomycetes are presently classified more or less on form, and there are four such families. Most from colonies consisting of a mass of branching filaments, some growing into the food source and some growing into the air. Many colonies have an earthy smell derived from acetic acid, ethyl alcohol, isobutyl alcohol, acetaldehyde, isobumyl acetate, and a bit of hydrogen sulfide thrown in for good measure. This gives healthy soil most of its odor.

The chemistry of their food is nearly as strange. In addition to the usual sources of carbon (sugars, starches, etc.) some actinomycetes digest oils, fats, pesticides, or even steroids, benzene, and cyanide. For a source of nitrogen, salts of ammonia are preferred and nitrates are acceptable. Some species use nitrites and carbomates, but give a choice, actinomycetes will pull apart proteins for nitrogen. One particular genus of actinomycetes has the ability to digest keratin, and as a consequence can break down hoof and horn material. Others can use oxalic acid as a source of carbon and thus detoxify the residues of such plants as spinach and rhubarb. Still others decompose the chitin in the skeletons of insects.

Thus transforming a wide variety of carbon compounds to humic acid, actinomycetes play an indispensible role in the carbon cycle. This is true not only in soils, but in manure piles and compost where higher temperatures are involved. In fact, when they die, many actinomycetes dissolve into a substance greatly resembling humic acid. On the whole, they are good plants to have in the soil or in one's composting toilet in spite of the fact that a few cause diseases such as potato scab.

One product of actinomycetes is generally well known—antibiotics. Many species of *Streptomyces* form medically and industrially important compounds in large amounts when reared under optimal conditions. Many, such as streptomycin, neomycin, and aureomycin are produced on a large scale and have made life easier for us and our livestock. Much of the vitamin B_{12} used as a feed additive is also produced by these plants. In the soil, the amounts of vitamins and antibiotics produced are quite small, having only a local action, but the antibiotics are often used effectively as a sort of chemical warfare against predatory bacteria.

Algae

Even though they are ubiquitous in soils, algae are not terribly important to the overall soil ecology. They are interesting, however, in that unlike all the other soil organisms they can use sunlight to photosynthesize their own food. Since they need sunlight they are found only in the top few centimeters of soil, and plowing can mean death to billions of algae. Rain water and earthworms also carry algae down into the soil, and many algae have a limited ability to return to the surface if not buried too deeply.

Like most other soil microbes, algae are sensitive to pH and other soil conditions. Most species prefer a near-neutral environment, but one species is known which will flourish at pH 1.0 in peat.

One of the curious features of algae is the ability of some species (blue-green algae) to fix nitrogen, especially in arid soils. In the topics, the amount of nitrogen fixed by algae can be significant: algae can usually be a substitute for fertilizers such as ammonium sulphate, and superior to nitrogen in a bag on marginal tropical soils. In most soils algae, whether alive or dead, function as fertilizers by providing organic matter and some nitrogen. On arid soils they can be a major source of organic matter.

Viruses

Smallest of all the soil microbes, viruses are so small that they are invisible under any light microscope. They have been photographed with an electron microscope, however, and shown to consist of a glob of genetic material, surrounded by a hard protein coat. While they are living beings, virsus are just barely alive, and will quite happily crystallize and sit in a jar on some lab shelf for 50 years. When conditions are to their liking they become "alive" once again. For a virus this means that a host must be present, and in gratitude the virus proceeds to dismantle the host cell in order to reproduce itself.

The virus-host relationship is very specific—often one species of virus must have one species of host to reproduce. In general, there is a group of viruses which attack plants, another which attack animals, and another which attack microbes (particularly bacteria and actinomycetes). Viruses are not known to attack fungi or algae. Although they cause diseases in many crops, it is rare for a virus to persist or overwinter in a temperate or boreal soil. Many of our viral plant diseases in Canada blow in every spring from warmer soils in the U.S. where they do overwinter, so viral ecology is certainly not a localized study.

One group of viruses potentially very important in agriculture makes it living by pulling apart *Rhizobium* bacteria to reproduce. *Rhizobia* are the bacteria responsible for the fixation of nitrogen on the roots of legumes. Build-ups of these viruses may be one reason why the yields of alfalfa and red clover decline if the crops are grown continually in one field.

The virus diseases of plants and animals are many, but beyond the scope of this article. Viruses, while providing a check on bacterial overpopulation in the soil, can cost you a crop once in a while. The best you can do to defend yourself against most viruses diseases of crops is to follow a good crop rotation.

Protozoa

Protozoa differ from all the other soil microbes by being animals. They eat and move in response to stimuli. Their life cycle is typically divided into an active phase when the animal feeds and reproduces, and a resting, or cyst stage. Most will reproduce by simple asexual division, but some species will periodically exchange genetic material in a sort of sexual reproduction.

A few protozoa have the remarkable ability to photosynthesize their own food, and these chlorophyll containing animals are the only members of the entire animal kingdom which aren't required to eat in order to survive. The vast majority, though, are dependent on pre-formed organic matter either as organic bits and pieces or whole microbes. Eating microbes is the usual habit, especially of soil protozoa, and the ability to move becomes quite handy when that luscious bacterium is just out of reach. To eat its victim, the hungry protozoa simply sidles up to the bacterium and surrounds it. Primitive, but very effective. When tasty bacteria are no longer available protozoa enter the cyst or resting stage and may thus persist for many years.

The population of protozoa is rich and varied (see Fig. 1-15), there being often 100,000 per gram of soil. Although bacteria are much more numerous, the protozoa outweigh them, individually, and will often outweigh the bacteria as a population. The population dynamics of the protozoa expectedly follow those of the bacteria rather closely and below the top 15 cm of soil they are rare. Despite their abundance, little is known of soil protozoa beyond their function as predators. It seems logical that they serve as a check on the total bacterial population, though this has not been conclusively proven.

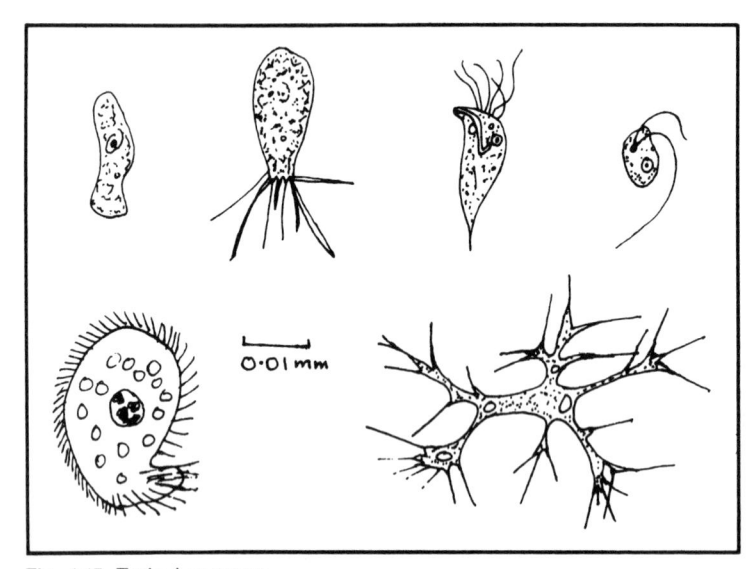

Fig. 1-15. Typical protozon.

Thus we see in some small way the ecological complexity of our soil. All microorganisms function together in ways that we understand only slightly. We cannot fully comprehend this precious balance in a magazine article or a lifetime—we can only try to preserve it and stand in awe.

Chapter 2

Organic Farming

In recent years a great deal of controversy has raged over "organic farming," but in too many cases the discussions have generated more smoke than light. As a result many people—including most farmers and even some organic gardeners—don't really know what organic farming really is.

Recently there have been several suggestions from as many sources that the word "organic" be dropped. The main reason among organic farmers is the connotation of the word, the feeling that it conjures thoughts of health food freaks and other strange faddists and thus makes their position look faddish. The word "organic" in the chemical sense is said to be meaningless in terms of organic farming. And the FDA thinks "natural" and "organic" foods are a ripoff.

The farming system now known as organic was originally called humus farming. Today, some publications prefer the terms eco-farming, natural farming, or biological farming. Other terms that have been suggested fall into the same general category: a system of farming that relies on working with nature, not against it.

We think the word "organic" is just fine, and here's why. In the first place, a word means what people think it means. In 1956 "sputnik" was gibberish in America. In 1957 virtually every man, woman and child saw an image when they heard the word.

Organic farming went through something similar. People confused it with organic chemistry, or it brought forth the image of long-haired hippies running naked through the woods. But today, most people are at least beginning to have a better understanding of what organic agriculture really is. It now has a place in the dictionary.

Moreover, organic also means "forming an integral element of a whole" or "having systematic coordination of parts." And that says a lot more than just "a system of farming that does not use chemically formulated fertilizers or pesticides."

For organic farming is a way of thinking about everything, a way of life. It relates not only to fertilization, even though organic fertilization involves the systematic coordination of all the factors of fertilization, not only the chemical ones. Organic farming looks at the entire universe, and fits food production into a niche that is coordinated with the rest of the universe: energy, health, transportation, marketing in general, true economics (as opposed to temporary economics based on temporary conditions such as the abundance of fossil fuels) and many others.

While we occasionally use such terms as biological farming and natural farming, we think "organic" is a term that has come of age, and one that best describes not only the farming method, but the lifestyle, that *Countryside* believes in and promotes.

THE SOIL

What is organic farming? Why has it become so popular in some quarters and so berated in others? Why do some people believe in it so strongly while others fight it so vigorously?

If there really is something to the arguments in favor of it, does it really work? Just as importantly, is it really practical and economical?

There is evidence that very few people involved in the controversy—on either side—actually know what organic farming is all about. Yet, if what proponents of the system say is true, the topics is of immense importance to every creature that depends on the soil for life—which is to say every living creature.

It should be particularly interesting to readers of *Countryside:* homesteaders who are already convinced of the value of organic methods but who often aren't quite sure why or what management practices to follow; and small farmers who were undoubtedly intrigued by the widespread publicity given the Barry Commoner study which showed that working organic farms are as profitable as similar operations using chemicals.

Contrary to popular opinion, organic farming is not merely farming without chemicals. It is not merely using manure for fertilizer. It is not "going back" to old-fashioned and outdated methods.

True organic farming is a highly scientific system which does not turn its back on technology, but which also is not blinded by the marvels of that technology. Organic farming looks ahead, unlike the farmers of the frontier who could plow virgin land, wear it out in three years, and move west.

The frontier is gone. We must husband what we have.

Organic advocates say the modern agribusiness complex is akin to the frontier homesteader. It is exploiting current resources for profit and endangering not only future generations, but the health and welfare of the current crew of Spaceship Earth.

Agribusiness advocates say we would all starve to death with organic agriculture, and that the form in which the plants receive their nourishment doesn't matter anyway.

Who is right?

In order to understand organic methods, we must have a basic understanding of the soil. While most of us learned something of the soil in school, and perhaps long ago, we must not only refresh our memories: we must re-examine it in the light of more recent experience, new information, and new concepts.

All soil came from rock, but the worth of that soil for agricultural production depends upon the nature of the parent material, the climate which weathered it, the type of life which contributed to its formation, the topography in which it is located and the time that elapsed since its weathering began. See Fig. 2-1.

Depending upon these factors, it may take 1,000 years for one inch of topsoil to form in southern Indiana; 2,000 years for one inch to form in northern Michigan, or more than 10,000 years for one

Fig. 2-1. The pale soil on the left shows the deterioration of 40 years from continuous cropping in contrast to the sample on the right from land in good grass rotation.

inch of soil to form in central Canada. But man can destroy that inch in a generation.

The implication is clear. When the topsoil is gone or depleted, it will take 1,000 to 10,000 years to replace even one inch of it. No doubt technological man, a flippant and braggardly creature, intends to dine out at McDonald's during that period?

The great variations in soil began with the variations of the parent rock, and each variation in rock was further subdivided as the other factors of soil formation did their work. In some places, magma from the interior of the Earth was pushed upward by heaving of the planet, resulting in granite. Sandstone was deposited in other places, and shale or limestone in still others. These were the basic raw materials Nature had to work with . . . the basis for our own bodies and our very lives.

The exposed rock was worn away by climatic forces. Changes in temperature from day to night and summer to winter broke rock into scaly pieces. Rainwater dissolved limestone and softened other parts of the rock. Wetting and drying caused expansion and contraction of particles, water freezing in tiny cracks and depressions further expanded and broke the rock. From the decay products of the rocks, new chemicals were formed and in the cracks and depressions there was now enough moisture and nutrients to support primitive plant life.

Under such harsh conditions, the lower forms of life such as lichens were first to appear. But as often happens with progress, it snowballs: the original processes which accounted for the first feeble step are aided and sped up by newer, more powerful forces. And so it was when the first lichens emerged.

The weathering of the rock continued, of course, but the lichens and mosses helped dissolve the rock more quickly, and as generations of these primitive plants grew, reproduced and decayed, they added organic matter to the forming soil. Eventually higher forms of plant life could survive, sending out roots to probe into the tiniest fissures, exerting forces that while technological man considers them puny and insignificant helped to make an entire planet habitable. These higher plants deposited organic matter downward as their roots decayed, the roots brought nutrients from the rock to the surface; and the above-ground growth (being more rank than that of the lichens and mosses) hastened the deposition of organic matter even more.

The process sped up and grasses and shrubs followed rapidly, in relative terms. And eventually, a hardwood forest stood on what once had been barren limestone rock.

Somewhere along the way a similar process was being made in the animal kingdom. Bacteria, fungi, insects, reptiles, birds and animals all helped form the soil. The lowest forms agitate, mix, and digest soil. Their bodies and wastes provide additional organic matter, or food for higher forms—whose bodies and wastes provide even more organic matter.

While this is the general form of evolution of soils, there are many contributing factors that have a bearing on the finished product ("finished" also being a relative term, as the processes are obviously still going on). On hilly land, the water will run off and even the very first step will be greatly retarded. Wind and gravity will help to remove the particles that may be formed. One flat rock, the process will be faster but if water is actually left standing on the rock surface the process will be slowed.

As noted in the difference in soil formation between central Canada and southern Indiana, temperature and climate also affect the speed of formation. This is in part a reflection of the types and activities of soil life, which is dependent upon certain optimum temperatures.

Soil, then, varies widely in its structure and chemical content according to the conditions under which it was formed. While nearly all the elements that are found in nature are found in soil, there is a wide variation in the chemical composition of soil.

A cubic foot of productive topsoil contains about two pounds of organic matter. About half of this is former soil life: the other half is actually alive. The live part consists of plant roots, bacteria, earthworms, algae, fungi, actinomycetes, nematodes, and many other forms of soil life.

This is just a quick summary of some of the basics of soil formation which most Americans learned in trade school. But they've either forgotten, or the facts have become so clouded over by later complexities, that they ignore the whole point: Life comes from the soil.

In normal times, urbanites could conceivably be forgiven for leaving such basic thoughts to the agribusiness complex. But these are not normal times. Misuse of the soil could of itself cause man's extinction, but in conjunction with other "minor" problems we face today, even an extremely slight misuse could have results of catastrophic proportions. Remember, nature does not work on the bulldozer principles which fascinate weak and puny man: she affects awesome changes with tiny fragile root hairs and delicate snowflakes.

Besides, there is reason to believe that our misuse of the soil is **not** slight or insignificant.

To follow the reasoning here it will be necessary to exercise a bit of humility, something modern technological man often finds difficult. Bear in mind not only the root hairs, with the tensile strength of filmy spiderwebs, reducing granite boulders to dust, but also the seldom acknowledged fact that smart as we may be, we don't know everything. The greatest minds in the world have not been able to tell us what electricity is.

Add to that the facts we have learned from the recent interest in ecology: everything is connected to everything else, often in subtle and mysterious ways that would never occur to us. True, there are still those who fail to see the connection between the California condor or the brown pelican and mankind's survival and thus scoff at one argument in favor of banning DDT, but their number is diminishing.

Man set himself above the gods and slashed away the forests, thinking, in his shortsightedness, that he was merely cutting down trees. It took generations to learn that the simple act of cutting down trees affected the oxygen-carbon dioxide cycle; soil erosion rates; ground water levels; and caused extensive flooding. And each of these results had further results.

Who can predict the results of exterminating the tiniest, most insignificant bacterium or nematode? The difference is only one of degree . . . maybe. But remember the root hair and the snowflake with which Nature wrought such cataclysmic changes.

Because of man's very real lack of knowledge; because of the subtle ways in which Nature works; and because we already know of the tremendous side effects of some seemingly minor events and actions; deviating very far from Nature's examples on the basis of unlimited knowledge is dangerous foolishness. Applied to something as vital as soil science, it could well be mass suicide.

We have seen that soils vary widely in their composition. Most U.S. soils, for example, are extremely low in phosphorus; potash content is low in sandy soils but fairly high in silt and clay soils, and is especially plentiful in regions of low rainfall. The other elements also vary according to the conditions under which the soil was formed.

Plants need certain elements, and in turn, we also require certain elements not only for health but for survival. If the nutrition isn't in the soil, it can't be in the plant and we won't get it either. In addition, as plant material is removed from the soil where it grew, the elements are removed too. Recall that under natural soil formation the plants decayed where they had grown, and that the body wastes and rotting corpses of animal life were also returned to the soil. Modern agriculture takes away the minerals in the form of crops, and instead of the end products returning to the same soil, they are flushed into sewer systems or buried in lead boxes in cemeteries. Such a system lives off capital and cannot go on forever.

For most of the history of man as farmer, the natural cycle was not much disturbed. Draft animals were used for power and at least their wastes and the night soil of the farm family were returned to the earth. But this did not take into account natural soil deficiencies, of which nothing was known.

When tractors replaced horses and oxen in the U.S., the need for fertilizer became more acute. About the same time, chemists began analyzing the soil and plant tissues and felt they had come up with the secret of growing more food in the same space with less labor: they would simply add to the soil the elements the plants took off.

Of the more than 100 elements found in soil, only 16 were considered important to plants. Most of these were in trace quantities. The primary ones were nitrogen, phosphorus and potassium.

Even if we who know more about the significance of seemingly insignificant phenomena—of root hairs—overlooked the neglect of the other 80 or 90 elements, there was still reason for concern. Because the manner in which the elements that were added to the soil neglected to consider the wonderful and wonderfully complex laws of nature.

The elements were added, not in their natural forms, but in souped-up versions which we'll examine later. The chemists had confidence in their knowledge but little regard for the preferences of Mother Nature. They were going to "help" her by pepping things up but they never stopped to consider that the help might be akin to pepping up a human with barbituates.

The original results were encouraging—just as the early experiences of a drug addict give him no indication of the torture to come later. Plant growth improved and yield per acre increased. Total fertilizer use in the United States increased 97 times in little more than half a century. And new and "better" sources were found. Anhydrous ammonia, for example, was first used in 1947 as a source of nitrogen; today over 4 million tons are spread on our land.

Fertilizer use was encouraged not only by the first flush of success, but by the increasing demand for food, and perhaps most importantly, by the increasing need for farmers to be competitive. Even if a farmer didn't "believe" in chemical fertilizers (and few could have argued with the same insight we have today), he had little choice in the matter. His neighbors used it. They produced more than he did. If he didn't compete, he was out of business. Fertilization became so commonplace, such an accepted part of agriculture, that very few questioned any of its effects. Didn't it increase yields? Didn't it reduce costs and increase efficiency and not only help Americans spend less on food than any other people but also feed millions of starving souls around the world? Why look such a gift horse in the mouth?

Like any drug, it became addictive. The value of fertilizer started to come under fire as the hangover symptoms began to appear. The addiction of the soil is apparent, since if chemical fertilizer is eliminated the withdrawal symptoms are impressive: production dwindles, in quantity and quality. Obviously few farmers are prepared to or are financially capable of coping with the withdrawal symptoms. The only answer was to use more and more of greater and greater potency.

The time has come to take a closer look. The food supply of the world is in a precarious position, putting our very existence in jeopardy. Fertilizer prices have doubled in recent years, and while new plants are being built, many of the most important fertilizers are based on petroleum, so not only will the cost continue to increase but one day, inevitably, our supply of oil will run out.

While these are imminently practical considerations, of even more importance to those in the forefront of natural agriculture or "organic farming" are some of the side effects of chemically based agriculture or toxic technology that have been glossed over in the interests of efficiency and resulting higher supplies and lower prices.

In the light of the lessons of the webs of ecology and the snowflake hypothesis, these side effects might be monumental.

Let's start with something very basic, which even the toxic technologists are beginning to speak of. The physical character of soil.

Go out and pick up a handful of soil. Crush some between your thumb and fingers and look at it closely. Does it look like a piece of good chocolate cake, or a fallen cake? Most of our cultivated lands will resemble the baker's fiasco.

This has importance for your health, the quantity and quality of food on your plate, and other considerations such as the availability of the water you drink and the control of floods.

The reason is that the soil that looks like good chocolate cake has small granules that are soil particles held together with the glues formed by the sticky juices of half-rotted grasses and the slimy excretions of earthworms. The soil granules could be compared to microscopic popcorn balls.

A good soil is composed of roughly 50 percent solids (minerals and organic matter) and 50 percent pore space. When soil moisture is adequate for good growth, about one-half of the pore space will be filled with water, the rest with air.

Plant roots need both air and water. If there is no pore space due to lack of the natural glues, as in the example of the fallen cake, the soil will not be able to provide sufficient amounts of either water or air. Because there is no pore space, rain will not soak into the ground, but will run off. This not only results in the lack of a water reserve for growing plants, but causes flooding as rain runs off suddenly after a storm rather than slowly over a period of time; it affects the water table because water does not soak into the ground; and rapid runoff causes erosion which washes away soil that took thousands of years to form.

So organic matter is important to your belly in and of itself. But the webs don't let it stop there.

Soil life depends in large part on organic matter. The bacteria, earthworms, fungi, actinomycetes and nematodes all live on organic matter. Not only will they starve without organic matter, but many of the "hot" fertilizers of the agrichemists actually kill them off, so even what organic matter is present is not digested and rotted and worked into the soil.

It has been said that each acre of fertile topsoil contains about 11 tons of biological life. Modern farms using toxic technology often have less than two tons. Fertile soils may have as many as 5,000,000 earthworms per acre (Fig. 2-2). Modern farms using acid fertilizers often have as few as 100,000 per acre.

There are practical considerations here. Flood control is important. The water table is increasingly gaining in importance. Controlling erosion is important. And the availability of water to plants during the growing season is obviously important for the production of food. All of that makes the incorporation and assimilation of organic matter of practical importance.

But there are also some unanswered questions. What affect does

Fig. 2-2. Earthworms abound in soil that is in harmony with nature.

that 11 tons of soil life per acre have? Destroying it or failing to cultivate it obviously means a loss of natural fertility which has to be made up by using more applied fertilizer. But what else that we might not even know about is happening?

The people who shrug this off as pure theoretical rhetoric or balderdash can be asked, "What is electricity?" Like the court fool who asks cosmic questions, we say "What about the snowflake?"

It could be that the theoretical questions really are of no importance, although even then the practical aspects should be considered at a time when the world faces mass starvation. But if theories should happen to prove right and we're continuing to sterilize and kill our soil at a prodigious rate, by the time the facts are in there will be precious little ground left to either plant or reclaim.

Even if reclamation is effected on nature's own terms, it will take time. If the food situation worsens, the time it takes can only add to the catastrophe. Already agri-chemical advocates use this as an argument for continuing the addiction; production will fall off so drastically with a return to natural agriculture that great numbers of people would starve. They're probably right, which means we're hooked already. It may already be too late.

It's important to recall the relatively brief time span covered by chemically-based agriculture. Anhydrous ammonia, as mentioned, was first used in 1947. Because its spread was gradual, any effects it might have would have been confined to a rather small percentage of the Earth's inhabitants. But of more significance is the fact that many very subtle changes are wrought only over generations. Toxic technology has run rampant only for one generation of man, and then only in certain areas. It would be better to look to shorter-lived animals for possible signs.

They're there, but we cannot use them as "proof." Because there are not supposed to be any ill effects from toxic technology, according to modern science, there is no point in modern scientists looking for any. Without research the statement becomes a self-fulfilling hypothesis.

Of course we must remember that not only do certain scientists have tunnel vision because of their extreme specialization but that their work is often based on the work of others who naturally follow similar inclinations and on very practical terms, the research grants come from chemical companies, not earthworms and nematodes.

It's quite interesting to listen to "old timers" talk about modern farming methods. The average farmer is more than 50 years old, which means many of them were farming long before toxic technology came on the scene. Many a farmer of 60, 70 and 80 years can tell of the year his pappy cleared that field down by the stream and got the best crop of corn he ever saw. It lasted about three years, then the land was "worn out."

These fellows can also talk of the year they started fertilizing hay and noticed subtle changes in their cows. They claim we have diseases and conditions now which were virtually unknown in their youth: even some vets admit that things like displaced abomasums seem to be increasing with the increase of toxic technology.

Problems and conditions that are very subtle don't show up in the computers, but only as gnawing hunches on the parts of the men who know each of their animals on an individual and personal basis. There's nothing much to go on, no proof, nothing definite to check out even if the scientists were willing to or interested in checking it out.

There's one more aspect of this that should be explained. We've only touched on organic farming and toxic technology as parts of a much larger and more complex situation which endangers our soils. There was no intent to explain the details of either system, but to point out the possible hazards of over-reliance on technology. But since organic farming is actually little understood, in spite of the masses of arguments presented against it by people who don't even understand what they're arguing against, let's go back over one point.

If it's true that plants take minerals from the soil (and it is), how do organic farmers put them back? We often hear the chemically-oriented scientists ridicule organic farming because "adding compost will in no way add the required nutrients." This is partially true, although as we have seen, sufficient organic matter is necessary if the soil is to effectively get any nutrients out of the soil; the compost does contain certain amounts of minerals; and it makes available many more than humus-poor soil cannot release. But compost or organic matter is only part of the story.

Where specific minerals are needed, it is far better to provide them in natural forms. Organic farmers do use fertilizers in the form of rock dusts, but the rock dusts are not souped up like that of the toxic technologists. The toxic technologist gets faster results, and for the short term at least greater yields, but his fertilizers are shorter-lived (meaning he needs more every year) and they have deleterious effects on the soil biology. While the initial results of the organic farmer's fertilization program may not be as dramatic, the slow action of his natural products means that less is required each year, and moreover, he is not sterilizing the soil which means that soil life is also contributing to his land's fertility.

Toxic technology considers the soil only as something to hold the plant roots while a predetermined nutrient mix is administered. Organic farmers speak of feeding not the plant, but the soil: they endeavor to return to or maintain the natural processes which have been tried and proven by Nature herself over the millenia.

Seen in this light, there really isn't much difference between organic farming and chemical farming. (Incidentally, neither term is etymologically correct, but people who argue about the misuse of the terms invariably forget about the real issues.) But if there is seemingly little difference in the methods and little or none in the end result (so far as present experience will take us and according to most authorities) there may very well be a tremendous difference not only over the long haul, but in the food you're eating right now, today.

The case for organic farming is a good one. But a return to natural farming presents a number of very real and serious practical problems.

First, even if farmers were forced into it, there will certainly be a lag between cutting off the drugs and harvesting respectable yields on a natural basis. The soil had to "dry out," just like the human drug addict; it must go through a withdrawal period.

I have plowed fields that had been doused with chemicals

without seeing a single earthworm in a furrow 80 rods long. Cornstalks that had been plowed under three years earlier showed no signs of decomposition: the soil was so sterile due to lack of biological life that the organic matter was as good as embalmed.

Adding such natural workers as earthworms to such soil would be pointless: the environment isn't right and they couldn't survive. The environment must first be rectified, and only time can accomplish that, even with good management practices.

Therefore, even if organic farming were to become the norm overnight, it would take three to five years before yields would even begin to approach present levels. If stockpiles are feeding us only on a hand to mouth basis now, and in fact the world is presently consuming more food than it grows, then any reduction in output will be intolerable. The question then becomes one of intolerable shortages in the near future, or devastating shortages, and perhaps other side effects caused by plants grown on unhealthy, dead soil, at some point in the future. Incidentally, in the future there will be even more people, even greater need for food: shortages will be even less tolerable with each passing year.

The world's inhabitants have no way of surviving without food, without soil. Beans and rice, tea and crumpets, burgers and fries, all originate with the soil. Our soil is not only in very real danger of losing its ability to produce, but on a far more subliminal and insidious level, it may be losing the capacity to supply us with the proper nutrients required to maintain physical and mental health. The crisis in our soil would therefore be more than enough to spell the doom of mankind.

FERTILIZATION

It's a common misconception that "organic farmers do not use fertilizer." Or that their only fertilizer is manure. Small wonder so many people think organic farming is only a game for backyard garden-food faddists, or a small and freakish cult of farmers who won't be around for long.

Yet, we have observed over the years that even people who proclaim a dedication to organic methods have little knowledge of what's really involved.

A Question of Semantics. One of the first and most vexing problems inherent in a discussion of conventional vs. organic farming methods is terminology. Some people spend so much time arguing about definitions that they never get to the heart of the matter.

"Organic" framing is a confusing, even a ridiculous concept, because "organic" refers to the carbon compound found in all living beings. By the same token, "chemical farming" says nothing, because the chemical elements that living beings, plant and animal, are made of, are present no matter what kind of fertilizer was provided.

Therefore, in this series (and indeed in all of *Countryside*) we take organic to mean farming or gardening without the use of chemicals that are toxic in the amounts normally used for plant growth: and chemical to mean farming with synthetically produced materials aimed at feeding the plant without regard for the effects of the material on soil life.

While this is just the basic concept of each term, each has further implications. Organic farming, for example, also entails special tillage procedures aimed largely at enhancing the environment of soil life (Figs. 2-3, 2-4, and 2-5), it frowns on the use of hormones and antibiotics and other commonly accepted components of animal husbandry; it eschews herbicides, fungicides, defoliants and other chemical products. And it takes these views, not from a desire to return to the Dark Ages, not simply because they think some chemicals might cause cancer, but for a complex host of interrelated reasons we are examining in this chapter.

THE NITROGEN FIXATION

Soil fertility is the quality that enables a soil to provide compounds in sufficient amounts and proper balance to promote plant growth, providing that other factors (temperature, moisture, light, etc.) are favorable. Few soils are "naturally" fertile for the crops we insist

Fig. 2-3. Organic fertilization.

Fig. 2-4. Enhancing the soil.

Fig. 2-5. Organic farming.

on growing on them, and in any event the removal of crops results in the removal of specific nutrients. Since these nutrients are essential for plant growth, they must be replaced.

Fertilization has been practiced since ancient times. The Greeks limed their soil; manure and human excrement have always been used to improve the soil; early agricultures observed that crops grew better where a fire had burned and thus began adding wood ashes (potash) to their fields; and everyone is familiar with the Indian practice of burying a fish in each hill of corn. Other fertilizers that were used long before test tubes were even invented include ground bones, dried blood, saltpeter and guano. No doubt their discovery was accidental: they improved crop production, and although no one knew why, no one likes to argue with success.

The scientific study of plant nutrition began about 1750, but it wasn't until 1840 that Justus von Liebig of Germany proved that treatment with strong acid increased the availability of nutrients in bones to growing plants. Von Liebig, therefore, generally gets the credit—or the blame—for fathering chemical fertilization.

It wasn't until the mid-20th century that fertilizers such as phosphoric acid, salt solutions and anhydrous ammonia began to be used in liquid form. It should be of more than passing interest to note that what we call conventional agriculture is actually a very new science—certainly in comparison with the history of agriculture. It's really no older than most people reading this.

As with most of technology, tremendous increases in knowledge and understanding of plant chemistry have taken place only in the past few decades. Medieval farmers might have concluded that the addition of dried blood or ground blood to their crops resulted in improved growth due to some form of magic, or perhaps alchemy. Today we know that dried blood is a good source of nitrogen, and bones contain appreciable amounts of phosphorus.

We know that fertile soil contains more than 100 elements, but only a fool would say we know everything there is to know. Is it possible, for example, that the 16 elements found essential to plant growth are the only ones needed, and if so why has nature provided the other 80 or 90? As ecological awareness grows, we become increasingly cognizant of the fact that nothing is wasted in nature; nothing is useless. It would seem childishly presumptive to say that while only a short time ago we knew nothing of the nutritive requirements of plants beyond that they responded to certain time-honored treatment, today we know all there is to know. We cannot write off those dozens of elements. Therefore, research continues.

Of the 16 elements considered essential to plant growth at this time, only three get much attention: nitrogen, phosphorus, and potassium, or N, P, and K. In fact, if you buy fertilizer you buy a product labeled with three numbers such as 10-20-10, indicating that it contains 10 percent N, 20 percent P and 10 percent K. Other elements are sometimes taken into consideration for certain crops under certain circumstances, including boron, zinc, manganese, magnesium, sulphur and a few others. But N, P and K definitely hog the spotlight so far as conventional chemical agriculture is concerned.

According to chemical theory, the application of N, P and K merely replaces that which is removed by the harvested crop. This theory holds that the form of the nutrient provided to the plant makes no difference to the growth and health of the plant. In brief, it considers the soil as nothing more than a medium to hold the plant roots while the required nutrients are provided by the farmer.

Proponents of organic agriculture see things a little differently. Because of the myriad of entangling webs, and the possible importance of seemingly insignificant factors and conditions, it will be helpful to examine various fertilization practices one at a time before drawing any general conclusions. And because of their widespread use and acknowledged importance, we will concentrate on nitrogen, phosphorus and potassium, and attempt to show the differences—methodological and ideological—between chemical and organic fertilization practices.

Nitrogen to plants is like water to a shipwrecked sailor. Nitrogen is essential to plant life, as water is to the sailor. And just as the sailor is surrounded by water he can't make use of, the plant is surrounded by nitrogen it can't use.

The atmosphere contains nearly 80 percent nitrogen. In order for plants to make use of free nitrogen, it must first be converted to soluble compounds of nitrogen such as ammonia (NH_2), nitrite (NO_2) or nitrate (NO_3). These soluble compounds can be taken up by plant roots and converted into amino acids and plant proteins. (Interestingly enough, the Earth's primitive atmosphere apparently contained ammonia, which made nitrogen fixation unnecessary).

Nitrogen fixation, or nitrification, is performed by several species of soil microorganisms. In other words, these tiny living creatures have the power to take nitrogen from the air and convert it into forms usable by plant life.

The reverse process—the reduction of soluble compounds of nitrogen to molecular nitrogen—is performed by other species of microorganisms. This is called denitrification. There are also microorganisms that decompose the remains of plants and animals, reducing the amino acids that contain nitrogen to ammonium ions and other products.

Some will consider it significant that the rate at which nitrogen is removed from the air through nitrification is balanced by the rate at which denitrification returns nitrogen to the air—and that the large-scale and widespread use of nitrogen fertilizers may be upsetting this balance.

There are two main types of bacteria and algae involved in nitrogen fixation. One lives in symbiosis with higher plants; the other is free-living and derives energy directly from sunlight and indirectly from plant materials. The *rhizobium* species are the most familiar to farmers, and the most abundant of the root-nodule symbiotic bacteria. These make it not only unnecessary to provide nitrogen fertilizers to legumes such as the clovers, alfalfa, peas and soybeans, but they actually leave the soil richer in nitrogen for the next crop. In addition to the legumes, these bacteria also work with the roots of such plants as alders and buckthorns.

The complexities of the webs of ecology become apparent when we see that, not only do these plants depend upon nitrifying bacteria to fix nitrogen from the air, but these bacteria seem to have a critical need for certain trace elements and do not function effectively without them. This is the reason that cobalt is considered an essential trace element for alfalfa: it's not the alfalfa that needs it, but its nitrifying bacteria.

Another nitrogen fixing microorganism that is becoming more widely known (especially among organic farmers) is a nonsymbiotic aerobic soil bacteria known as *Azotobacter*, which supplies fixed nitrogen in grasslands and other ecosystems where symbiotic microorganisms are absent. Several products containing such nonsymbiotic nitrifying microorganisms are now commercially available, making it possible for nonlegume plants such as wheat or oats, or even the nitrogen-gobbling corn, to "produce" their own nitrogen just like the clovers and other legumes.

It is estimated that 92,000,000 tons of nitrogen are fixed annually by natural means. It is entirely likely that Man's use of fertilizers is causing more nitrogen fixation to occur than the biosphere can return through denitrification, in which case there would be a gradual buildup of nitrites, nitrates and ammonia.

The nitrogen cycle is extremely complex, extremely important, and not very well understood. But this doesn't stop agribusiness from pouring millions of pounds of additional nitrogen onto our agricultural lands.

Most nitrogen fertilizers are in the form of synthetic ammonia, used either as a gas or in water solution, or converted into salts such as ammonium sulfate, ammonium phosphate and ammonium nitrate. Sources less favored by agribusiness, but more favored by eco-agriculture, include packinghouse wastes, tannery wastes, treated garbage and sewage, cottonseed meal, and manure. Fertilizer production doubled twice between 1950 and 1971, reaching a worldwide total of 60,000,000 tons, and a large portion of that was nitrogen in the form of ammonia.

Ammonium gas was first produced from ammonium chloride in the late 18th century, but it wasn't available in quantities until the invention of the Haber process in 1913. In the Haber process, atmospheric nitrogen is combined with hydrogen to make ammonia. Since the nitrogen comes from the air and hydrogen can be produced from water theoretically there is no limit to the amount that can be produced. As a practical matter, it should be noted that it takes 1,500 cubic feet of natural gas to produce the nitrogen used on one acre of corn, and no one needs to be reminded of the precarious future of that resource. (The process requires high pressure and high temperatures.)

While it has nothing to do with agriculture per se, it's interesting to note that Fritz Haber, developer of the Haber process, was "strongly imbued with the conviction that the basic purpose of science was the betterment of mankind." Moreover, he was something of a maverick: he didn't last long in his father's business; he took up organic chemistry but soon tired of its "orthodox methods," and turned to physical chemistry, a subject in which he was self-taught. Haber was awarded the Nobel Prize for Chemistry in 1918.

Somehow, he also played a major role in the development of poison gas as a weapon during World War I. That is a role organic farmers will see as not incongruous with his development of agricultural ammonia. In fact, although agriculture is far and away the leading user of ammonia, another major use is in the manufacture of explosives.

The most common nitrogen fertilizer is anhydrous ammonia, a pure, dry ammonia used in liquid form under pressure. It changes to gas when released in the atmosphere. Anhydrous is highly flammable, corrosive, it can cause burns and frostbite, blindness, and inhalation can cause death. Application equipment is quite specialized and operators must exercise extreme safety precautions. One essential item to be on hand while working with anhydrous is a jug of water, for in case of accidental contact with the skin or eyes the area must be flushed with water in a matter of seconds.

This is what we're putting on our soil—soil that, in its natural state, can contain as much as 11 tons of life per acre. The predictable result is that many of our "best" soils today contain two tons of soil life, and we'll examine the implications in that later.

Anhydrous contains 80 percent nitrogen; other forms of ammonia somewhat less. Most manure contains less than one percent. Furthermore, the nitrogen from natural sources is not as fast-acting as that from ammonia. Therefore, those interested primarily in bushels and dollars only for the short term rely on ammonia. But here's what happens.

Under natural conditions nitrogen fertilizers are in the form of proteins. The proteins are broken down into their amino acids through decomposition, and then into ammoniums in the form of nitrite. This becomes nitrate which is the form plants can take up. It all happens with the cooperation of soil life, creatures just doing their jobs whether we appreciate it or not, and even if we don't know they are there. If they are encouraged, if the materials and conditions they need to work with are provided, they can produce better.

If they're killed off they can't do a thing.

When the ammonia forms of nitrogen are added to the soil they must be properly applied. They can't be too close to root systems or damage to the plants will result. Soil moisture conditions must be right or the nitrogen will escape into the atmosphere directly. A heavy rain soon after application will leach out much of the nutrient value, and feed already algae-choked lakes and streams instead of the soil. And because of the readily available nature of the material, it has a shot-in-the-arm effect rather than a slow and steady release.

By the next planting season (actually long before) it's used up, and more must be added. In fact, because of its effect on soil life which normally provided nitrogen, an increased amount must be used each year just to maintain the per acre harvest.

Under natural nitrification the slow release of plant nutrients continues throughout the growing season. There is less leaching, partly due to the form of the nitrogen and partly due to the amount available. There can actually be a nitrogen buildup, as in the case of legumes: less is needed from outside sources each year on a well-managed organic farm, with strong implications for costs and labor.

And most importantly, being in a natural form instead of a deadly, corroding, inflammable poison gas, nitrogen on the organic farm does not harm the biosphere, which includes not only the nitrogen fixing bacteria but other microorganisms with other functions we'll examine in other contexts later.

Of course, from the practical standpoint, working farmers as well as all others accustomed to eating want to know if it really works: is organic farming practical? Is it possible, not only to grow food without synthetic nitrogen, but in the quantities to which we've become accustomed? The reservations of the agribusiness community are usually based on the assumption that organic farming means going back to fertilizing with manure, and to yields that were a half to a third of today's yields.

Such is not the case. Established organic farmers are racking up yields that compare favorably with their neighbor's and in some cases exceed their neighbors' who are using toxic chemicals. And they're doing it with less input, as well as less damage to the soil (which is part of the biosphere we live in).

There are several reasons that skeptics find it difficult to reproduce the results dedicated organic farmers get. One is virtual neglect of the soil life which their chemicals have destroyed. It doesn't work to simply quit using chemicals and expect the soil to perform, because it's dead: there is nothing to perform with. Yet, this is the "test" agribusiness all too often gives organic methods. Whether through ignorance, or through strong ties to a rich and powerful agribusiness petrochemical complex, is difficult to say, but the results are the same in either case.

It takes from three to five years, and in some cases even more, to convert sterile soil into the living, healthy medium plants can grow and thrive in under natural conditions. The conversion is a biological process, which means first of all that the environment must be corrected, and second that is takes time.

While all of the processes are interconnected, we can make some specific observations on how organic farmers manage to "get along without nitrogen."

The first step is to stop killing off the nitrifying bacteria by burning up them and the humus they live on with ammonia. A hospitable environment for these natural producers of nitrogen must be provided. This includes proper soil management so they have sufficient light and air (as opposed to the aenerobic conditions that persist in some of our dead soils); incorporating humus and organic matter into the soil so these microorganisms have something to work on; including legumes in the crop rotation to make use of the more productive nitrifying bacteria; making use of *Azotobacter* and other nonsymbiotic nitrifying agents; innoculating compost heaps with specific microorganisms available commercially; etc. (Even sizeable farming operations must use compost heaps instead of sheet composting, contrary to popular opinion, in order to make maximum use of the fertilizing value of manure. This will be covered in future issues of *Countryside.)*

Natural forms of nitrogen fertilizers are available commercially, although they are terrifically expensive. Proponents point out, however, that the organic materials such as dried blood and leather tankage go farther and last longer than ammonia, and therefore actually cost less. Moreover, there is a build-up of reserves so future crop years require lesser amounts rather than more, which is the case with ammonia products.

It should be apparent from the foregoing discussion that organic farming is not simply going back to old-fashioned methods. It is not using manure or no fertilizer. Organic farmers are not ignorant clods with their heads in the compost heap while the rest of the agricultural world has been making new discoveries in radioisotopes and microbiology. The proponents of organic farming are the ones who have been the most open minded, the most progressive. if nothing else, as the price of petroleum continues to increase it might well follow that in the years ahead, organic farming might be the only kind of farming.

P & K

We have seen that the effects of just a few drops of nitrogen in the form of ammonia on the soil that is teeming with life can be compared, numerically at least, with the explosion of a nuclear bomb in the heart of a large city. The result in both cases is the wholesale destruction of life. And in both cases, those lives fan out and touch on the lives of countless other creatures, and entire ecosystems.

While N is the chief culprit in the big three of chemical fertilization, P and K are not exactly clean, either.

On the surface it would be legitimate and logical to ask how this can be, because both phosphorus and potassium (P and K) fertilizers come from "natural" materials. Unlike the nitrogen fertilizers, which are obtained from synthetic ammonia, phosphorus comes from phosphate rock and, to a lesser extent, bones. Potassium, namely potassium chloride and potassium sulfate, is mined from potash deposits.

However, neither is often used in their elemental or natural form. Just as with nitrogen, chemists have discovered ways to speed up the soil's delivery of these elements to plant life and . . . again just as with nitrogen . . . with no regard for the consequences to soil life.

Phosphorus

Phosphorus is not plentiful: it constitutes less than one-tenth of one percent of the earth's surface. But it is of extreme importance because it is necessary in all plant growth, it assists in cell division and the formation of fats and proteins. (The nucleus of each plant cell contains phosphorus, so cell division and growth aren't possible without it).

Of that 0.1 percent phosphorus in an average soil, only a small portion is available to plant life at any one time. There is no efficient mechanism on clay crystals or on humus particles for holding exchangeable and available phosphorus. In nature, and under ideal conditions, as plants take in phosphorus from the soil solution other phosphorus ions replace it from slowly soluble compounds in the soil.

In strongly acid soils, phosphorus availability is even lower because of the formation of iron and aluminum phosphates. Plants are not able to readily use the phosphorus in this form. The situation is somewhat similar in alkaline soils, where tricalcium phosphate forms to reduce the availability of soil phosphorus to plants. In other words, a soil with a balanced pH will do the best job of making naturally occurring phosphorus available to plant life.

Phosphorus affects plant growth in several important ways. It stimulates root formation and growth, aids in seed formation, and hastens maturity. Of importance to the next step in the food chain, phosphorus increases the protein and mineral contents of grasses and legumes and its availability to the plant increases the percentage of phosphorus and calcium in crops, and therefore to the animals that eat them.

Phosphorus also makes plants more winter hardy, it enables legumes to compete better with grasses and aids in legume nodule formation.

Most phosphate fertilizers are compounds containing calcium and sulphur although the fertilizer guarantee is given in terms of phosphoric acid equivalent, or P_2O_5. But there is no P_2O_5 in phosphorus fertilizer, and for that reason some people prefer the term phosphate.

Most phosphate ore in the U.S. comes from Florida, but there are reserves in Idaho, Wyoming, Utah and Montana with more recent mining areas being opened in North Carolina and Arkansas. A lesser source is phosphatic iron ore, from which the phosphorus is obtained as a by-produce from the slag.

Phosphate rock was formed on the ocean floor, and consists largely of insoluble tricalcium phosphate. To be used as a fertilizer, this rock must be converted to a form that is water soluble, even if only slightly so.

The conventional commercial approach is to convert the rock phosphate to superphosphate with the use of sulfuric acid. The process involves converting tricalcium phosphate (which has the three hydrogen atoms of phosphoric acid, or H_3PO_4, replaced by calcium) into monocalcium phosphate, in which only one hydrogen atom is replaced by calcium.

The process is often carried further, as much for the economic considerations of fertilizer production as for the availability of phosphorus to plants. The reason is that tremendous amounts of storage space are required to store fertilizers, and because of its weight, shipping costs are an important factor in the price. But the weight of superphosphate is greater than the amount of the original phosphate rock by the amount of sulfuric acid added, and it also carries the dead weight of the calcium sulfate that is formed in the manufacturing process. The solution used is to replace the sulfuric acid with phosphoric acid, which itself is obtained by the action of sulfuric acid on phosphate rock or by an electric furnace process. This results in triplesuperphosphat. The useful content of the fertilizer (expressed as the percent of phosphoric acid) is increased from 20 percent in superphosphate to about 45 percent in triplesuperphosphate.

There are other variations. Instead of using either sulfuric or phosphoric acid to treat the phosphate rock, nitric acid can be used. One of the resulting products is calcium nitrate, which is also used as a fertilizer.

Phosphorus is becoming of greater importance as our soils become increasingly depleted of organic matter. It's important because it so commonly is the limiting factor to plant growth; that is, other elements may be abundant but with any single one missing the others are useless. The analogy of a barrel with broken staves is often used. If just one stave is broken halfway down the barrel there is no way you can fill that barrel with water even if the other staves are intact. The broken one is the limiting factor. And if phosphorus is lacking, that is the limiting factor in plant growth regardless of how much nitrogen or potassium is available.

In an article titled, "Let's Look at Nutrition... From the Ground Up!" (Polled Hereford World, 1964) Dr. William A Albrecht mentioned that during the early period of increasing use of agricultural limestone and other fertilizing materials, many farmers observed that livestock seemed to prefer clover grown on fields or sections of fields where phosphorus had been applied.

Dr. Albrecht looked at phosphorus from another angle in a paper written in 1948, and reprinted in *The Albrecht Papers.*

"That human health may be related to deficiency in the soil has come to be more than mere speculation when animal troubles are localizing themselves more and more according to soil fertility deficiencies. If one looks at the map of poliomyelitis in 1946, for example, it is significant that this health trouble was more severe in those states where the less acid soils give deficiencies in phosphorus for the plants and animals. It is all the more significant when we remind ourselves that the brain and nerve tissues—most seriously affected by "polio"—represent high concentrations of phosphorus."

We can continue quoting Dr. Albrecht when we examine why the more highly soluble phosphorus of commercial fertilizers is less desirable than the slower-acting forms favored by organic farmers. The reason is humus. For there is evidence, he claims, that phosphorus in organic matter is more efficient in the soil than phosphorus in other forms.

He cited the experiment at the Missouri Agricultural Experiment Station by Vernon Renner using radioisotopes.

Barley was grown on sand cultures using controlled nutrients, including radioactive phosphorus. The barley was dried, pulverized, sampled for chemical analysis, and then mixed into soil at a ratio of one part of the pulverized organic matter to 500 parts of soil. This represented a rate of two tons per acre.

Soybeans were planted in that soil. They were harvested after 60 days and analyzed. The plan was to determine the total amount of phosphorus in the plants as well as the radioactive phosphorus. The total phosphorus minus the radioactive part would be the phosphorus coming from the soil, a mass 500 times greater than the organic matter containing the radioactive material.

The analysis showed that one part of the phosphorus was radioactive, while five parts were not, meaning that the phosphorus from the soil organic matter was 100 times more effective in feeding the insoluble, but available, phosphorus to the soybean plant, than was soil which was "high" in phosphorus according to a soil test by an extracting chemical reagent.

Thus, we again see the importance of organic matter in soils. And the acid and salt fertilizers have a detrimental effect on organic matter by destroying soil life. In the case of superphosphate, there is also a high sulfur content, which serves to show again the dizzying—but fascinating—complexities of the webs of ecology.

The sulfur causes sulfur-reducing bacteria to multiply. But part of the diet of these bacteria is a fungus whose function is to break down cellulose in the soil. Without the fungus, the organic matter is not as rapidly decomposed and without the organic matter more phosphate is needed to give similar results in plant growth. So, like all of chemical agriculture, it becomes a vicious circle.

However, not even the organic farmers are in full agreement on the matter of how to supply phosphorus.

Rock phosphate has long had the best acceptance. It is not highly water soluble (the attribute chemical agriculture doesn't like about it) and is lost only through cropping. The beneficial effects of rock phosphate far outlast those of the more soluble forms such as superphosphate.

The benefits of rock phosphate have been enhanced in recent years by the introduction of more sophisticated machinery, which is capable of grinding the material much finer (and therefore making it more available but without the side effects of the superphosphates.)

According to the Brookside Farms Laboratory Assn., Inc., the subject of rock phosphate has long received unfavorable consideration by universities and experiment stations. However, "We feel that such unfavorable impressions have resulted from experiments where a coarse rock phosphate material, usually ranging from 20 to 70 percent fineness through a 100-mesh screen, was used.

"In 1952, our laboratory, for purposes of experimental research, made an arrangement with a major phosphorus producing organization to provide our members with a Florida soft-pebble rock phosphate material that should analyze at least 33 percent P_2O_5 and ground to a fineness of 85 percent through a 200-mesh screen.

"Subsequently, we have made thousands of rechecks on soils that have been treated according to our recommendations with this special material and have found that our results were satisfactorily accomplished. At the same time we have rechecked many soils where other materials of coarser grind and lower P_2O_5 composition were applied with results that were far from satisfactory and almost negligible in many instances."

In converting from a chemical system to an organic system, the best method seems to be to work into the soil the total amount of rock phosphate recommended in the soil report, and then apply from 20 to 80 pounds per acre (according to the phosphorus values) of a water soluble P_2O_5 fertilizer in the first season, and 10 to 40 pounds per acre thereafter until the soil analysis shows that the desired level of active phosphorus has been attained. At this point the farmer may live on the interest only, not touching the principal.

Potassium

Potassium is the seventh most abundant element in the earth's crust . . . about on the same order as sodium, which it resembles very closely. Potassium, however, is contained in small amounts in a large number of mineral formations from which it cannot be economically extracted.

The use of potassium salts as fertilizers began in the second half of the 19th century and at that time it was thought that Germany had a monopoly, but many other workable deposits of potassium salts have been found in other parts of the world. In 1970 world consumption of potash was about 20,000,000 tons a year. Saskatchewan, Canada has large deposits, and worldwide reserves used at this rate are adequate for thousands of years.

Potassium averages about two and one-half percent in surface soils and is in adequate supply almost everywhere. Available supplies are often low, however (especially in more humid areas) and soils with as much as 20 tons total potash per acre often get additional potash to supply it in a readily available form for plant growth.

As with other elements found in chemical fertilizers, in its pure form potassium is a highly active, caustic, and dangerous element. While this doesn't scare the chemical agribusiness folks much, it scares the pants off organic farmers who are thinking in terms of that invaluable soil life—which, if properly nurtured, will supply all the potassium plants need.

Muriate of potash (60 percent K_2O) is the most common potash fertilizer, and accounts for 80 percent used.

Potash is the element that concerns itself with carbohydrate manufacture (starches and sugars). Potash is not included in the carbohydrate molecules, but all starch and sugar making stops when potash is not available.

Potash is also important to counteract excesses of nitrogen. High nitrogen may cause plants to lose their resistance to disease, but a good supply of potash can assuage that.

While mined potash is "natural" in that it is not processed in the same way that artificial nitrogen and acid phosphorus is, the fact remains that it is an ocean deposit and has more in common with ordinary salt than it has with natural and productive soil. Farmers will do well to recall that in ancient times, it was a common practice in some conquering cultures to sprinkle salt on vanquished farmland to make sure nothing would grow when the conquerors moved on. Notice also, the effects of road salting on vegetation along highways in northern climates where the practice is now coming under scrutiny. Plants just don't grow in salt.

Theoretically, or ideally, the abundant potash in most soils will be made available by a well-balanced, organic soil. But because so few soils attain this ideal, outside help is often necessary. The best source is natural mineral sources such as granite dust and greensand, both of which are available through sources of organic fertilizers. Manure and compost, and plant residues, will also be found to be satisfactory sources of potash.

The customary application of rock potash is 1,000 pounds per acre, or two and one-third pounds per 100 square feet of garden area.

Radioactive potassium techniques have shown that as much as one-third of plant potassium is fixed as plant protein. Potassium also helps to maintain cell permeability, aids in the movement of carbohydrates, keeps iron more mobile in the plant, and increases disease resistance.

In general, potassium can be said to impart plant vigor and disease resistance: aid in moving foods from the leaves to the roots: produce stiff stems and thus reduce lodging in grains: increase grain plumpness, and impart winter hardiness.

In a naturally well-balanced soil, potassium—like all other elements—is present in adequate amounts and is available to plants. The main problem with its application under toxic technology methods is that it's a salt, which has detrimental effects on soil life, and results in a vicious circle.

LIFE BENEATH YOUR FEET

The next time you're in a field or the garden, reach down and pick up a small sample of soil: a teaspoonfull will do. Hold it in the palm of your hand and examine it very carefully. And while you examine it, think of this:

A single teaspoonful of good soil can contain as many as 4,000,000,000 bacteria; 40 to 100 meters of the mold filament of fungi; 144,000,000 actinomycetes . . . plus assorted other living things that grow, consume, excrete waste, reproduce, and die.

There are as many bacteria alone in that one spoonful of soil as there are people on the face of the Earth.

What role does this teeming population of living protoplasm play in the production of our food, and what is the effect of our food production techniques on these inhabitants of the biosphere? Before we can come to any conclusions, we must know something about these life forms.

Soil life consists, in the main, of plants and animals that are able to exist in darkness, "feeding" on the crude elementary substances dissolved from rocks, and the elements of the atmosphere. Such simple life was probably the first to exist on Earth, and these organisms probably inhabited the sands of the cooling new planet for untold ages before there was sufficient accumulation of combined plant food to support the growth of higher plants. Progess must have been excruciatingly slow, for surely much of the product of their work was washed out to sea by torrential rains and floods which geology shows to have prevailed in primeval times. See Fig. 2-6.

Such organisms are at work today. They are attached to soil particles by the billions, drawing the mineral elements required for their growth from the rock powders ground by sun and frost, wind and rain. From the air and water circulating in the soil they take oxygen, nitrogen, hydrogen and sometimes carbon, necessary to complete their tissues.

And when their term of existence is completed, they leave a substance in which elements have entered into the first stages of transformation essential to their service in the nutrition of higher organisms. As Thorne, in *The Maintenance of Soil Fertility,* says, "This appears to be the initial stage of bacterial action, the first step in the multitude of transformations through which the elements must pass before they are finally combined in the support of that highest form of earthly existence, the 'living soul' of man."

From early times, agriculturists have been familiar with the idea that decomposition of animal and vegetable matter takes place in the soil, and that that process is somehow connected with soil fertility. But, while early Man studied the movements of the heavenly bodies and other things over this head, it has only been in the past hundred years that he bothered to pay much attention to the mysteries that lay under his boots. Even today, the life of the soil is largely neglected: how many farmers, even, think soil life means earthworms?

While earthworms are not the beginning and the end of soil life, our systematic observations of soil life began with them. Aristotle

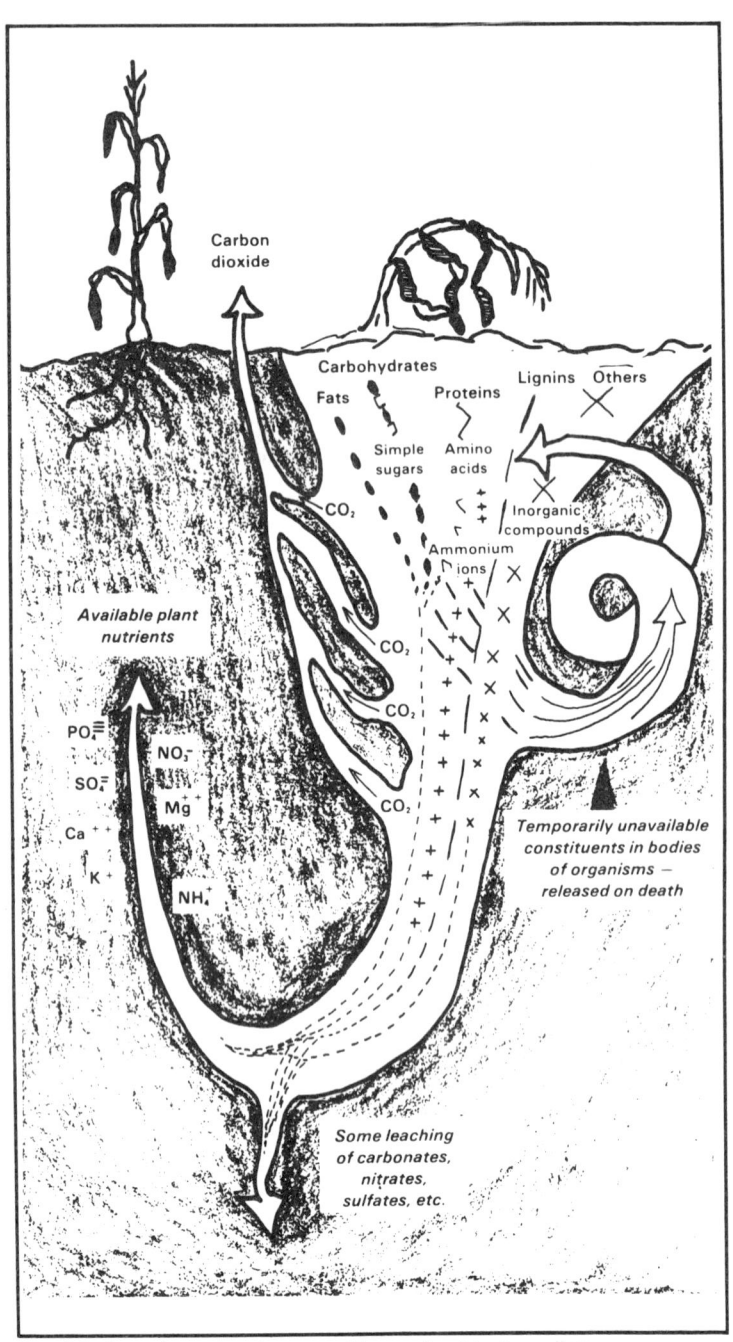

Fig. 2-6. Organic matter decomposition and nutrient recyling.

called them "the intestines of the soil" and their value was recognized in ancient times.

But it wasn't until 1881 that naturalist Charles Darwin published his monograph, *The Formation of Vegetable Mould Through the Action of Worms with Observations on Their Habits*. What should have been a classic in scientific literature caused no stir at all, at the time. Darwin's fame was to rest on apes, not worms.

Little more was done with the subject until some 60 years later when the fledgling school of organic agriculture republished the paper with the somewhat neater and more modern title, *Darwin on Humus and the Earthworm*, with a forward by Sir Albert Howard, titular head of the humus school.

However, also in the 1880s, other brilliant work was being done, all in France and all directly traceable to Pasteur. His discovery of bacteria paved the way for the discovery that these tiny plants lived and functioned in the dark recesses of the soil.

For many years, bacteria were thought to be the only microorganisms inhabiting the lithosphere. Only in recent years has the list of soil flora and fauna been expanded to look like this:

Microflora

A. Heterotrophic
   1. Bacteria
      a. Nitrogen fixers
         Symbiotic
         Nonsymbiotic

   2. Fungi
      a. Yeasts and yeast-like fungi
      b. Molds
      c. Mushrooms

   3. Actinomyces

   4. Algae
      a. Blue-green
      b. Grass-green
      c. Diatoms

B. Autotrophic
   1. Nitrite formers
   2. Nitrate formers

3. Sulfur oxidizers
4. Iron oxidizers
5. Those that act on hydrogen and various hydrogen compounds

Important Soil Animals

Protozoa
 Amoebae
 Ciliates
 Flagellates

Worms
 Nematodes
 Earthworms

Mollusks
 Snails
 Slugs

Anthropods
 Wood lice
 Spiders
 Mites
 Millipedes
 Centipedes
 Springtails
 Insect larvae
 Ants
 Termites

Vertebrates
 Reptiles
 Moles
 Gophers

Bacteria: the Most Abundant Soil Organisms

Bacteria, which are single-celled plants, exceed all other soil organisms in kind and numbers, although it is no longer held as it once was that soil life is primarily bacterial.

The most common soil bacteria are about a micron (1/25,000 of an inch) in diameter and up to a few microns long, which is certainly a reasonable explanation of why they could go about their business for so long without attracting any attention. A gram of fertile soil can contain as many as a billion bacteria, and an acre may have been more than half a ton of these plants.

Scientists divide bacteria into two main groups. The heterotrophic bacteria get their energy and carbon from complex organic substances; the autotrophic bacteria can obtain energy from the oxidation of inorganic elements or compounds, their carbon from carbon dioxide, and their nitrogen and other minerals from inorganic compounds. This latter group includes the nitrite formers, the nitrate formers, the sulfur oxidizers, the iron oxidizers, and bacteria that act on hydrogen and its compounds.

Most soil bacteria are aerobic, which means they get their oxygen from the air in the soil. Others cannot live in the presence of oxygen, and are anaerobic. Because of these and other environmental and nutritional requirements, the kinds and numbers of bacteria present in any soil depend on available nutrients and the soil environment.

The Fungus Among Us

Fungi are heterotrophic plants of great variety, ranging in size and structure from single-celled yeasts to molds and mushrooms. They typically grow from spores by a thread-like structure. These threads (hypha and mycelium) are easily fragmented, so it's difficult to determine the amount of fungi in soil. But researchers have observed that soils contain anywhere from 10 to 100 meters of mold filament per gram, and on this basis they claim that fungal tissue equals or exceeds bacterial tissue on most soils . . . which is about a thousand pounds per acre.

Fungi are important in all soils, particularly in acid forest soils because of their tolerance of acidity.

Actinomycetes are often called "fungilike bacteria" in that they resemble bacteria in some respects and fungi in others. Actinomycetes may be present in numbers anywhere from 0.1 million to 36 million per gram of soil, and under optimum conditions may exceed 700 pounds per acre.

Algae is a plant of great diversity, ranging from single-celled organisms to ocean kelps that are more than 100 feet long. While algae are the most important water plants, it is thought that their importance in soil is minor. However, they are universally distributed in the surface layer of the soil wherever light and moisture conditions are favorable and the most abundant (blue-green) contribute organic matter to the soil because of their ability to fix carbon. Some can also fix nitrogen. Algae are the simplest chlorophyllous plants, and their ability to photosynthesize puts them at the top of the heap in terms of the primitive plants being discussed here.

Important Soil Animals

The smallest and most numerous of the soil animals are protozoa, which are single-celled animals that live in the film of water which surrounds soil particles and are, therefore, really aquatic animals. When the soil dries out protozoa encyst, to become active again only when conditions become favorable.

Soil protozoa are predators, feeding on bacteria, and some also eat fungi, algae, or dead organic matter.

Worms that inhabit the soil include not only earthworms, but also microscopic nematodes. But because of the importance that has been attached to earthworms in agriculture soils, we should pause to examine some of the observations of Darwin.

Earthworms eat raw and half-decayed organic matter, and also pass through their bodies considerable quantities of earth. In this intermingling process they produce a rich vegetable mold which is constantly being added to the upper surface of soils. To quote the original Darwin monograph: "Worms have played a more important part in the history of the world than most persons would at first suppose. In all humid countries they are extraordinarily numerous, and for their size possess great muscular power. In many parts of England a weight of more than 10 tons of dry earth annually passes through their bodies and is brought to the surface of each acre of land, so that the whole superficial bed of vegetable mold passes through their bodies in the course of a few years . . . Worms prepare the ground in an excellent manner for the growth of fibrous-rooted plants and for seedlings of all kinds. They periodically expose the mold to the air, and sift it so no stones larger than they can swallow are left in it. They mingle the whole together, like the gardener who prepares fine soil for his choicest plants. In this state it is well-fitted to retain moisture and to absorb all soluble substances, as well as for the process of nitrification."

One respected current authority has written that earthworms don't add anything to the soil that wasn't already there, and that as a consequence, their effect on plant growth is minimal or of no concern. "Attempts to increase plant growth by increasing earthworm activities in soils have been disappointing," he said.

However, the same authority acknowledges that there are between 200 and 1,000 pounds of earthworms in an acre of soil. Every chicken knows the food value of a delicious, fat and juicy worm, and since worms don't live forever it would seem that their carcasses ought to contribute something of value in the way of plant nutrients. In addition, it is widely recognized both that worm castings are more fertile than the original soil, and that the mixing of the soil referred to by Darwin is of great importance to healthy plant growth.

Some researchers suggest that the activities of ants are of even greater importance than earthworms. Some ants are pests, such as the Harvester ants of the southwestern United States and of course the Fire ants, but there is evidence that the incorporation of subsoil material from as far as five feet below the surface, as well as a concentration of nutrients in the form of stored plant material and fecal material, produces effects comparable to earthworms. In one study, the entire land surface of a prairie was estimated to be reoccupied by ant hills every 600 years, with an increase in clay content and thicker, darker-colored A horizons (the top layer of soil).

This, of course, is only a brief and superficial review of some of the types and forms of life in the soil, and in the future we will examine many of these plants and animals, there requirements, their actions and their reactions, in more detail. But even at this point we should be aware of several facts about the living soil . . . and we should ask ourselves several questions.

In the first place, we know that earthworms are only a minor part of soil life, in numbers, weight, and activity.

We know that with proper conditions of food supply, moisture and temperature, soil organisms can be found in the soil in huge quantities: 1,000 pounds of bacteria per acre; 1,000 pounds of fungi per acre; 700 pounds of actinomycetes; 1,000 pounds of earthworms; plus lesser amounts of other plants and animals.

We know that these organisms can break down plant waste and other organic matter, and even rock, and convert it all into plant nutrients.

And we know that these are all living creatures, adaptable only to limited environmental changes.

What then, we may ask, is the real role of these tons of living protoplasm in each acre of healthy soil, in the production of food for higher animals? What effects do our biocides have on them? Our tillage and other management practices? Are they unimportant, or is there some yet-uncharted web that binds them to mankind . . . as we have learned every other form of life is bound to ours?

Over billions of years, these organisms adapted to changing conditions and acquired the ability to decompose all compounds formed directly or indirectly by photosynthesis. This is known as "the infallibility of soil organisms." But in the space of a few short years this concept has become endangered, for Man is now an important contributor of synthetic compounds to the environment, and many of these are not biodegradable, including many products used in agriculture. Nature is not as adaptable as Man appears to be for the short run, but isn't Man a part of nature too? Could our "adaptability" without regard for the rest of nature be a curse, instead of the blessing we take it for?

There are no scientific answers to these questions yet, which often makes those who ask them appear more mystical or philosophical than practical. But when you consider some of the possible answers, they are practical for what could be more practical than concern for the continued existence of mankind?

CHEMICAL FARMING: FAD THAT CAN'T LAST

Every farmer and gardener, of any size, or persuasion, wants fertile soil, because by definition that's the only kind plants flourish in, and flourishing plants are the reason for farming and gardening.

But, for two reasons, maintaining or increasing soil fertility (Fig. 2-7) is not easily accomplished. Soil is a very complex organism and soil fertility is even more complex. And this results in a second reason for the difficulty of knowing what to do and how to do it: there are too many conflicting opinions, too much complicated knowledge, and we too often embrace the simplest solution offered. The simple solution may be attractive because of economics, or because the farmer hasn't the interest or knowledge to follow a better course, but that doesn't make it the ideal.

The simple path of least resistance may be followed either chemically or organically. Both will often result in the desired goal—higher crop yields.

Chemicals are more attractive, certainly on an agricultural scale. They provide simplicity in many forms. They are easy to apply. Since farmers are not chemists, the use of chemicals that they feel they will never understand anyway makes it easy for them not to even make the attempt and to rely on the authority of others. And in the recent past, the economics of chemical fertilization have overwhelmingly favored its use.

Fig. 2-7. Increasing soil fertility.

In brief, if you approach a subject of extreme complexity and discover a method of reducing it to a soil test, the application of certain materials according to a formula, and if those materials are relatively inexpensive, easy to handle, and produce good results, this method is obviously attractive. Its attraction is attested to by the fact that this is what we call "conventional agriculture."

On the other hand, organic agriculture can also be simplified in the extreme. Simply apply copious amounts of manure and compost. While this has drawbacks in terms of labor and economics on large plots, its value has been amply shown in millions of organic gardens . . . including those of commercial farmers who use chemicals on their fields as a matter of routine but who wouldn't even consider fertilizing their home gardens the same way.

Thus we see a pattern emerging: organic methods are fine for gardens and small areas, but too expensive and time-consuming for larger tracts of land.

For the most part (but with some notable exceptions) that's just where the situation has rested for a number of years. But recently, the progress of events has broken down this simplicity, necessitating a re-evalution of both sides. An explanation is in order.

An examination of the history of agriculture reveals that what is now "conventional" embraces only a very brief span of that history. It's not hard to see how chemical fertilization came about, and developed, as a result not only of a rapidly expanding body of chemical knowledge, but as a result of increasing population and a lack of virgin soils to exploit.

As we look back on the birth of chemical agriculture, it's interesting to note the lines of divergence it took from the conventional agriculture of its day, which of course was old-fashioned organic agriculture. The differences were slight at first, but they grew exponentially until in the very recent past chemical developments grew like a cancer, and the line of chemical farming is now moving away from the line of natural plant growth at nearly a 90 degree angle.

Although much of the relative simplicity went out of chemical methods as technology progressed, they were still simple for the farmer. And they were cheap, not only in price but relative to increased yields. The result was that more and more reliance was placed on all forms of chemicals, (fertilizers, pesticides, fuel, etc.) and less and less on natural methods of fertility maintenance, insert control, etc.

This had two results. One was that the common ground between chemical and organic methods, which certainly existed in the beginning, was blurred as more and more of the credit went to chemicals. We have reached a point today where many farmers can see no similarity at all between the two.

But more importantly, the use of chemicals over a long period of time actually did lessen the need for natural forces and at the same time eroded those forces: humus, soil life, tilth and so on. Without those natural forces more chemicals were needed, of course, but that was no serious problem, technically or economically. More potent fertilizers were easy to develop, and with them herbicides, insecticides, and other products of technology. This progressed until, today, most agricultural soils are so poorly suited to organic methods that chemicals have provided a self-fulfilling hypothesis. It's true that most of those soils would not respond to purely organic treatment in the short run: but it's true only because the natural forces of fertility have been neglected and destroyed.

Some people say this is of little consequence, because increased knowledge and technology have made the old ways, the old need for natural factors, obsolete. And so it might be, except for several very disturbing developments. While some of these were foreseen several decades ago, they have only become highly visible in the past few years, due to increasingly potent chemicals as well as the accumulative effects both of chemicals and of neglect of natural factors.

The humus content of most soils has deteriorated to an alarming degree. While studies of a generation or two ago demonstrated that chemical applications were beneficial and had no deleterious effects, those studies were made on soils that had two or even three times as much organic matter as they do today, and organic matter, or more properly humus, acts as a buffer and a catalyst as well as providing mechanical benefits to agricultural soils. Moreover, the chemicals were in forms that had less effect on the life of the soil than those commonly used today. And they did not include pesticides.

More alarming is the dawning knowledge that many substances interact. This is true of the soil as a whole, of course: various elements, soil organisms, water, temperature, soil particle size and many other factors work together in harmony. One cannot be studied or treated alone, because its alteration will affect the others, and ultimately plant growth. But this has been drastically complicated by "unnatural" alteration of the soil environment.

One very recent example is the theory (of Dr. Philip C. Kearney and his co-workers at the USDA Pesticide Degradation Laboratory) that when atrazine and chemical fertilizers are simultaneously applied to the soil, as they are in "no-till" farming, a chemical reaction produces a nitrosamine known as nitrosoatrazine. The theory was developed to attempt to explain a fact: the concentration of nitrosamines found in American soil is 10,000 times greater than the concentration found in bacon, and no pork producer has to be reminded what a furor that caused just over a year ago. Nitrosamines are one of the most potent cancer-producing agents known.

While this is only one example, there have been many others. Chemicals can be tested for "safety," but it's virtually impossible to test the safety of chemicals in combination. There are thousands of chemicals, with astronomical numbers of potential combinations.

Yet another factor which only recently struck home to most people is ecology, the interrelationship of all forms of life and their environments. There can be no denying that conventional agricultural practices change the environment of the soil. The often-used retort that all farming, even the most primitive and organic, changes the environment, is beside the point: a small amount of salt in the diet is necessary for survival, but too much is lethal. Because a certain amount of environmental manipulation is necessary doesn't indicate that a great amount is better, or even equally beneficial.

There are many other disturbing factors involved, some of which can be proven scientifically, but many more which are still only hunches, or wisps of theories indicated by isolated experiences which have not as yet been thoroughly investigated. These include the highly disputed claims that food products grown on chemicalized lands are less healthful, less nutritious.

There are several possible explanations for such controversies, the most plausible of which is that this field of inquiry is so new and uncharted that we don't yet know precisely what to look for. Perhaps this can be likened to the famous experiment of Van Helmont (1577-1644) who planted a willow shoot weighing five pounds in 200 pounds of oven-dried soil. He added nothing but water, and even kept the shoot covered to prevent atmospheric dust from reaching it. And when, five years later, the tree weighed 169 pounds and three ounces, and the soil (dried again) weighed only two ounces less than at the beginning of the experiment, he concluded that water is the sole nutrient required for plants.

Today we might regard that as bordering on the comic, but despite the impressive body of knowledge that we are heir to, there are still many areas where we are as unsophisticated as Van Helmont was regarding plant nutrition. The role of air, and the missing two ounces of soil, didn't seem significant to Van Helmont, just as the role of microscopic or invisible forces seem unimportant to many of today's best scientists.

It's also important to remember that natural plant production has progressed through millenia on a fairly straight line. The chemical theory is the one that has curved away from that line, slowly at first, then with increasing rapidity until it is almost at right angles with the natural curve. This has two implications.

The first is that in its early stages, chemical theory and practice was not very far from natural practice. Humus was extremely important to both, and chemical use was limited both in quantity and potency. Only as conditions changed to enable chemicals to become more competitive did the two become more widely separated. These conditions included not only increasingly sophisticated chemistry, but also the decrease in importance of livestock farming due to the introduction of tractors and more recently, the rise in importance of cash crops and concentrations of livestock in feedlots and other confinement situations. Chemical fertilization became more important as world population burgeoned, concurrent with the end of new arable lands to develop.

The second implication is that as this chemical curve zoomed upward and away from the natural straight line, the more difficult it became to return to that straight line: it's much farther away than it was only a few years ago.

The interest in returning to that straight line of natural plant growth is evident today, and not only for the reasons already cited. Farming is an economic enterprise, and economics is at the very base of it. It's true that food is fuel, and health, but we must admit that these, too, are subject to economics.

Therefore, when farmers gave up their horses and oxen, their diversified farming methods, and many of them even left animal husbandry altogether, the use of chemicals was the only possible method available for maintaining soil fertility, for producing crops, and income. This has reached its apex today, and as we have seen, the reliance on chemicals in past years has created a dependency on even more chemicals and more potent ones. Insecticides, rodenticides and herbicides provide the most dramatic examples: everyone knows that strains of rats and flies have developed that are immune to poisons that were considered deadly only a few years ago. Therefore, today's conventional farmer is committed to chemicals, stronger chemicals and more of them, for economic reasons. He is part of a curve that seems to be too far off the base line to return to.

And yet, if problems such as those listed (and many others related to animal and human health) are only now beginning to appear, there comes a very serious question as to just how far this curve can continue. And it also becomes economic.

The rat and fly poisons mentioned provide an example on one level. If new strains that are immune to our poisons are constantly developing, is there any logical reason to believe that we will one day catch up? Might it not make more sense to adopt natural controls rather than to continue our attempt at complete eradication? This is a particularly important question in view of our new awareness of ecology and balance.

It should also be pointed out that this train of thought doesn't mean that we just let rats and flies proliferate: it merely means using our experience—with poisons, with natural controls, with the importance of ecology—to re-establish a balance we can live with.

The same is true of soil fertility, weeds, and plant pests. It's becoming obvious that we're fighting a losing battle, and that we'd be better off, maybe not way down on that base line, but certainly somewhere closer to it.

One of the final arguments in this chapter gets down to nitty-gritty economics.

Many farmers are finding that their increased reliance on chemicals of all kinds is becoming uneconomic, which is just the opposite of their original purpose. This is due partly to the fact that originally, chemicals were intended to be used in conjunction with natural fertility, and partly because of rising application rates and costs. The latter—costs—can only skyrocket, because most agricultural chemicals are highly dependent upon fossil fuels (most of them are derived from oil) which, even the most optimistic will concede, are going to increase in price. Along with that is the increasing cost of processing, transportation and selling, due to such factors as rising fuel expenses all along the line, rising wages in industry, and many other such factors. Therefore it follows that the farmer who intends to keep on farming, at a profit, is going to be forced to take a long, hard look at his purchases of chemicals—even if he attaches no particular importance to the other arguments put forth by organic farming interests.

The big question then is, how do we go about it?

This is not strictly a matter of method: it's intertwined with the economic health of the farm operation, and on a large scale it very likely will also affect the total world food supply.

When former secretary of agriculture Earl Butz (and others) said that we'd all starve to death if all farmers adopted organic methods, they weren't entirely wrong. But they were partly right for the wrong reasons.

Butz was correct in pointing out that there isn't enough manure in the entire country to put that land back in shape—although he didn't say it quite that way. In the majority of cases it's quite true that yields will fall drastically, at least until the soil is brought back to a point of natural fertility.

For the individual farmer, this need not be a concern, if only because input costs can often more than match the drop in production. Farmers live on their net income, not their gross. Many who now spend tens of thousands of dollars annually on chemicals could afford a sizeable reduction in yield and wind up earning as much. Of course, if all farmers did this, food prices would climb to reflect the reduced supply.

However, this is not the inevitable outcome because today there are highly sophisticated programs of organic farming available that need not reduce yields. And it is to these, the combination of the technological and the natural, that the modern progressive farmer is turning.

THE REAL DIFFERENCE BETWEEN CHEMICAL AND ORGANIC FARMING

It often seems that organic farming is full of "don'ts." It's all negative. "Don't use chemical fertilizers, don't use pesticides, don't use antibiotics and hormones." This is strange, because the real organic farming message is not negative at all: it's 100 percent positive: do everything you can to promote life in the soil, and avoid anything that destroys the life in the soil.

Significantly, this is the only place where organic farmers have any argument with "chemical" fertilizers.

Organic farmers sometimes speak derisively of the NPK syndrome. That isn't to say they're against chemicals, against N, P or K. We have seen in this series that plants need nitrogen, phosphorus and potassium, so it naturally follows that farmers and gardeners, even organic ones, need them too.

What organic farmers are really objecting to when they speak of the NPK syndrome is the common belief, implied or otherwise, that nitrogen, phosphorus and potassium are all that plants require. They can't object to the introduction of these elements to soils because all fertile soils have them and plants need them: but they can and do object to the forms in which they are applied, for many of those forms destroy life.

What is the most important factor in organic farming? As the name itself implies, organic matter. (More correctly from a roots' eye view, humus, which is decayed organic matter. Early organic farmers, in fact, were called humus farmers.)

It's interesting that we couldn't find a single book or article, even by the most vociferous opponents of organic farming methods, that even suggests that humus is not necessary for successful farming! On the contrary, virtually every agronomist insists that humus is vital for crop production. They may not always speak of soil life or impute much importance to it, but they mention factors like tilth and absorption and retention.

Now we are at a most interesting crossroad. Both organic and chemical farmers believe in and depend on N, P, K, and the other elements we looked at earlier. Both chemical and organic farmers agree on the need for humus in the soil.

So where (on this admittedly somewhat elementary level, at least) does the difference lie, and why?

The difference is merely one of degree. Every farmer and gardener relies on both humus and on chemicals. They must, because that's how plants grow. But some rely more on one, some rely more on the other.

What happens then demonstrates just how overenthusiastic and unbalanced people can become when they espouse a cause, or reap immediate benefits from a given way of thinking and acting. Like the new husband in the laundromat, they think that if one cup of detergent gets clothes clean, two is better and it's some time later that they are embarrassed by oceans of suds billowing out of the washer—with no way to stem the flow and no place to hide.

What happens on the humus or organic side is that certain important elements turn up short, because the so-called "pure" organic gardener or farmer absolutely refuses to utilize soil amendments of any kind. The die-hard organicist is so convinced that "chemicals" are bad, that he refuses to acknowledge that the crops he removes from his land are removing chemicals. Some of these people say all chemicals are present in rocks, and organic methods make these available. But not all rocks are the same chemically, and even when they are it often takes intensive organic methods to make them available—methods more suited to small areas.

Actually, most of these people are gardeners, who can take the produce of 10 acres and apply it to half an acre. Their system often works, which says something for organic methods, but they seem to ignore the nine and one-half acres they've left barren. It's no long term or widespread solution.

The other side of the beam is more drastic. Those who believe in chemicals often see such astounding results that they give all the credit to their applied fertilizers. In the extreme, they lose tilth, they lose topsoil, they lose natural fertility, and they lose their farms. Why? Because the chemicals that produce such fantastic yields are the very ones that destroy organic matter and humus, and with it, soil life. Yet, chemists and agronomists and soil scientists all know that humus acts as a catalyst for the chemical fertilizers: without humus, the fertilizers are less effective.

This means that the chemical farmers are between a rock and a hard place. The more chemical fertilizers, fungicides, insecticides, and herbicides they use on their land, the less organic matter they will have. And the less humus they have, the more chemical fertilizers, fungicides, and insecticides and herbicides they need. Like the soap in the laundromat, it doesn't happen immediately.

In fact, in the soil it takes a great deal more time because there are so many other factors involved: more potent chemicals prolong the illusion, for one thing. In addition we have developed many hybrid plants since the inception of chemical fertilization, we have adopted new tillage practices, and the weather has been abnormally favorable for crop growth on our portion of the Earth, just coincidentally since the beginning of the widespread use of chemicals.

What we're suggesting, then, is that so far as broad-scale and long-term agricultural production is concerned, few are 100 percent right or 100 percent wrong. The wisest course lies somewhere between these two extremes.

If this is true, what is the best and most practical method of making soil fertile?

Just skimming the surface we can see that it's important to have enough N, P and K in the soil to enable the plant to grow and flourish, and it's important to have enough humus in the same soil not only to react with the chemical elements but to provide many other benefits that may be less in volume but not less in importance. Adding humus does not diminish N, P or K.

However, adding N, P or K in certain forms does affect humus, by affecting the soil life which acts upon organic matter to transform it into humus. Therefore, the logical place to start in improving a soil is to increase the organic matter.

You will recall from earlier sections of this series that many of the common forms of chemical fertilization have deleterious effects on soil life. Anhydrous ammonia provides the best example, because it's especially dangerous even to the farmer applying it: it's easy to imagine what it does to the life in the soil. Remember that a teaspoonful of fertile soil contains more living organisms than the entire human population of the Earth: if inhaling anhydrous ammonia can kill a man, what will a drop of it do to that teaspoonful of life?

But this life represents thousands of pounds of the plow layer of each acre of land. When it's diminished, it cannot reproduce, defecate, and die, in the same numbers as when it is abundant. What's more, it cannot do the work which is its state in life, some of which was touched on last month and more of which we shall examine in greater detail later.

It has been pointed out that Man, through carefully formulated vegetarian diets, could live without livestock. But, it is highly doubtful whether Man could live without the animals in and on his own body. It is even more doubtful whether Man could live without the animals in the soil, because of their importance to even a vegetarian diet.

If this soil life—plant and animal—is so important, to both organic and chemical farmers, our first order of business should logically be to preserve and enhance it. And the most urgent call is to eliminate the factors that destroy that life, and to increase those that enhance it.

This embraces the toxic chemical fertilizers: the acids and salts that, in excess, destroy soil life. It also includes tillage practices: burying crop residues below the depth where soil organisms can turn them into humus. It involves management, such as completely denuding a field so no organic matter is present; plowing down a slope so rain can carry away topsoil; continuous cropping so the same elements are constantly sucked from the land.

Organic farming is no one-shot solution. It's an integrated system of farming. And the main difference between that system and the use of chemicals is that one is permanent while the other is only temporary. And that means Earl Butz was wrong: chemicals, not organic methods, will result in mass starvation.

PRACTICAL ORGANIC GARDENING

Most of what has already been covered in terms of commercial farming also applies to gardening. But gardens are much more labor-intensive, and therefore are more conductive to organic methods.

The principles are the same: soil testing, repairing the broken staves in the barrel, and building up organic matter. You can more easily afford the expense of quickly building up garden soil with organic fertilizers and soil amendments such as blood meal, not only because you'll encounter costs of dollars instead of thousands, but because the garden is much more productive than your fields due to the value of crops grown and the additional labor expended on it.

Likewise, adding organic matter is a much simpler task. Anything obtainable that is compostable, anything organic, is meat for the garden soil. Manure, leaves, straw, wood chips, sawdust, egg shells, coffee grounds . . . you name it. If it's organic it should be composted. (Composting is much more desirable and beneficial than merely spreading such materials, because fertility depends not on raw organic matter, but humus. In some cases the raw materials may actually decrease fertility temporarily.)

In addition, the gardener can also make use of such practices as companion planting and mulching, both of which are more "natural" than not making use of them, and both of which will pay dividends. Too much has been written about these practices elsewhere to warrant covering them here: but we hope that the information presented here will make it more clear why these practices are a good idea, and how they fit in with the total concept of soil fertility.

Now, to illustrate just how all these varied factors mesh together and are treated by the practical agriculturist, we can examine a case study. It involves both successes and failures, both of which can be educational. The example is the farm operated by *Countryside,* both as an economic enterprise and as a working laboratory for the magazine.

This is the Belanger family farm. It should be mentioned that we formerly worked a small place—one acre total. That ground had never been worked in terms of modern chemical agriculture, and moreover, it had lain fallow for several years.

When this ground was worked, you could plunge your arm into it up to the elbow.

The homestead at that time consisted of two pigs, half a dozen goats, a few sheep, 50 chickens, half a dozen rabbits, plus geese, pigeons and dogs and cats. All of the resultant bedding and manure went on about a third of an acre. No wonder that soil produced so abundantly! It yielded enough to can 200 quarts of tomatoes plus a surplus; 300 pounds of fine potatoes; sweet corn, peppers, broccoli enough to make the family sick of it and enough dry beans to feed six people for a year and still have some left over for bean bags. It produced mangels for stock feed, Jerusalem artichokes, comfrey, eggplant, salsify, carrots and beets, and more than a year's supply of acorn squash, even for acorn squash lovers. It produced strawberries and raspberries, currants and gooseberries, and basil, majoram, and enough caraway seed to garnish a thousand buns. And more besides.

And all of that manure, with the bedding (and feed) hauled in, with leaves retrieved from the village park and the lawns of citizens who weren't inclined to compost, with sawdust hauled from the sawmill, we were sure that organic gardening was the answer to the world's problems. For goodness'sake, why fertilize with yields like that? Why worry about weeds that were too few to notice or about insects that didn't exist?

Then we "graduated" to an 80-acre place. It was heavy clay that had been heavily cropped . . . to corn, yet. (There is a saying among organic farmers that the two worst evils in the countryside are hybrid corn and compound interest.)

The first year, we planted 30 pounds of potatoes and harvested . . . not one. All other yields were off discouragingly. Field crops fared somewhat better (except for corn), but the yields would have made any experienced farmer grimace.

If we had enjoyed the benefit of more knowledge and experience, we would have done many things differently. As it was, we were spoiled by our experience with a completely different soil situation and handicapped by a lack of resources, including knowledge, experience and cash. It's one thing to speak of building up a third of an acre (which wasn't in serious trouble to begin with) by hauling in leaves, sawdust, and by making copious amounts of compost, but it's quite another to look at 80 acres with the same ideas. Convinced of the importance of organic matter, all the bedding and manure from 100 pigs, 20 beef cattle, a small flock of sheep and about 30 goats, from chickens and horses . . . all of it went on a special five-acre field we intended to improve first. Three years later, the organic content was still less than three percent. And that left 75 acres to go.

In those early days, we could plow a furrow (we didn't have a chisel plow then) in our largest field, which was about a quarter of a mile long, and not see a single earthworm. We plowed a field that had lain fallow for three years (due only to the set-aside program in effect then) and unearthed cornstalks that were untouched by decay in all that time. All of this made us even more determined to turn the place into the veritable garden of Eden we had known before. But how?

In retrospect, we would have made much more progress, much more rapidly, by being less greedy. With our methods it probably would have been more profitable, too. We should have devoted much more ground to green manure.

As it was, we virtually eliminated corn (and regretted the little we did plant). Corn was responsible for most of the waste-landlike situation we found ourselves in in the first place.

Corn is profitable, because of its yields. But it is also a very heavy feeder, especially of nitrogen. These two factors result in the overuse of nitrogen, and usually in forms that have devastating effects on soil life and on humus.

Continuous corn results in weed and insect problems, which results in bringing on the pesticides—which only increase the problems. The profitability of corn results in plowing up hillsides that can only erode under row cultivation, and marshes that can only be worked when too wet and therefore have their tilth destroyed.

The sum total was a farm that was virtually worthless for crop production, except for ever-increasing applications of fertilizers and other chemicals. There was no organic matter, not only because of the chemicals that killed off the soil life but because the former operators harvested the corn stalks for fodder and bedding . . . a penny-wise but pound foolish measure.

The first years, small grains languished, due not only to the lack of fertility but to the residues of herbicides which the corn left as its legacy. All the land was planted to hay, or small grains and clover, as a means of increasing nitrogen and organic matter. Various organic fertilizers were used, fertilizers which contained not only some of the important elements of soil fertility, but microbial life as well. The chisel plow was adopted as the standard tillage tool.

The books say that buckwheat is great for poor soils, it will flourish where nothing else will grow, and that it reaches "30 inches in 30 days," Ours had trouble making 10 inches in 90 days.

But in time, things started to improve. The field that wouldn't grow buckwheat was planted to sorghum-sudan, which was chopped and chiseled in, treated with 200 pounds per acre of an organic fertilizer that the government doesn't allow to be called fertilizer, and planted to winter wheat. It yielded 30 bushels per acre. Another field yielded 50 bushels of rye. And within four years, more than a few neighbors commented that we had the best-looking barley they'd seen. See Figs. 2-8 through 2-11.

Fig. 2-8. Organic gardening.

Fig. 2-9. Organic gardening can increase yields.

Fig. 2-10. Corn fields can be chopped and chiseled.

Fig. 2-11. Organic matter is the key to soil fertility.

Just over a year ago, we took over another 90 acres, with most of the same problems as the original 80. It too had a history of corn and more corn, with the attendant fertilizers and herbicides. The herbicides made the growing of small grains impossible, so we had to adopt a long-range plan.

Because of the herbicides there was little choice but to grow corn the first year . . . but with a difference. The only fertilizer was 200 pounds of an organic soil amendment (in this case Shur-gro Mor-K, from Canton Mills, Minn.) and 80 pounds of urea. You will recall that urea is not a recommended soil treatment, but in this case it was the lesser of two evils. Because of the previous treatment it was impossible to grow anything but corn; corn requires a great deal of nitrogen, not only for the growth of the current crop but to break down the previous year's residues, which would actually take nitrogen out of the soil and rob the current crop. This was, in other words, a half-way measure, neither chemical nor organic, but a means of converting to organic while still making a crop and meeting expenses.

The corn stubble was chopped, and the land chisel plowed.

The corn was rotary hoed 10 days after planting, and cultivated twice. No other fertilizers, and no herbicides or insecticides were used.

Although there were problem areas, we got a respectable crop, especially in that drought year in the Midwest.

Two smaller fields were planted to barley, and one to oats, based on information from the former operator that they had not been subjected to Aatrex. One barley field was a virtual failure while the other wasn't bad. The oak field was on a long slope, and while the lower portion grew grain that reached the tractor tires when combining, the higher ground produced sickly little stalks that the header couldn't even reach when it was in its lowest position. The reason is obvious when plowing: after so many years of moldboard plowing and row cropping, and on the slope instead of on the counter, all the topsoil was washed down to the lower portion of the field. There was no organic matter and no fertility left on the crest.

Having a good suspicion of this beforehand, that field was planted to sweet clover along with the oats. Some farmers despise this plant and consider it a weed. It is thick-stemmed and makes poor hay and forage, and it's difficult to eradicate once it gains a foothold. But it is probably one of the best soil improvement crops we have. Its thick, fleshy roots probe deep into the soil to bring up nutrients, to relieve compaction and provide organic matter. Being a legume, it provides nitrogen.

Mammoth red clover was sown on the other fields, to be plowed down the following spring.

The corn fields were again chopped and chiseled, and next year the herbicide residues should be diminished enough to enable small grains to grow. Naturally, they will be sown with clover.

Then, instead of attempting to produce a saleable crop on every acre every year, we will adopt a practice followed on the other farm after several years of experimenting, and it's certain that results will be more dramatic and will come more quickly. And that is the old-fashioned practice of green manuring.

There can be little doubt to the serious observer that organic matter is the key to soil fertility. On these lands at least, that is definitely the broken stave in the barrel.

There isn't the slightest possibility of getting enough manure to treat 170 acres here. Local sewage sludge has all been spoken for for years. Composting leaves and similar materials is out of the question, from the standpoint of time and economics. While there is a local cabbage processing plant which spreads waste on farm lands, it comes at a time when corn is still standing . . . and there is the question of residues of insecticides in the cabbage leaves. (We have, however, applied several hundred tons of certain fields, with very good results—the aforementioned barley field being one of them.)

The only choice left would seem to be "grow it yourself" organic matter. While we could go into the economics of this versus chemical fertilization, it hardly seems appropriate here: we have seen the devastating results of chemical farming on this soil, and we're determined to correct that devastation whatever the cost.

The soil test also plays an important role. We need some nitrogen, but the legumes and soil micro-organisms provide that on land that is already being healed. We're low on calcium, so although the pH is acceptable, we lime heavily with high-calcium lime. The small amounts of P and K required were added via organic fertilizers. And that's about it.

On some fields, we can expect to add as much as 20 tons of organic matter to each acre in a single year. Depending on variable factors, we use buckwheat, clover, sorghum-sudan and winter rye for green manure. Clover-grass mixtures are mown and left on the surface. New growth pushed up through the residue. We can repeat this three or four times in a year, then work it all in with the chisel, and still plant winter wheat or rye. On other fields we have clover or rye growing during the fall and the next spring, and that is plowed in July and planted to buckwheat for a grain crop. On still others, we plant buckwheat early in the spring, then plow it down and plant sorghum-sudan (which is drought resistant) in the summer. The possible combinations and methods are endless, and are determined by the soil, the weather and the workload. Such lands are also amazingly weed free in comparison with continuously cropped fields.

The idea, then, is to incorporate as much organic matter as possible; to work land only on the contour and to avoid planting slopes to row crops; to chisel and subsoil; and to soil test, but to avoid using materials that will wipe out the hard-won gains in humus and soil life. Crop rotation is imperative for us.

There is probably an ideal that could be applied to large and small acreages alike. We haven't applied it on a large scale because of the familiar laments of farmers who have to make a living, and can't afford to divert sizeable portions of their land, or even to experiment on a grand scale. But we do have enough experience with that ideal—or the closest to the ideal that we've found . . . to be able to recommend it to anyone willing to try.

The farm or garden should be divided into four areas of roughly equal size. One of those four areas should be in green manure, preferably a legume. If planted with a small grain, there is no cost for tillage or planting: the only expense will be in seed, and in letting the land lie "idle" for a year. And combined with other organic practices that cost will be recovered in savings on chemical fertilizers and pesticides within a year, in most cases. It's not an expense, in other words, but an investment.

And that, perhaps, describes the rationale behind organic farming better than any other single word: investment. You might be young enough to have hopes for cashing in the dividends on that investment yourself. But even if you aren't, the one concern that binds all organic farmers and gardeners together is the thought for the future: our children and our children's children who will inherit the legacy we leave them. Will greed and blindness make us squander that inheritance in hopes of quick profits now—or will we pass on an Earth that is rich and fertile enough to feed all of mankind for all times to come?

The choice is ours.

ORGANIC FARMING REALLY WORKS

There are many ways to finance a dream, and Howard Beeman Jr.,

Fig. 2-12. Organic farming works.

Rt. 1, Box 155, Woodland, California, has been putting his pennies into the pot for five years.

A conventional farmer with 340 acres he rents from his father, Howard also grows certified organic *Inia* wheat on his own 200 acres and is working toward the day when all of the crops he grows will be organic. See Figs. 2-12 through 2-19. Since 1971, when he became

Fig. 2-13. Howard fabricated this 24-foot grain drill in the family machine shed.

Fig. 2-14. Howard and Susan show off their turkeys.

one of the state's first certified organic growers, he's paid for half of his own land.

Howard is a member of the third generation to farm the land, and with his father and brother, operates the Three Howard Beemans' Farm. His father and brother are strictly conventional farmers, and Howard's out to prove to them and to the world in general, that organic farming is economically feasible at his scale, despite many reverses and adversities.

"We're in the transition stage," the 35-year-old farmer says. "We're working hard and biding time to get our scene together so it makes sense. And if we can make it organically on our comparatively large operation, it will be a model for other farmers."

Fig. 2-15. The "workhorse" of the farm is a 125-hp Caterpillar tractor. It is half-owned by Howard.

The "comparatively large" needs clarification. Howard's place is in the fabulously rich Sacramento Valley—a lush irrigated land dominated by vertically integrated agribusiness corporations. Farms of 40,000 to 60,000 acres are not uncommon; "average" farms in the valley run 2,500 to 3,000 acres, and 1,500 acres is considered "small."

Within that frame of reference, it's easy to see why Howard considers himself "tiny" as a valley farmer, even though 200 organic acres is a sizeable chuck of land in other parts of the country. As an illustration, Howard is a member of an independent tomato canning cooperative and with 100 acres in the crop, he's the smallest

Fig. 2-16. Getting enough clean manure is a never-ending challenge for Howard.

146

Fig. 2-17. The "ranch house" was nearly gutted by fire, but it is now almost completely restored.

grower. The other members average around 500 acres in tomatoes.

In 1976, Howard split his acres into the tomatoes, at 100 acres; 240 in wheat; 75 in sweet corn; 65 in rice; 25 in alfalfa; and 40 "lost" acres in a field without irrigation equipment. Last year California experienced its worst drought in recorded history, with the Woodland area receiving just 41 percent of its normal rainfall.

Giantism, Howard explains, has been the way of California agriculture since the Spanish land grant days. Then came the land barons, and the energy interests after mineral rights, and the corporate and conglomerate farms. The land was worked in a long tradition of near slave labor—first the Indians, then the Mexicans and the Chinese, Japanese, the Filipinos, and now the machine.

Fig. 2-18. Precious water comes from a country surface system (above), a well, and a run-off slough.

Fig. 2-19. Howard surveys his first crop of sweet corn.

Howard is the kind of man who'll take a visitor on a tour of the town of Woodland and point out things that the Chamber of Commerce is apt to ignore. He'll go out of his way to gaze fondly at a splendid Victorian home and he knows and shows the location of every surviving towering valley white oak tree.

"Bigness is abhorrent to me," he states. "I just dread it. And yet they say that the byword around here is to get big or get out. I'm closer to getting out than getting big. I have to be out on the land every day instead of sitting at a desk with an account book. But I have to face reality. I'm surrounded by giants and I have to compete with them."

Yields in the valley are monstrous—two and one-half tons of rice to the acre; five tons of corn, three tons of wheat; 30 to 40 tons of tomatoes; between 25 to 30 tons of sugar beets. "There's a lot of bounty here, and that, of course, helps make the land so expensive." Howard says.

His area did not escape the land boom. When he bought the 200 acres which used to be his grandmother's homestead he and his partner, Susan Pelican, made the deal for $500 an acre.

"That was about the time the wheat prices doubled," he recalls. "Now corn's up, tomatoes have just about doubled as have most other things and production costs have tripled, so now the assessor tells me our land's worth around $1,500 an acre for its Number Two and Number Three soil. People are paying around $2,500 an acre for Number One soil like my father's land, especially in parcels of around 80 acres. There's a person near my parents' home who paid over $100,000 for 30 acres and a house. Wow! So the land with the most return is being gobbled up by professional people with money to invest, and they can't go wrong around here. And how does an organic farmer bumble his way through it all? It's hard to stay afloat sometimes."

Howard has what he calls his "little diatribe about what's painful and wrong about California agriculture" and why he sees organic agriculture in the state as a tough, but not impossible nut to crack.

The state has a law on the books called the Williamson Act, whereby approved land is placed in an "agricultural preserve" for tax purposes on a 10-year, self-renewing basis. A person wishing to withdraw his land from the preserve is supposed to give a 10-year notice. There are loopholes and the land can be withdrawn, albeit with penalties. The act is designed to give a tax break to farmers and to keep the land in food production, but it contains a "catch-22." Land within the preserve is taxed according to how it produces on a basis of its "highest and best use" according to the type and class of soil.

"This," Howard explains, "has terrific implications. If you have Number One soil and you're taxed according to what the state figures your income should be, this means the land is literally too valuable for livestock. It must be extensively farmed, often in vegetable row crops. This in turn means that you don't have the mixed animal-plant culture that's highly desirable for organic farming. And the act also causes the land values to spiral ever upward so that the theoretical maximum yields you're taxed upon are required in actuality to keep the banks and/or landlords at bay.

"This means maximum efficiency, coupled with a great deal of experience in order to stay afloat. It means you have to be super-efficient. There's no slack for a non-crop year, so only the fittest have survived.

"The hardest part of farming around here is the psychological fragmenting of yourself to the bankers, the buyers, and even your neighbors when you try to make a go of it organically. You can't afford to foul up in any way and still keep your land. There are a lot of pressures.

"We have to generate our operation which can generate enough money to secure the land for us. Because land is such a scarce resource, how you are going to get it is the question. You have to have more than just a few acres to justify the overhead to generate that much more capital—and that is the sort of tail-chasing exercise we're in now."

Politics and organizations also enter the "diatribe." Howard, who has been organic in sympathy and action "ever since we discovered honey wheat bread," was a founding member of the Rodale Press sponsored California Certified Organic Growers (CCOG), which culminated in what he calls "an organization disaster" when it tried to become independent.

He feels that the state has "huge vested interests to quash organic farming," including a usually agribusiness oriented university, most of the press, including the *Los Angeles Times,* a major landholder, and the agrichemical people themselves.

"Then we had Ronald Reagan for governor and his appointees who could care less. Now we have Jerry Brown and his people who are interested, but still, they're not knowledgeable. They don't have a real tie to agriculture. They're academia or the new hip leadership potential, and besides they're so busy with so many projects they can hardly appreciate organic farming. So we're left with no real force behind the organic movement here, except for the California Organic Growers (COG) which is less than a year old. It seems to have a healthy chance for success, though."

Of the previous organization, the CCOG, Howard says, "the input that I tried to make was all denied. I was mostly an outcast and my ideas were pooh-poohed so I lost interest in trying to bang my head against the wall."

He is a charter member and an active participant in the COG (see *Countryside,* September 1976, pages 19, 20). He explains that some of COG executive Don Foote's ideas are similar to his own, which were previously put down. For example, Howard doesn't think there should be only black and white classification of organic and non-organic.

"There are shades of organic," Howard maintains. "Some people really do have organic soil and others don't. Why sell produce that's coming out of haphazard soil as representative of the same as produce from genuine, fertile, well cared for, organic soil? It's not fair to either the consumer or the farmer. There should be allowances for shades of differences, for transistions."

Howard also feels that self-certification along with tissue tests has certain limits. "You would have to sample the product within hours of being sprayed with the stuff they use now, because it isn't detectable later," he maintains. He cites as an example an occasion when one of his fields was sprayed by mistake. The next morning, samples were taken from the sprayed tomatoes and the tissue tests disclosed no biocides. "Now how are you going to have a certification program when somebody sends in a couple of leaves at a random time? There's no validity there."

He would rather see the government involved providing source material in the validation process. "In California, we have a government-operated, computerized poison permit system. The county agent oversees where the chemicals go: who buys them, who applies them—and it is tight. You have to have a license to sell them; you have to be trained to apply them; you have to have rigid safety controls and train anyone on your farm who might apply them. And every poison that's sold has a permit which goes on the computer. There's no reason why you couldn't catch supposedly organic people who are using it if the government would open up the computer access to the organic certification committee. You could positively check up upon who is or isn't using the chemicals. To have total validity, we need that kind of help."

When *Countryside* visited the Sacramento Valley last summer, pesticides hung like a shroud in the still air as crop dusting planes dropped their loads. The acrid smell permeated everywhere. The distant mountains to the south were murked with pollution from the Bay area. Howard used to be able to see them distinctively every clear day.

He considers the amount of pesticides and herbicides used with such crops as tomatoes and sweet corn as appalling. "In tomatoes, the poisons are used at seeding, when the plant emerges, when it grows a little they spray for the first bugs that might appear, and gain after the plant grows a bit more. Then they rototill the whole bed and apply herbicides to it all. The poisons used to raise that crop are phenomenal," he says. With sweet corn, it's herbicides at the beginning and the plant is sprayed with pesticides every three to five days while the silk is out. "The sweet corn is terrible and I think the tomatoes are without taste, " he states.

"That's another reason I'm interested in turning agriculture around and making farmers aware of the benefits of using less poison on the land, and also doing out bit to help change the food distribution system."

Howard and Susan are almost totally self-sufficient in food they produce for themselves, their son, Ezra Beeman, 3, and their "two and one-half employees," mostly students serving as paid apprentices. They have seven goats, including four milking does, some sheep and lambs, a cow, geese, ducks, chickens and turkeys. They have a summer and winter garden for all of their vegetables, and rice and wheat which Howard grows. Susan grows "eating tomatoes" preferring them to Howard's near-organic canning tomatoes.

They're now living in a slightly down-at-the-heels plantation-style manse complete with pillars, a huge foyer and an exposed staircase. The house was built after the Gold Rush by a wheeler and dealer who hit it rich outfitting the miners. They have been slowly restoring Howard's grandmother's homestead ranch house which was almost razed by fire and was open to the skies for four years. They hope to be able to move to "the ranch" this year.

The soils they're working with are high in natural nutrients, geologically much younger than the lands east of the Rockies and therefore more fertile. Howard calls his rented Number One soil tough and resilient.

"You can dig down for 8 or 10 feet and it's the same quality as topsoil," he maintains. "But that rich layer is much thinner on our own land which is Number Two and Three. On this Number One soil, because it's so fertile, people can brutalize it. They can tear it up and plow it down 12 inches, flip it upside down and start over again, forgetting about soil life. That's common practice. If they go into new ground, the first thing they do is plow it as deep as they can and turn up unused soil. And they can do that over and over again. It takes a long time to exhaust soil like this. They know that, so they don't worry about it. But eventually . . ..

"But the land at the ranch is sandy and its very difficult to keep the humus content up. It has to be renewed every season. Even though we don't put anything on it to burn it up, there's hardly any humus left after a summer. It's all eaten up, decomposed."

Tomatoes are Howard's favorite crop, giving him "instant gratification" as he munches one of the ripe fruit. They are not the square-around or tennis ball variety found in your local supermarket, but a variety developed for machine picking by the University of California-Davis. They're tasty and juicy, being different from the ordinary garden variety only because of their thicker skins. They're picked when ripe and red, not green as is usual in tomato row cropping. The fruit does have the ability to stay on the plant for 30 days until rot sets in, so they can be harvested in bunches.

Their taste and freshness is important to Howard. He recalls when he went to a reception in Pasadena. "There was a big bowl of fruit on the table. The peaches and apricots were tasteless. The only thing that retained its taste were the cherries. I guess we're spoiled, but I wonder what New Yorkers eat. Now when apricots leave from around here bound for New York City, they're picked when they're lime green. There's no chance for them to develop flavor."

Tomatoes are also the backbone crop or the "mortgage lifter" for Howard. He grows them without pesticides or herbicides, except for bacillus and a ripening agent, on chemically fertilized soil if he must, or organically fertilized soil if he can.

A good harvest a couple of years ago gave them a large influx of cash which they put right back into equipment and loan payments, although he somewhat ruefully admits "we might have been better off if we'd gone to Europe instead of buying that second tomato harvester."

Howard and Susan started with down payment money from her parents and from his mother, owing them both about $40,000 plus $7,500 remaining on their one-half interest in a $44,000 crawler tractor and some "little stuff" to his father.

They have been unable to get bank financing through the Production Credit Corp., even on the strength of their wheat contracts although they have tried four times. "We know and the banks know that the money will be coming in, but they still wouldn't lend it to us, because our statistics don't meet their books."

They've had two bad years in tomatoes, losing 40 percent of the crop one year, about $50,000, and last summer's cannery strike caused all sorts of complications.

The strike went on for weeks while the tomatoes, which have only a 30-day holding capacity on the vines, were steadily ripening in the hot, dry weather.

When the strike was settled, the growers were raring to go. But the cannery, because of the fact that everyone was starting at once, put the growers on quotas. Howard, who harvests five to six truckloads a day, was allowed two trucks a day, and was sometimes allowed three trucks every other day. So he was harvesting at less than half of capacity.

After the first week of the harvest, the tomatoes had reached their holding limit and began to deteriorate. At the beginning, at most 15 to 20 percent were culled; at the end, the situation was nearly reversed and he was able to harvest about one-third of them.

"So although we began the harvest with 27 tons per acre, at the end we were harvesting 12 to 15 tons at the most. And we figure it takes 20 to 22 tons to break even. Then while this was going on we had heavy rains and marble-sized hail—rain at the wrong time in a year of drought. I applied a fungicide for the first time. That was a waste of time and money. So, we took a beating on the tomatoes this year."

Howard feels that it's going to be a struggle to recover from the two bad tomato crops. "That's where the margin in efficiency comes in; you have to be successful all the time. If that would happen again, I would just have to declare bankruptcy and say I've had my shot. It's just not worth it to spend my whole life paying off a dept. We'd give the land to Susan's mother, and call it square."

Despite the two unprofitable tomato years, Howard says that "just an average year" will pull them out of debt. Because the land is half paid off, he hopes to qualify for a government "Cal-Vet" loan for $80,000. They had to pay off that half before they could qualify.

But even with their losses, they've wound up with just one big bill that "we're handling." And an average year would mean an end to the drought which has forced them to pump more than usual. Last year the pumping bill for the rice was $1,500.

There are three choices of water—a deep well pump, a surface county system, and a drainage slough. Howard can tap any and all of those sources, but he's very concerned about the biocide residues that are apt to be in the slough, so he tries to rely on the other, purer but more expensive, sources as much as possible.

Howard says he became a farmer because his father's a farmer and he had access to his operation and access to his land. His father has a machine shop of nearly commercial size and outfit, which is convenient and necessary for making parts and repairing equipment.

Howard has even fabricated a 24-foot grain drill, which is not all that surprising considering he's a mechanical engineering graduate of the University of California-Berkeley. He was an ROTC member at Berkeley, and admits that "Vietnam scared me into studying." (He wound up there anyway as an officer in the Army Corps of Engineers. After a divorce from his wife, Mardee, the mother of his son, Howard III, 12, he met Susan and got caught up in the organic movement.)

The machine shop is quite necessary in California because the state has an inventory tax and it's difficult to get parts, especially at harvest time.

"The dealers don't want to keep any more parts on the shelves other than the bare minimum. They're always 24 or 36 hours away out-of-state at depots in Nevada. I've run around the countryside all day just trying to locate 20 lug nuts. This is something you have to get used to and try to circumvent."

Howard declared, "I'm machine oriented. I grew up on a farm that was mechanical with big, powerful, sophisticated equipment. Part of my farming technique is from watching my father farm. I don't know anything else, and both of my sons go nuts over equipment. That adoration of equipment gets in early and it stays."

So he has a disc that cuts a 24 foot swath in fifth gear and can knock out 40 to 50 acres a day. He has his half interest in a 125-hp. Caterpiller crawler tractor, a 50-hp wheel tractor "that's a little under what we should have—about 90-hp." There's a combine with both rubber tires and tracks. For tillage he has a ripper, a plow, a disc and lots of cultivating equipment including rolling cultivators and 16-foot tool bars to which specialized equipment may be clamped. There's the grain drill, a vegetable planter, and two tomato harvesters, one of which is being phased out.

All told, Howard has about $100,000 in equipment for a farm that's considered "tiny." The tax bill on that equipment last year was $1,700. He considers his equipment minimal for his operation and is glad he has what he does. That $44,000 tractor could not be replaced at double the price now.

Howard practices a couple of different systems of crop rotation. On the rented land he alternates dry crops like wheat with the irrigated crops like tomatoes. He isn't using the system he would like to use on that land "because the landlord objects." That would be to put the land into alfalfa for five years, then tomatoes followed by wheat, then corn and/or tomatoes, and then back into long-term alfalfa. He'll use this plan on his own land when it's paid for, and is starting now with a small field of alfalfa.

For fertilizer on the conventional land which tends to be alkaline, he uses standard dry fertilizers along with some ammonia sulphate, and adds sulphur and zinc. He taps a mountain of lime from a nearby sugar factory only as a soil conditioner, not for pH.

On the organic land he spreads a minimum of eight yards, about four tons, to the acre, alternating buckets of chicken and sheep manure onto the spreading truck. That's when the manure is available. Then he works it in with a disc harrow and seeds bell beans, which are similar to fava beans, for nitrogen. He either plants the beans or vetch. But the beans will grow in the winter and the vetch won't, so it depends upon the season.

"You may get a little more nitrogen from the vetch," he says, "but you have to wait until May for it to grow, whereas the beans will be done and the field ready to use at the end of March."

He likes to use both the beans and the manure, but sometimes he can only get enough manure for part of the land and settles for the legumes. Tomatoes will then go into the prepared land.

He put on 400 to 500 pounds of rock phosphate per acre a couple of years ago, and his annual soil tests show that there's still enough on the land. The first rock phosphate he used came from a mine in Florida, and the second, all the way from the Sahara Desert.

"That was from a natural dried-up lake bed deposit that had 35 percent phosphorus. It was really hard to get, and I had to convince the co-op to sell me the raw stuff before they treated it with acids so it would break down quickly—just what I don't want. They really don't like to do that, because they can make more money on it after it's treated. It was like pulling teeth."

He uses two tons to the acre of gypsum; he's tried seaweed and would like to again when he can better afford the expense.

Securing an adequate supply of manure is a never-ending problem. There's plenty available from area feed lots, but Howard is suspicious of it because of the chemicals fed to the animals.

Howard explains that he's invested a considerable amount of time and money in hauling manure for his own land, starting with a sheep slaughterhouse owned by Armour in nearby Dixon. It was fine manure, and although he's never been cheated, he got left out several times in favor of a bigger operator—a man who's business is manure. Howard then started to pay for the manure and his men were forced to wait for several hours until they could load up. The manure scavenger still got the best product. So he quit again.

In the meantime, he'd bough a truck to haul it with and had amassed a couple of mountains of manure. Another farmer agreed to spread it for him with his huge spreader truck, but the repair department at the slaughterhouse had tossed used conduit, spikes, chunks of concrete and sheet metal into the manure with great abandon. The farmer's spreader got jammed by the bolts and boulders, so Howard tried to spread it himself, picking out the debris by hand. He finally managed it, meanwhile looking for a manure cleaner.

He discovered a chicken farmer with lots of manure and a cleaner for sale for $1,500. The chicken farmer would sell the manure, but he hedged on the cleaner, taking a $750 check on deposit, finally. That check still hasn't been cashed, but at least Howard has his manure. He got so much manure that it took a crew two days to spread it all with a 30-ft. truck, a job Howard estimates would have taken him months with his little spreader.

The costs for that manure, however, have more than doubled in the past couple of years. As Howard says, "it's like anything else. It's garbage until there's gold in it. And sometimes when you deal in manure you get treated like it."

The problems he's had, he feels, "all go back to not having a mixed animal-plant culture. We have to have extra equipment to haul the manure in from elsewhere, and we have to depend upon other people's often careless treatment of the manure. We could go into the animal business, and on our own land it would be justifiable. But until we do, we're at the mercy of others who may or may not be sympathetic to what we're trying to do. We're still in the transition stage, and developing these sources ourselves and finding the right equipment is a terrible task, especially when we're busy all of the time."

Howard's main organic cash crop is a relatively hard winter wheat from the Mexican *Inia* strains, which has a protein content of above 14.69 percent. He sells wheat from the farm, bagged with his own label, or from the field to distributors.

He's trying a different tack with some of his wheat this year, growing foundation stock for the Yecora and Rojo *Inia* strains. He explains that when the wheats are developed, the California Certified Seed Assn., composed of growers, the university and people associated with the seed industry, will grow the very first seeds that are brought in.

From those there may be only one desirable mutant, so they wind up with one seed head. The next year there'll be a sack, then 60 sacks, and so on. And when the pure strain is isolated and then gets to production level, it's called foundation stock the very first year it's available to outside growers. The crop out of the foundation seed is called registered seed, and the crop out of that registered seed is called certified. The fields growing the seeds are all inspected for having only that variety and for not having any of certain noxious weeds growing in the fields.

"The bottom has fallen out of the wheat market—about $2 a hundred-weight since July," Howard explains, "so we're hoping to protect ourselves by growing the foundation seed. Last year we got a dollar extra for our Yecora-Rojo and we hope to be able to do it again. This seed wheat should help ensure our getting an adequate return."

Howard's rice crop did well this year, despite the high cost of irrigation and high winds washing out some of the banks and transfer boxes. He did comparatively well in his first year of sweet corn, finding that the single cross he planted wasn't bothered by the corn smut that sharply cut yields in triple cross corn this drought year.

And although he can't afford another year like this one with its drought and cannery strike, he's already looking forward to the next year.

He says he's "committed to growing foods that are natural—that are involved with life. And I hate the thought of so many people eating foods that are dead, embalmed. And that's without even considering possible contaminants or mutagens in the foods."

The ranch house is all painted so they'll be moving in soon. Its yard is all cleaned up, ready for the orchard and vineyard they'll plant to replace his grandmother's which was destroyed.

He's very excited about what he calls his "insect preserve"—a 25-acre alfalfa field he put in in October on the ranch.

"People from the university are interested in our little plot because there's hardly any other place in the valley which hasn't been sprayed and isn't going to be. They're going to conduct experiments and introduce some beneficial insects and try to get them established. And besides it's nice having all of that green in the winter. We will now have our own organic hay and will have some to sell to the others who need it.

So he's starting in alfalfa—the first step on his long-range plan on rotation. All he's looking for now is "just an average year" and the dream is that much closer to reality.

HEALTHY, WEALTHY AND WISE

Four years of being plagued with skin rashes and depression, plus a $12,000 medical bill, finally convinced Ralph and Rita Englekens to stop farming with agricultural chemicals and to try another way. "The reason we decided to try organic farming was a desire for improved health," Ralph recounted in an unassuming voice that has become familiar to many. In recent years Ralph has often traveled far from his secluded Iowa farm speaking to various groups about his success farming organically.

"I worked for three years custom applying 2,4-D and after a while developed a serious skin rash. Soon Rita and the children began to break out as well. After quite a few visits to the doctor, the source of the problem was finally identified." Traces of 2, 4-D had spread from Ralph's clothes through the laundry, contaminating all the family's clothing. Besides the skin rash, Ralph also suffered from internal irritation as well, but he got off easy. One of his brothers died after a severe two-day reaction to 2, 4-D.

Converting to organic methods involved much greater risk and required a good deal more courage 19 years ago when the Englekenses made their decision to convert. "We reached the point where it was either give up farming or give up farming with chemicals," Ralph explained. Information, advice and moral support were scarce; organic fertilizers and integrated pest management virtually unheard of. Fortunately for Ralph and Rita, there was one person sympathetic to their plight—their parish priest, Father Louis White, an organic gardener since 1946. It was his encouragement and willingness to teach that helped the Englekenses get started.

Once having decided to make a fresh start, Ralph and Rita in-

Fig. 2-20. Ralph Englekens (left) and Richard Thompson are both active proponents and practitioners of farm-scale composting of manure.

Fig. 2-21. A field day conducted at the Englekens' farm.

vested in a new 200-acre farm. "The previous owner had used chemicals and the year before he sold out he hadn't even made enough to pay the property tax." Having regained his own health, Ralph set about restoring the health of the farm. Naturally, he began with the soil. See Figs. 2-20 through 2-23.

"It took me two years to build up the soil and another two years to cultivate an adequate population of soil bacteria. But things had improved enough by the end of the first two years, that we were

Fig. 2-22. Fall sown rye is fed as silage in the spring. The residue is plowed back as a green manure for the following corn crop in one of Ralph's experiments with double-cropping.

160

Fig. 2-23. Each year the Englekenses feed out about 500 head of feeder cattle on their homegrown grains and hay.

able to invest in another 300 acres." Through carefully planned crop rotations and the addition of copious amounts of organic matter, Ralph created what rightfully deserves to be called an agricultural masterpiece. Success breeds success it is said, and eventually the Englekenses purchased another 200-acre tract.

Though much of the Englekens' 700 acres is in difficult to cultivate slopes, through the years this family has developed a good working relationship with their land. Four shiny blue Harvesters are the most obvious indication of their success. It's common knowledge in the corn belt that a man's monetary worth is directly related to the number of Harvesters on the property. The new house is further testimony that organic farming has proved profitable for this family of 11.

Upon closer inspection, however, the real wealth of the Englekens' farm becomes apparent—a thick layer of rich, sweet smelling topsoil. In return for Ralph's respect and thoughtful management of this capital resource, the soil returns dividends such as 125 bushels of corn per acre (up to 185 bushels on his best land) which has tested as high as 11 percent protein. Hay fields have yielded as much as 12 to 13 tons per acre dry matter, testing between 18 and 25 percent protein. When cut for haylage the protein content runs about 18 percent with a TDN (total digestible nutrients) of 49 percent on a dry matter basis.

These dividends are then invested in the Englekens' herd of feeder cattle. Ralph "backgrounds" on the average of 500 beef cattle per year. About 70 percent of the herd is sold to feedlots for finishing at a profit margin of two cents per pound. The remaining 30 percent are retailed from the farm. He is also experimenting with exotic crosses, to see if weight gain can be improved.

Ralph prefers to feed haylage as the bulk of the ration. "The protein content of our haylage is so high that I have to water it down with corn," he grinned. The herd also receives a mineral supplement.

Corn is by far the biggest cash crop in the state of Iowa and it's one of Ralph's favorite crops as well. It's the lead off crop in his rotation of corn and oats followed by three years of hay. And just for fun, he's got one plot that's been in continuous corn for nine years with no reduction in yield. "I'm going to keep this plot in corn just to see how long yields can be maintained," he chuckled. Each year this plot receives applications of Calphos, gypsum, high-calcium lime and 15 tons of manure per acre. Ralph also innoculates his seed with liquid seaweed (Fieldgold) and calculates it results in a 10 bushel per acre increase in yields.

Ear corn is harvested when the grain has cured to about 28 percent moisture. After the grain is taken off, the stalks are chopped for silage. Ralph prefers his Harvesters to the pit silos as a greater amount of nutrients are preserved. Silage tests run in February of 1973 showed a protein content of 6.78 percent in the pit silos compared to 8.66 percent in the Harvesters. The Englekenses get most of their field testing done by A & L Agricultural Labs, 2176 Dunn Ave., Memphis, Tennessee.

Problems with root worm and corn borer have been nonexistent on this farm for the last 12 years. Ladybugs imported from California have all but eliminated corn borers. "The combination of a strong population of ladybugs and a healthy soil is the best insect control program we've found," according to this seasoned veteran.

Nor is there any appreciable weed problem. When Ralph first started farming organically, he would cultivate the corn four or five times and still not be satisfied. But with each passing year the number of necessary cultivations declined until now he only cultivates twice. It's been Ralph's experience that "the strong and rapid growth of the crop more than takes care of any weeds."

Two years ago Ralph decided to experiment with double-cropping corn fields. Rye was sown in the fall of '75 and harvested for haylage in May. That was fed at the rate of 12 pounds per cow per day until it ran out. The stubble was turned under for green manure and within about 10 days the field was planted to corn. Ralph was pleased with the results and commented that "the neighbors can't grow rye in the fall because of herbicide residues in their field."

None of the feed grown on this farm is sold. Even so, there have been occasions when it was necessary to buy feed. In these instances, the Englekenses were very careful to buy only those supplements necessary to round out their homegrown ration. "We were short of hay for a while in 1975," Ralph recalled, "and I bought some from a neighbor. But it ended up costing me an additional $110 a day to supplement that hay because it was deficient in zinc, cobalt, iron and sulfur."

It's been over a decade since the Englekens acreage has felt the cold steel of a moldboard plow. Like many other organic farmers, Ralph advocates the use of a chisel plow as the optimum tillage tool for enhancing humus content and soil life. "Modern tillage methods kill the aerobic bacteria in the top layer of soil," according to Ralph, "and that hinders the decay of crop residues." Before changing to a chisel plow, Ralph remembers plowing up two-year-old corn stalks. Now they have disappeared by the first cultivation. Problems with winterkill have also ceased as there is no longer any plow pan to trap water.

Soil test are conducted each fall to monitor the flow of nutrients through the soil. Ralph has found that his system of crop rotation, returning organic wastes to the soil and supplemental mineral fertilization as indicated by soil test has more than adequately maintained the soil fertility he's worked so hard to achieve.

With an operation this size and the vagaries of the marketplace, it's necessary to be on the lookout for new labor and energy conserving methods. In this regard, Ralph has been experimenting with the use of composted manure. He has been running tests for General Compost Corp.'s Paybac compost stater for about a year. According to Ralph, one of the big reasons for composting manure rather than spreading it raw is that more of the available nutrients in the manure are preserved. Consequently, fewer tons of composted manure need to be spread per acre. In terms of plant nutrients, two tons of composted manure is equivalent to about 15 to 20 tons of raw manure. This translates into fewer trips onto the field, and that saves time and energy as well as reducing compaction.

Ralph estimates that he's composting about 3,000 tons of raw manure a year. It's piled in 40-ton windrows and then inoculated with a mixture of water and compost starter. The windrow is allowed to "work" for seven days and then turned. Depending on how well the composting process is proceeding, it may be inoculated again. After another seven days, the windrow is turned once more, and again at 21 days.

It's then ready to spread, though it can be allowed to mellow for an additional six weeks. Ralph uses his front end loader and manure spreader to turn the windrows. He figures it takes about 45 minutes to turn one 40-ton pile of composting manure. He has also tried composting just corn stalks with good results and has discovered that the addition of sawdust to the composting windrow helps reduce the moisture content. Managing the compost piles doesn't cut into the time available for other farm chores. According to Ralph, it's an activity that can be attended to during inclement weather.

The end result of the composting process is humus. The decayed organic matter is provided by the manure and the beneficial microorganisms from the compost started—55 cultivated strains to be exact. The regular application of humus on the Englekens' fields have enhanced the quantity and availability of nutrients as well as tilth and friability. And as humus is capable of absorbing four times its weight in water, there has been a significant increase in the moisture retention capacity of the soil. This is of singular importance during the current widespread drought conditions.

In 1975, a drought year, Ralph got three cuttings of hay. His less fortunate neighbors got only one. That same year he averaged two ears of corn per stalk, compared to half that amount from fields just down the road. Though some of his neighbors have been critical of "all the work" Ralph seems to do, his efforts have been more than amply rewarded.

In addition to the benefits accrued to the soil and to crop and livestock production, Ralph has found organic methods to be a real energy saver as well. "I figure we've had about a 32 percent saving in energy use. The tractor doesn't have to work as hard and we've completely eliminated petro-fertilizer costs. Some of my neighbors are having to use from 70 to 80 pounds of anhydrous ammonia per acre to maintain production, plus an additional 10 horsepower per acre." And it doesn't take a genius to figure out that as the price of fossil fuel products rises because of scarce supplies, so will Ralph's profit margins compared to his petro-powered neighbors.

Ralph and Rita also know that they can produce higher quality food at less cost for their family as well. With seven out of 11 children still at home, the monetary savings of home food production is particularly great. The Englekenses large organic garden is Rita's domain for the most part. It produces all the fruits and vegetables the family can eat, plus some extra. Nearly 1,500 pounds of potatoes were harvested from the 2,220 square foot potato patch, and Rita sold over $250 worth of strawberries the summer of '75. The 100-hen laying flock produces more than enough eggs with plenty left over to sell. Two Holstein cows provide an adequate supply of milk. The principles of organic agriculture have proved equally successful for the Englekenses on the gardening and field crop sale.

It would seem that with a nearly textbook-perfect example of the merits of organic agriculture right in the neighborhood, more farmers in the Greeley area would be interested in finding out just how Ralph does it. Quite the contrary. For years, many of the Englekens' neighbors were openly hostile and often ridiculed his efforts. However, in recent years those attitudes have begun to soften somewhat.

Ralph noted, "We had one neighbor who was very critical and he still can't admit to the errors he makes. But, he's been coming over here more and more often, now, to find out how we do things. He's beginning to change."

Ralph is particularly amused by the predicament of his local extension agent. "On the job he spouts the official line," he commented, "but he comes out here and has an entirely different opinion as a private person." And as seems to be so often the case, the public schools are the last bastion of archaic ideas. Ralph's son reports that not only do his peers frequently laugh at the way the family farms, but that the agriculture instructor is just as bad.

This comes as no surprise to Ralph, though. He considers advocating organic agriculture as being tantamount to revolution and "revolution is hard for people to accept." But neither he nor Rita are daunted in their efforts. They know only too well the grave consequences of chemical agriculture. Strong family ties and a deep commitment to their purpose provide solidarity and helps soothe any hurt feelings.

Ralph Englekens is not a crusader, but he is a man with a purpose and a message—to nurture lasting soil fertility while providing high quality food for animal and man, and to exhibit on-the-farm proof that organic farming is a viable alternative.

GROWING CORN ORGANICALLY

By now our corn should be waist high and the spaces between the rows will have disappeared under a canopy of dark green leaves. By moving our planting time to the third week of May, our corn is usually well ahead of the old axiom which had it "knee-high by the Fourth of July." We have done everything we can do to get the corn off to a good start, now it is up to the whims of weather to determine the success of the crop in the fall.

Corn growing techniques have changed in the last few years here at Valley View and the future will see still more, I suspect.

When I started farming, I was not into the "organic bit" and my procedures showed it. I was growing corn up to three and sometimes four years on a plot before seeding down, fertilizing with 300 pounds of 0-25-25 as a broadcast and planting with another 300 to 400 pounds of 15-15-15. Weeds were sprayed with a couple different products since there was no time for cultivation.

The results? Besides a corn crop, my efforts were rewarded with harder and harder fields to plow, soil so low in organic matter that erosion was becoming the rule no matter what the slope. Even the fields with growing corn wouldn't hold the soil effectively. The chemical buildup of herbicides created a carry-over situation which on our soil type made seeding alfalfa and grass after corn a risky proposition. The only area I could feel at all good about was that I had never got into the use of any kind of insecticide on the land.

The realization that I was rapidly developing a merry-go-round which would soon be spinning too fast for me to get off, helped lead me to the decision to cut back on the scope of my operation to the 35-40 cow level in 1972. As a result of this I was subsequently able to cut back on the acres of corn and concentrate more on my grassland farming. My corn acreage is now at 30 acres (or less) with about 20 acres chopped as whole plant silage and the remainder picked as cob corn after drying down on the stalk to 30 percent moisture which then allows us to crib it in wire cribs five feet wide, 12 feet high, and fifty feet long. The rotation now has a maximum of two years of corn and I am working to reduce this to one year if possible.

Now that we have the manure stacker and the past winter's manure is stored on concrete, we have the option of returning it to the land whenever I choose. Of course, this attitude does not always set with the grain of the milk inspector, but this is a situation where the environmentalist carries a bigger stick than health, at least in the overall view. Anyway, back to manure.

My plans include removing the manure to the hay field that is destined to be fall plowed for corn in the following year. August is a good time to do this; haying has wound down and we are not thinking about the fall harvest season. Spreading the manure on sod after the second cutting has been baled will allow little loss of nutrients in spite of not being plowed in immediately. The grass in the field will be stimulated by the manure and by the time we do plow in late fall, not only will we be plowing down the manure, but also a good green manure crop. In the spring we disk the land once and then we use a spring-tooth drag harrow or a roller harrow about once a week until planting in an attempt to ruin weed seedlings as they struggle to gain a foothold.

Fertilization at planting is still in the experimental stage. On the acreage which is in its second year I use 160 pounds of 15-15-15, primarily because I haven't devised a way to positively get manure back on this land without losing timeliness and fighting the fall rains. In 1978 I tried planting on the plowed down sod, without commercial nitrogen. I used 160 pounds of 0-25-25 and harvested about 125 bushels per acre of corn that was dried down literally weeks before heavily fertilized corn was. Apparently some of the bad things I have heard about nitrogen fertilizer are true and the results from this particular field were very gratifying. In 1980 my plans call for first year corn with no commercial fertilizer. I feel the fertilizer situation is well under control and I would guess that in three years at the most, I will not be handling a single bag of fertilizer. I also am not using any other soil amendments since at the present the soil tests, the crops, and the animals' response to the feed grown on it, show the quality of the land to be on the increase. I should mention too that this is helped along by the large amounts of straw I purchase every year for use as bedding and which of course ends up in the soil.

Weed control in my corn is a different story and it is here that I need more input. Two years ago I was finally able to purchase what I consider the ultimate in cultivators, a Lilliston Rolling Cultivator. With this two row machine, it was my hope to eliminate the herbicides. Our first use of the machine was on our experimental plot. This is a two acre plot right in back of the barn which has had no artificial additives in about six years. My logic for picking this odd shaped lot was to be able to give it maximum care and attention and to be close by for frequent observation.

Two years ago I plowed down a heavily manured sod. I planted corn with no fertilizer and used no sprays. Cultivation was the only form of weed control and it was a qualified success—everywhere except in the row. We did lay-by on the third and final pass where we adjusted the spiders to throw soil into the row and bury the weeds that were starting there. Possibly we did it too late for the size of the weeds but at any rate, by harvest time we had pig weed that matched the corn for height, with the growth only in the row between the rows it was clean. Needless to say the yield was considerably lower than in our sprayed fields, so much so that I have been reluctant to try a no-spray program in our bigger fields. We do cultivate even the fields we spray now, usually twice whereas in the test plot we cultivated three times.

Some folks have suggested that our soil may have still been out of balance and that is why we got the rank growth of a monoweed. Others say the straw, which at the time was local straw and not the cleanest, was to blame, that I am buying everybody else's weed seeds and my manure does not compost long enough to render the seeds sterile. (I now buy my straw from Canada and it is absolutely clean, golden in color and a pleasure to work with.)

I do not expect clean, weed-free corn fields, like the sprays give us, from cultivation, but neither can I tolerate a 25 percent reduction in yields. I will keep trying, but at this point I do not see anything short of a man with a hoe being able to mechanically rid the rows of their weeds. I seriously doubt that my hired man would take too kindly to my suggestion that we had 30 acres of corn to hoe. Therefore in the interest of keeping him on the job, (and me too!) this can be considered an open solicitation for ideas.

"DEVIL'S ADVOCATE"

"A devil's advocate. That's what I'd like to think I am," says Bud Wallace, (Figs. 2-24 through 2-29) a farmer from North Leeds, Maine. "I want to know the questions behind the answers and the answers behind the questions. I like to draw out the facts on both sides of a debate well enough so people can form their own opinions.

"That's how I feel on this whole organic vs. chemical agriculture controversy," says Bud, an organic farmer himself. "We don't want to belittle the chemical farmer. After all, he's only doing what he's

Fig. 2-24. Bud Wallace, energetic organic farmer and vo-ag teacher, stresses the need for "book larnin," especially in fertilization.

Fig. 2-25. About 75 percent of the Wallaces' customers are regulars who snap up their organic produce.

been told is right by all the 'experts.' But we do want to keep the door open to the chemical farmer and help him keep his mind open to some of the advantages of ecological agriculture."

Bud practices strict ecological agriculture on his own 45 acres "because I want the certification. It's important to me, but I personally don't see much harm in using a little 5-10-10 fertilizer occasionally if that's what happens to be available"

Bud, who's reclaimed his 20 tillable acres from alder and scrub lands in the past four years and leases a few more acres across the road has his doubts that organic agriculture as it is today is the answer to the world food crisis.

"With the present state of technology and research, I don't think the world can feed itself by organic methods exclusively. If it takes

Fig. 2-26. Bud Wallace often picks produce while the customer waits.

Fig. 2-27. According to Bud Wallace, research is the most glaring need in organic agriculture today.

the organic matter from three or four acres to support intensive food production on one acre, I just don't see that there will be enough land available," he says.

But even with his doubts, Bud feels that organic agriculture is the best way today to produce food while caring for the soil the way it must be cared for. "You've got to feed the soil if you want to feed the people," he maintains.

Bud and his wife, Barbara, grow "everything from asparagus to zucchini" and sell their produce from their roadside stand on U.S. highway 202 about halfway between Lewiston and Augusta. "About

Fig. 2-28. Bright orange pumpkins catch the eye of travelers on busy Highway 202.

Fig. 2-29. Diversity leads to near total self-sufficiency for Bud Wallace.

75 percent of our customers are regular, but only about 15 percent come here specifically because we're organic." Most of the people who come from as far away as Brunswick and Portland drive many miles to get their fresh, quality produce at reasonable prices," he says. "People can see and taste the difference between a healthy organic tomato and an anemic-looking synthetic one."

He'll even pull carrots and beets or pick sweet corn and tomatoes to order while the customer waits. In the first two years of operation their sales doubled and have been increasing every since. "We can't grow enough of a lot of things now, the demand is so great," he beams.

A highly energetic man who chain smokes while he picks and weighs vegetables or shells beans while he talks, Bud has been "looking at the facts and questioning the answers" for a long time.

A 1949 agricultural engineering graduate of the University of

Maine, Orono, he was a vo-ag teacher in Aroostook County, Maine, and in New Hampshire for five years. He then "went the way of so many Maine farm boys" and worked for Pratt and Whitney Aircraft in Connecticut for 18 years where he was a jet engine overhaul inspection foreman.

The family always had a large garden, and while there, Bud switched from chemical to organic methods "because of the bugs"—the horrendous warnings on the insecticides. "If you couldn't handle it or breathe it, and had to keep it out of your eyes and the reach of children, how could you go ahead and put it on the food you're going to eat and the soil that's going to grow it?" he asks.

Bud got himself some books on the then fledgling organic movement and after a few years of reading and doing, his organic vegetables were so outstanding that his neighbors and boss began copying his methods. But "Connecticut was too hot and humid and there were too many people and my son wanted to farm, so I cashed in my chips and moved back to Maine," he grins.

The fate of Aroostook County, where he first began teaching, has had much to do with swaying him toward ecological agriculture.

"The County," he explains, "is within a few square miles of being as big as the state of Massachusetts. The part of it that borders New Brunswick is a big potato growing area. It's so isolated, though, that in a hundred miles there are only a couple of towns that amount to anything. The potato land is surrounded by barrens and infertile swamp and woodland, good only for recreation, pulpwood and logging.

"They used to say about the County that God created the best country in the world, then pushed it so far north so nobody would fight over it. Then they mined the soils for 70 years and began using nothing but chemical fertilizers while taking out the hedgerows. It's in deep trouble now. Potato yields had increased steadily until 1958 and now they're going down, down, down. The farms grew larger—from about 50 to 500 or 1000 acres. The family farmers who practiced crop rotation and contour farming grew fewer.

"In some areas they've lost 30 inches of topsoil and there are some fields down to bedrock. In many places they're down to one-half to one percent humus. We've got the beginning of a Great American Desert up there now," he says, almost grimacing in pain.

It may be that the tragedy of "the County" has given the ecological agriculture movement its good start in Maine. In 1975, the Maine Organic Farmers and Gardners Assn. (MOFGA), had around 300 members. Now its members number nearly 1000 and the association, through a foundation grant, is able to employ a full-time executive director. Chaitanya York of Union, Maine, and a newspaper editor, Tym Nason, Kennebunkport, Maine. Bud calls Chaitanya the "spark plug" of the organization, and Bud is a director, working specifically on the acquisition of fertilizers.

One MOFGA co-sponsored conference, called "Spring Growth," was held at a dot on the map, Hinckley, near Waterville. They only expected a thousand people at most, but 2500 came to learn. It was sidewalk to alley people and very heartening, according to Bud. Another conference last September at the College of the Atlantic in Bar Harbor, was originally scheduled for 250 people, then boosted to 400, limited only by the space available. Several hundred, who did not make advance registrations, had to be turned away.

Ecological agricultural methods are also catching on with the "establishment" in Maine, Bud says. The University of Maine Variety Trial Farm just down the road from him is conducting five-year trials on organics under the aegis of Dr. Frank Eggert, former professor of horticulture and former dean of the graduate school at the University of Maine. He is devoting his time to research and development of economical and ecological practices for part-time and small farmers.

Bud feels that there is beginning to be a "tremendous meeting of the minds" between university agriculturists, secondary school educators, and organic farmers. He talks about Charles Gould, a county extension agent, who conducts workshops with Chaitanya York and others at teachers' conventions, with other extension agents, and with just about anyone else who's willing to listen. Bud has appeared on a local cable TV series which explored the pros and cons of organic methods.

All this exposure is paying off, Bud feels. "From about 1955 to 1970, the enrollment in the agricultural school at the University of Maine declined to around 1200. This year it's 2700. It's more than doubled in the past five or six years."

As Bud sees it, one of the major reasons for this upsurge is because "the young people are completely disenchanted with the present food production system."

He uses apprentices on his operation and considers it a good idea. "But the young people have to have more than just work experience. They have to have 'book larnin' if you will. The days of 40 acres and a mule are gone. And there's a tremendous difference between the way grandfather farmed and the way we farm. Grandpa just used whatever he had available and knew through experience that some materials made some crops grow better. He didn't know why. Now we have the technology to know why we want to use various organic substances even though we don't have the research to show why it works. The entire ecological agriculture field demands more research," he states.

One of the glaring needs in education he feels, is how to use fertilizer. "For instance, Maine soils are generally deficient in magnesium, but here and there are pockets of high magnesium clay soils that are low in calcium and this will tie up the availability of potash. So I believe in testing each and every plot of soil before applying lime or anything at all to it."

On the low and very low magnesium soils he uses Sulphomag which has 21 to 22 percent potash with 18 percent available magnesium. "Now chicken manure is readily available around here. It's the cheapest possible nitrogen and phosphorus carrier for me, but it's high in magnesium and I don't dare use it in some areas. These are the kinds of things that one learns through books," he explains.

Bud's land lies in the south-central Maine area of rolling hills, lakes and rivers. Millennia ago, his 45-acre farm in Androscoggin County was at the outlet of a much larger Lake Androscoggin so there are wide variations in his soil types. His basic soils are Atlantic Sandy Loam, Belgrade Silt, Androscoggin White Clay and black swamp soil. Each and every type of soil demands a different fertilization program, modified of course, by his intricate program of crop rotation. He applies fertilizer with a heavy hand. Some might say too heavy, but it's bearing fine results for him.

"Now someone who's worked the land for just one summer and has had things work out reasonably well isn't going to know those important details I've been talking about. He's going to think he knows how to farm and he won't. He'll have some knowledge of farm life and farm work, but that is not enough. You can't give him the answers, because often the youngster doesn't know what questions to ask and you don't know just what he needs to know," Bud says.

Bud mulches and companion plants extensively on his "asparagus to zucchini" operation. Vigorous, glossy green buttercup squash and pumpkins fill every available nook between many stands of his corn. "In fact, they're so thick they present a slight problem at harvest," he says wryly.

He'll run two rows of corn, two of peas, then corn again, and do the same with beans. "I don't plant corn in the recommended four row blocks because I like to take advantage of the nitrogen fixing qualities of the legumes. I've never had any trouble with pollination on the corn, and Mexican been beetles, which used to be a scourge in this area don't trouble me at all," he says. He releases 70,000 ladybugs annually to take care of any aphids.

Bud cites some studies at the Variety Trial Farm on seaweed mulch as one of the reasons he's a believer in mulching. "In two weeks without water, the moisture content of the unmulched soil dropped from 100 to zero percent, while that of the seaweed mulched soil dropped to 90 percent. I suppose any mulching material would give similar results, so I try to get my hands on as much organic matter as possible."

"Cauliflower is a good pH indicator, preferring a pH from 6 to 6.8. In chemical gardening, if you don't stay within that range the plant either won't head out or you'll get half-dollar sized heads. But with soil that has an organic meterial level of five or six percent, that cauliflower will tolerate a pH ranging from about 5.5 to 7.2.

"The reason for this is that one of the greatest advantages of ecological farming methods is that you can get away with imbalances in nutrients in the soil to a far greater extent than you can with chemical methods. By keeping the humus content up, you have a great stabilizer. If you have any excess of any element, the humus will lock it up so it doesn't adversely affect the plant."

As an aside Bud adds, "don't plant your cauliflower near your asparagus. It won't head out. But if you companion plant tomatoes with the asparagus, the tomatoes repel the asparagus beetle and the asparagus deters tomato blight."

Since 1973 when he returned to Maine, the Wallaces have been slowly clearing the land, adding more tillable each year. Bud believes in heavy fertilization and has his soil tested each year at the extension laboratory at the University of Maine-Orono, but is getting disillusioned with what he considers mixed and sometimes conflicting results.

He is thinking of switching to a soil audit with either Advance Agriculture Associates of Boise, Idaho, or Atlantic Laboratories, Waldoboro, Maine, so he can get a more detailed analysis and a clearer picture of his soil's needs. "It will cost about $40 a sample, but they can recommend an exact and individual program for either chemical or ecological methods, and I think it would be worth it," Bud says.

Bud's season runs from the full moon of May to the full moon of September, "give or take a frost or two." Annually, he applies 20 tons of manure to the acre "that's very heavily on the chicken side. It's from cage-layer birds, so it's the pure, unadulterated product. There's no litter, only an occasional feather or broken egg. So I have to apply it with tender loving care because it runs so high in nitrogen with nothing to absorb it," he explains. He puts on 40 tons per acre the first year on newly reclaimed plots.

"Then I apply rock powders—rock phosphate, either granite dust or feldspar dust—keeping in mind that the latter is high in aluminum so I have to watch the pH," he continues. "With a low pH, too much aluminum will combine with the phosphorus and make the soil nutrition unbalanced. In areas of relatively high rainfall, such as the northeast, the soil pH of untilled, unfertilized fields will usually settle out around 5.0 to 5.2. Because of the low pH on old land and the aluminum problem with feldspar, I use granite dust where the pH runs 5.0 to 6.0, and feldspur dust at 6.0 and up."

He used 200 pounds of ground rock phosphate per acre annually, on the average. This varies, of course, according to the soil. "I'm flying in the face of the experts' recommendations here," he says. "They say the stuff will last for three years, but I feel better doing it annually because the crops seem to respond better. I don't need much where I'm using cage-layer manure."

Then comes 600 pounds of granite dust or 400 pounds of feldspar dust, and this is followed by an application of lime, when pH indicates a need. Bud does all of his plowing and fertilizing in fall, with the land left bare in winter except for cover crops and a half-acre hillside planted in perennials which he keeps in permanent mulch.

He sees to it that each field is planted to green manure crops every fourth or fifth year, except for some sections of corn which he's interplanted with beans and peas or squash and pumpkins for four years running.

He points with pride to one sweet corn patch. In 18 rows, 160 feet long of interplanted sweet corn, he harvested 400 dozen ears of marketable Agway's Buttercorn last summer.

Bud farms his land with two tractors, a 1948 Ford and a 1973 25-hp Sotah, both with three-point hitches. He uses a two-row seeder, a two-row cultivator, a 16-in. single bottom one-way plow and a 6-ft. cut-away double disc harrow. He also has a 10-ft. lime spreader and a manure spreader.

He and another organic farmer jointly own a tractor-operated brush chipper so they can make their own mulch and turn wood cuttings into animal bedding by running them through twice.

But his favorite machines are a 1967 Troy-Bilt rototiller and a years-old Esmay garden seeder. "My tiller can easily turn under thick squash vines in two or three passes and about everything else I have. It has pick and cultivator tines, not the bolo tines, which I think were a big mistake and I have so informed the company," he asserts.

The Esmay is his special delight. He says, "I can plant just about anything with it, even cucumbers by plugging up all the holes but one in the corn plate. I've got all the available plates, but there's no way to plant marigolds with the thing. They still have to go in by hand."

Bud grows some crops for a seedsman, and is particularly proud of his own strain of Jacob's Cattle Beans, which have been handed down from generation to generation. "They're an invention of the Northeast and are highly popular here as a dry bean, but they make fine shell beans for canning." He saves seed from the earliest harvested pods which have six or more well-shaped and deep-red mottled beans in the pod.

The Wallaces work full-time and then some on their farm. Because of their roadside business, evenings and weekends are hopping. Besides the business of growing, the produce has to be picked, weighed and bagged and the bags are individually stamped with the MOFGA organic certification stamp, and the Wallace Organic Farm stamp.

Along with the apprentices, the Wallaces are helped out by their daughter, Racheal. Their son, David lives and works in nearby Greene and comes to pitch in whenever possible. They have three other daughters, Ruth, Glen Falls, New York; Rebecca, Winsted, Connecticut; and Sandra, Augusta, Maine.

David started the Wallaces' goat herd which now numbers 13 with seven milkers. There are three registered French Alpines, one registered Nubian, one grade Nubian, one grade Toggenburg, one grade Saanen and three registered Nubians due to freshen any day now.

"But our best milker is a backyard Saanen who jumped the fence and got herself bred for the first time when she was nine months old and didn't even weigh 75 pounds," Bud laughs.

He like to tell the story of the time he had an apprentice who "was sure he wouldn't like goat meat even when you called it 'chevon,'" and viewed it with great trepidation. "He knew I'd taken an old and useless buck in to the slaughterhouse and kept waiting for this suspicious tasting meat to appear on the table. He looked kind of peculiar when I told him that what he didn't know was that

I'd had the buck ground and that he'd eaten it for dinner three times already!"

Bud interjects, "We're no purists. We'll eat white bread occasionally and do use white flour and sugar in cooking. We certainly don't belong to what I like to call the organic fringe movements—extremists in diet and food production. It's our feeling that the strict vegetarians I know have a pasty look. Even though they spend a lot of time outdoors, they just don't look healthy."

The Wallaces' chicken flock is even more diverse then their goats—three or four Wyandottes, four or five Leghorns, a few New Hampshires, a couple of Barred Rocks, several sex-linked crosses, some hatchery white laying crosses, and one Araucana. "They're from six months to four years old, and they do well enough for us, although some of the old ones are just broody hens and pets now," Bud explains.

They also raise "backyard bacon-type hogs." And as Bud says, "their ancestry is pretty mixed up. Last year, one sow had three white piglets, three red ones, and two with black spots all over them. I called them Dalmatians, after the coach dogs, whenever anyone asked me what they were."

The family beef supply comes from Holstein-Hereford crosses they raise, and the farm has a plentiful supply of friendly cats for mousing and petting.

As a result of all this diversity, the Wallaces are almost totally self-sufficient. In fact, the only thing they don't raise for their own consumption or that of their animals is grain. "And we don't have a root cellar yet," Barbara says, "So I can a lot between helping to man the stand. I also freeze a great deal, stocking up our two freezers."

Bud and Barbara are pretty well tied to the farm in summer because of the nature of their roadside business. He is most interested in MOFGA and does manage to get to the regular meetings of the Kennebec County group, of which he was one of the initial instigators, and to the Lewiston chapter.

He is currently working to set up a profit-making fertilizer supply arm of MOFGA and is struggling with replacing their dried up supply of granite dust with feldspar dust. The granite dust is difficult for them to acquire at the right price and quantity. The switch to feldspar will have other ramifications, because it contains twice as much potash as granite dust.

The family's income comes from the farm, the stand, from pulpwood Bud cuts from his woodlot, along with his personal sales of fertilizer and some substitute teaching he does.

Barbara feels they "aren't quite out of the financial woods yet." But Bud says that the summer of '76 was his best to date. "We may make a living out of it this year," he twinkles. And the way he says it, you know he will. And while he's going about that and thriving upon diversity, he'll still be questioning the answers.

IT'S A TRADITION

"Conversion may be a very slow process. Unless there's a sudden disappearance of fossil fuel, conversion will depend on volunteers. Furthermore, there are no monetary incentives for volunteers. All the volunteers I've know have been moved by a primary concern in quality and health. Of course, large numbers of consumers interested in quality and health can provide a great catalyst for conversion."

The speaker was Claude Aubert, noted French author on the subject of *l'agriculture biologique* and advisor for many members of France's largest association for biological farmers, Nature et Progres. His audience consisted for the most part of organic farmers and representatives of organic farming associations, with a smattering of university professors and students, as well as a few journalists. Officially called the "European Farm Tour for North Americans" (jointly sponsored by the Small Farm Research Assn. and the International Federation for Organic Agriculture Movements), the group was an overnight guest in the Aubert home. Having finished a classic organic repast of freshly baked bread, cheese, vegetables, fruits and French wine, everyone had gathered around the massive stone fireplace. Talking late into the night by the light of a few kerosene lamps, the discussion focused on the practical aspects of organic farming as well as its acceptance in both Europe and North America.

"It's hard to predict if and when organic farming will be in the majority." Aubert remarked "It's just not a technical question—gas weed control, etc.—it's philosophical as well. As long as the majority of the population is interested only in money rather than physical and mental health the change will take a long time. If consumers don't want better quality, there is little hope." The sharing of experiences by all present, only slightly hindered by differences in language, highlighted the striking similarities in problems encountered by the organic farming movement on both sides of the ocean.

As one of the very few biological agriculture advisors in eastern

France, Aubert is acutely aware of the status and problems of the movement. Though he has been working with farmers in the area for over three years, his own conversion to the principles of biological agriculture dates back 10 years to when he was working as an agronomist for the French government in Africa. "Much of the work done in Africa under the auspices of the government, including my own, was disastrous. I observed catastrophic results using conventional methods and thought that if it's not good for Africa, perhaps it's not good for Europe." To Aubert, a shy, though forceful, student of Gandhi, the agricultural disasters he witnessed in Africa represented a form of violence against man and nature. Searching for a different way, he came to view the practice and philosophy of the biological agriculture tradition in Europe as an expression of non-violence as taught by Gandhi. Aubert's conversion to biological agriculture was a very personal decision based on philosophy as well as practical agronomic considerations.

Besides his consultant activities and writing, Aubert is working to remedy what he considers to be one of the major problems facing the organic movement today—a lack of knowledgeable advisors. "It is difficult for farmers to convert without competent help," he lamented. To this end, he conducts two seminars a year (15 to 20 people) to train other agricultural advisors in the methods of biological agriculture. "Three of four years ago there was a seemingly insurmountable gulf between biological and conventional agriculturists. If there was any contact at all between the two, it was a fight. If one asked the conventional people about their attitude towards biological agriculture, they would say it was just a contemporary fad that would fade away. Contrary to what they thought, it hasn't faded away. And so, they've begun to pay attention." And what "they" are paying attention to are the results—the continuing success of organic farmers. See Figs. 2-30 through 2-34.

Knowledgeable in the numerous methods of biological agriculture prevalent in Europe, Aubert is not totally committed to any one, though he is considered especially expert in the ANOG method of growing fruit. The method originated in Germany with Leo Furst. ANOG is a specialized method of fruit and vegetable production which is organic in terms of fertilization, but which does allow the use of some pesticides.

Aubert explained, "It's extremely difficult to combat pests in the orchard. Obviously, you must have good soil but that's not enough. Great attention must be paid to the relationship between the variety, climate and form of the orchard. The key to success is

Fig. 2-30. The sign on the gate of the Carre farm.

growing varieties adapted to the particular soil and climate." One of the biggest problems encountered is the fact that most of the varieties currently being grown in France originated in America. "Certain old French varieties don't have the disease and pest problems experienced with the American varieties, and we're trying to start again with these old varieties. But new orchards are slow growing and production is less at the moment," he commented.

The chemicals which are allowed vary from region to region. Furazin is used for serious infestations of coddling moths and

Fig. 2-31. For convenience, Jean Marte ferments bedding on a concrete slab directly behind his three-sided pole barn.

Fig. 2-32. Carefully tended late plantings.

diazanon is also accepted in certain cases. Bacillus thurigensis has proved somewhat successful; however, ANOG orchardists have discovered that to be effective its use requires precise timing, which is not always possible unless sprayed every day. Trichogramma wasps released by ANOG orchardists in Switzerland yielded poor results.

Some of the farmers under Aubert's direction have also experimented with liquid seaweed. "But," he noted, "Experimentation is difficult because if it fails, the farmer may lose his entire crop. Usually they only want to use a sure thing. There are real problems with little or poor quality research."

Fig. 2-33. Jean Humbert proudly displays the rich humus manufactured in one of his many compost heaps.

Fig. 2-34. Gang leader Eliot Coleman gets a lesson on sharpening scythes from an expert.

Green manuring plays a key role in Aubert's orchard management programs. A legume and grass mix of vetch, oats and barley or rye is sown in the fall and tilled under in the spring. Green manures are alternated depending upon how the trees are growing—too much vegetation results in an acid soil. Every other year mustard is planted to bring minerals up from the subsoil. Chinese radishes are often interplanted with the mustard. Their long, thin roots are excellent for reaching subsoil nutrients. Continuous legumes are avoided as they result in excess nitrogen buildup. Rock powders are recommended according to the results of systematic soil tests conducted by Centraal Bodekundig Bureau Rispens in Deventer, Holland. Soil test analysis reports always include figures for trace elements and biological activity.

No doubt one of the reasons ANOG methods have been so successful is due to the flexibility and practicality of approach. "The ANOG method is changing as we receive new information and as new methods are developed," said Aubert. "At the moment, we know of no other but chemical solutions to some of the insect infestations, but when a new idea comes along, we'll try it."

One successful grower advised by Claude Aubert through Nature et Progres is Pierre Carre. M. Carre began farming biologically 12 years ago. The 35 acres that he and his son manage are located on the fertile, silt and sand deposit banks of the Loiret River at St. Helene/St. Messmin, not far from Orleans. The Carres consider themselves "market gardeners" and they grow a wide variety of fruits and vegetables for both the local and Parisian market, as well as for neighbors and the nearby Steiner school.

A bit taken aback by the excited curiosity of his American visitors, M. Carre soon warmed to the oohing and aahing over his luxurious produce. "In the beginning, many crops were lost for lack of advice," he commented. "I had too much faith in 'organics' and not enough information."

Testifying to the fact that this is indeed no longer the case are six acres of precisely cultivated biodynamic fruits—pears, kiwis, and cherries—plus three acres of ANOG apples. His vegetable plots are totally organic.

The Carre operation is very much a family operation. Father and son (Michel) are in charge of the commercial production; mother and (married) sister take care of the home food production. One remarkably jovial hired hand is employed as well. A centuries old agricultural tradition is reflected in the architectural and horticultural design of the Carre farm. Located just outside the barnyard are the compost piles and a supply of straw which is mixed with horse manure, guano and biodynamic preparations for composting. The horse manure is provided by the three and one-half-year-old Breton horse which earns its keep plowing, planting and cultivating. "I did use a tractor for a while after the old horse died," Carre laughed, "but the machines compacted the earth. The horse can tiptoe!"

Fertilization of the orchards and vegetable plots reflect the individual needs of the Carre operation. Vegetable plots receive 40 tons of compost per hectare each fall, along with 500 to 600 kilograms of dolomitic limestone. The asparagus patch, which has been in continuous production for nine years, is fertilized in the spring with compost, fish meal and hoof and horn meal. Wood chips are used throughout for mulching.

A cover crop of rye is planted each fall and then undersown with clover in the spring. This serves the dual purpose of pasture for the horse and green manure in the crop rotation. Chickweed and yarrow grow profusely everywhere and whereas many gardeners would expend considerable time and energy to eradicate the "weeds," the Carres were glad to see them. According to M. Carre, the yarrow indicates that there is no pesticide residue in the soil and the chickweed signifies that the soil is rich in organic matter and nitrogen. Since farming biologically, the Carres have also observed that the soil holds more moisture.

Companion planting in the vegetable gardens was tried, but the difficulties at harvest time more than outweighed the advantages. However, the fruit trees (except the apples) are intercropped as the practice reduces the seriousness of insect infestations.

The fruit trees are all pruned according to espalier methods "because it doubles the yields," according to M. Carre. Most of his trees are approximately 15 years old and he expects another 15 years of production out of them. The apples are grafted onto Malling number seven rootstock (from the Malling Experiment Station in England) and the pears are grafted onto quince rootstock.

The trees are planted about six feet apart in north to south rows and first year wood is soaked in copper sulfate. Support posts are placed about every 20 feet. The first wire is placed at 18 inches and all succeeding wires at 16-inch intervals to a height of six feet— "hand high." Each winter (December through April) the trees are pruned heavily to within one inch of the spurs.

The Carres follow a three-part fertilization program in their orchards. Vetch is sown for a green manure and every fall compost is spread around the base of the trees. When spring arrives, the compost is raked into the center of the rows and tilled in to a depth of four to six inches. A liquid fertilizer made from powdered seaweed is also used after leaf drop, harvest and sometimes even during the growing season.

The apples are grown by ANOG methods because of the serious problems with the coddling moth, as well as minor infestations of aphids. The trees were sprayed about eight times last year with copper sulfate. However, neighboring growers sprayed as many as 25 times. ANOG growers view the methodology as more of the transition period to clean fruit and use only those sprays of short term toxicity which are readily degradable and which are not harmful to bees and other beneficial insects.

The Carres either market their produce directly or through Nature et Progres. They receive a premium price for their fruits, celery and carrots. The remainder of their market crops are sold at competitive prices.

Not all the Carre vegetables are sent to market. Each year the family puts up a year's supply of vegetables and also enough white carrots, mangels and turnips to feed the horse and their home meat supply, rabbits. To supplement these root crops, the horse and rabbits are also fed the bran leftover from grinding grain from their bread, which is baked twice a week in clay ovens located in a room attached to the barn.

Appreciative of his visitors' desire to learn as much as possible about his experiences, M. Carre talked frankly about the reasons he decided to convert to biological farming. More and more it had become necessary to rely on "experts," which were hard to get in touch with and whose answers were less than satisfactory. Concerned over the fact that he had no system of monitoring the changes taking place in his soil, and feeling less and less challenged by the textbook chemical solutions suggested by the experts, the sensitive and thoughtful approach of biological agriculture was very appealing to this lean and vital Frenchman, who is now very obviously fully satisfied with the life he has chosen.

Three hours east of Orleans by car is the farm of Jean Marte, located just outside the village of Auxerre. Marte's 65 hectares, plus a few that he rents from his father, have been farmed organically for six years now. The foundation of the Marte operation is a herd of Holstein-Fresian cows—45 milkers and about 50 heifers. The herd provides milk for the cheese the Martes manufacture and whey for their 12-sow swine herd that supplies meat for the family and a few select customers.

A relatively new three-sided, 800 cubic meter pole barn provides shelter for the animals. They have constant access to pasture, but spend a good deal of time in the barn during the winter and inclement weather. Straw is used for bedding over the dirt floor, and Marte estimates that he goes through about 6,000 bales each year. Attached to this barn is the small milking parlor which can service eight cows at a time.

A proponent of the Lemaire-Boucher method of biological farming, Marte makes use of many of the company's brand name products. Five to 10 kilograms "Calmigal H," lithothamne calcareum and seaweed (calcium, magnesium and trace elements), is spread on the bedding to improve fertilization value. The shed is cleaned twice a year and the bedding "fermented" for two weeks on a concrete slab just outside. Marte generously applies the composted bedding at the rate of 15 tons per hectare every other year on pasture and 12 to 15 tons per hectare each year on cultivated fields.

Convinced of the effectiveness of "mineral fertilization," Marte spreads an additional 250 kilograms per hectare of Calmigal P, lithothamne calcareum with added phosphorus, every spring. Cereals are also fertilized with 500 kilograms per hectare of feather and blood meal.

The product of this carefully nurtured soil is a store of nutrient-balanced homegrown feed which fuels Marte's milk producing machine. The cows are fed a grain mix of field peas, rye, oats and barley sown together. The grain is either combined or chopped for silage depending on conditions. "Aromaligne," a Lemaire-Boucher mineral mix, is fed free-choice.

Reward for his thoughtful husbandry is an average per cow production of 4,500 liters per lactation. The herd is bred so the bulk of milk comes during the summer. At the peak of milk flow, two other people are hired to assist with the milking and cheese making. Marte's cheese resembles a mixture of yogurt and creamed cottage cheese in taste and texture. It is marketed directly through a small health food shop which occupies a remodeled corner of the old barn attached to the house. In addition to the cheese, the Martes offer a full range of organically grown foods and health aids.

A large vegetable garden encompasses the area behind the house. It provides the family with all their fruits and vegetables for the year, including enough for wind making. Chickens are underfoot everywhere. A few milk goats and rabbits are accorded preferential quarters in the old barn as well.

In an unprecedented display of hospitality, the Martes served the crowd of curious, talkative Americans a feast of cheese pie, pastry and a popular local drink of homemade wine and a fruit syrup. What better evidence of the merits of biological farming could be given?

The rolling hills around Auxerre rapidly give way to more mountainous terrain as one approaches the Swiss border. Deserving of being immortalized on a picture postcard, the farm of Jean Humbert lies at an altitude of about 1,000 feet. Boxes bursting with flowers adorn most every window and border the while stucco house. Canaries can be heard singing inside. Though a chorus of canines announced the arrival of the group, no one came forth. After a few minutes of trying to nonchalantly snoop around, we found Humbert seated behind the barn, sharpening his scythe with effortless precision. Closeby, the 30 some rabbits were being fed a breakfast of freshly cut clover, grass and dandelions.

After closely scrutinizing this literal gang of strangers, he began to discuss his conversion to biological farming. "I began farming biologically about 13 years ago. Farming with chemicals had caused the grass to harden and I was starting to have problems with mastitis in the herd," he explained. "So, I decided to try some lithothamne on 10 hectares. There were immediate results. The clover came back," he continued, "and when given a choice, the cows wouldn't even eat the chemically fertilized pasture. Also, the grains began to ripen about 10 days earlier than when I was using chemicals."

Humbert had started by trying to follow the Lemaire-Boucher method, but ran into some economic problems, the high price of Lemaire-Boucher brand name mineral products. "I was eventually able to find a cheaper source of lithothamne," he grinned.

Seemingly curious by nature, Humbert has also acquainted himself with some of the other methods of biological farming espoused in Europe, and has adopted some techniques of the biodynamic and Muller-Rusch for "bio-organic") methods.

How Humbert rotates the crops on his 50 hectares depends on the nitrogen content of the soil. "The rotation begins with two years of grain, barley and rye, followed by winter wheat. The third year is planted to a pasture mix of three types of clover and rye grass." The pasture is allowed to grow until dock and shepherd's purse begin to appear. According to Humbert the presence of these plants indicates there is too much nitrogen in the soil. Then he figures it's time to plant the grain. Like Carre and Marte, Humbert favors shallow tilling, 15 to 20 centimeters, to preserve the aerobic bacteria.

At any given time about 45 hectares will be planted pasture and the remaining five or so hectares will be divided into two and a half hectares of wheat, two and a half of barley, and the remaining usually in rye.

The biggest setback Humbert has had to face since converting to biological methods occurred five years ago when the house and barns caught fire and burned down. The structures were rebuilt in much the same way as the original ones, as centuries of architectural thought had perfected the design and arrangement of space in functional, yet attractive ways.

A wide aisle runs full length down the center of the barn, with stanchions lining either side. Directly behind the stanchions is a trench for liquid manure removal, and on the other side is another aisle wide enough to allow for the mechanical removal of manure. The swine are housed in concrete pens in an adjacent room. The trench also runs through this section of the barn before emptying in a cement storage tank buried behind the barn. The wash water from milking and cleaning flows into the holding tank as well. There are no problems with soap in the water because Humbert doesn't use soap for either of those purposes. The main reason is "because the chemicals foul the cheese making process."

Humbert also spreads lithothamne on his bedding and he claims it keeps odors down as well. The bedding is removed as necessary and composted. More lithothamne is added during the composting, along with biodynamic preparations. The piles ferment for 30 days and are turned once. Compost is spread as ready at the rate of 12 to 15 tons per hectare on pastureland and 10 to 20 tons per hectare on the grains. The liquid manure is sprayed in 25-meter swaths about once a month during the winter. The herd is confined to the barn from November 1 to April 1 and during these months it takes about a month to fill the 44 cubic meter liquid manure tank.

Humbert's herd consists of 27 milking cows, 13 heifers and 10 yearlings. There are Montbeliard cattle, a popular local breed. The herd average is 4,235 kilograms per cow per lactation, with an average butterfat content of 3.6 percent. Some cows have produced up to 6,000 kilograms, Humbert liked to boast.

All the milk is shipped to nearby Plaimbois where Humbert is a member of the cheese co-op. Small in comparison to most of the cheese plants in Wisconsin at least, the Plaimbois co-op has storage capacity for only 200 cheeses, each two and a half feet in diameter and four inches deep. The cheese is made every other day. The milk is curdled in three six-foot diameter, well-used copper vats, which hold enough milk for two cheeses. The cream is separated first and marketed separately, as is the left over whey. After the cheeses have been pressed, they are stored unwrapped at 100 percent humidity in the cavernous basement. The rounds are turned and salted twice a day for even curing. "Comte" is the name given this cheese, and it is one of the most popular hard organic cheeses produced in France.

Each of these men has given much thought to adopting those agricultural techniques most suited to his particular situation of climate, soil and personal desires. And though their common beliefs in the superiority of biological farming often manifest themselves differently, one thing they do have in common is "method." From the arrangements of space to the close attention paid to the number and kinds of weeds in the pasture, the amount of thought given the timing and execution of each task can only be called methodical.

In every instance, natural cycles and processes are emulated as closely as possible. The number of animal units per hectare is balanced to ensure the production of adequate supplies of manure for fertilizer. Minerals are periodically returned to the soil in the form of rock powders and green manures to supply more organic matter for soil biota as well as adding nitrogen.

In this country such a closed system of nutrient cycling is called a "a balanced ecosystem." To these French farmers it's the natural evolution from the traditions of their fathers. Years of experience have been passed from father to son, affording a proper perspective on their functioning in the total creation. They see their role as being part of the process, not as manipulator of the processes. While many today struggle to understand the science of biological farming, these Frenchmen are mastering the art of farming.

Just for fun, we didn't convert the hectares to acres and the liters to pounds or gallons in this section in order to give you a little practice is converting to the metric system. Here are the equivalences you'll need for making the calculations yourself:

one hectare = 2.47 acres
one kilogram = 2.2 pounds
one liter = 1.06 quarts

WHY DO ORGANIC FOODS COST MORE?

Dear Countryside:

This letter is an appeal to all Countryside readers who are organic farmers and see their products to the public. I recently heard on the radio that the FDA was considering a ban on the word "organic" on food items. Their first reason given, (which is untrue) was that organically grown food was no more nutritious than "regular" food. The second reason, which is unfortunately all too true, was that organic foods cost as much as a third more.

I recently read in Countryside about a farmer saying he wanted "a better price for a better product," "better price" meaning higher. That's crazy! For organic farming to compete with (not to mention replace) conventional chemical farming, organic farmers must price their products at competitive levels, or maybe even lower.

Look at it logically: when a working person who has several people to buy food for and a limited budget, with food prices rising all the time, goes to the market is that person going to buy organic whole wheat bread at 89 cents a loaf or the bland, white, nutritionless stuff at 29 cents a loaf? If you think they will buy the more expensive bread, you are dreaming. At today's prices only the wealthy can afford to eat organic.

I have often read in Countryside that organic farming produces larger and healthier yields with less overhead. If this is really true, then organic farmers can certainly afford to bring their prices down some. After all, I don't think anyone expects to get rich farming. On the other hand, you are likely to price yourself right out of the market altogether if you don't lower prices.

Organic farming is better. Don't let it be defeated by high, inflated prices. Get the masses on your side and they will tell the FDA where to get off.

Edward Hanson
LuVerne, Calif.

That seemed like a simple enough letter the first time we read it, and we decided to print it in our *Letters to the Editor* column along with a brief reply. Mr. Hanson obviously isn't a farmer, to judge from his letter, and we thought it would only be fair to look at the other side of the coin.

But the simple letter turned out to be a bucket of worms: the reply went on for eight pages.

Even at that, we weren't sure it was a good reply. So we decided to ask a few other people who are involved in the organic movement for their opinions. The list included journalists, researchers, organic food marketers, and of course organic farmers. Why, we asked them, do organic foods cost more?

The respondents were basically in agreement on several points (Figs. 2-35 through 2-38) which would serve to answer the question directly. But we think you'll be interested in some of the detailed, individual replies. For example, Jim Lukens, and the Kansas Organic Producers, Inc., provided the following thoughts.

"The pricing of all agricultural commodities is complex. I don't know much about what organic food costs in the stores, but from what I have heard, a person who routinely buys food in a health store must either be rich or desperate. In my opinion, food buying co-ops are one of the most exciting things happening and I would hope that, through them, the producers and the ultimate consumers will be able to meet. I feel that it is important for everyone to be involved with obtaining their own food and if a person can't grow it, a food co-op seems to be next best.

"Here are a few random thoughts from my particular perspective:

☐ Agricultural products do not accurately reflect their true

Fig. 2-35. "Agricultural products do not accurately reflect their true cost."

cost. We have been living off fertility and energy—both resources that are running out.

☐ Organic farms tend to be smaller than average conventional farms, and so need a larger profit per acre. Small farms of all kinds are in trouble in the U.S. The urban consumers need to realize that the continued adequate supply of good food depends on the con-

Fig. 2-36. "The consumer needs to be protected from phony 'organic' growers and sellers."

Fig. 2-37. "No farmer will lose money just to make it possible for a lot of cranks to get their food cheaper."

tinued economic viability of the small farms, be they organic or chemical.

☐ The period where farmers want to change their production methods from chemical to organic is when they find themselves in the greatest economic peril. Not only are yields likely to suffer to some extent, but the short-run costs of rebuilding the humus and

Fig. 2-38. "It is only grains and some vegetables that are expensive."

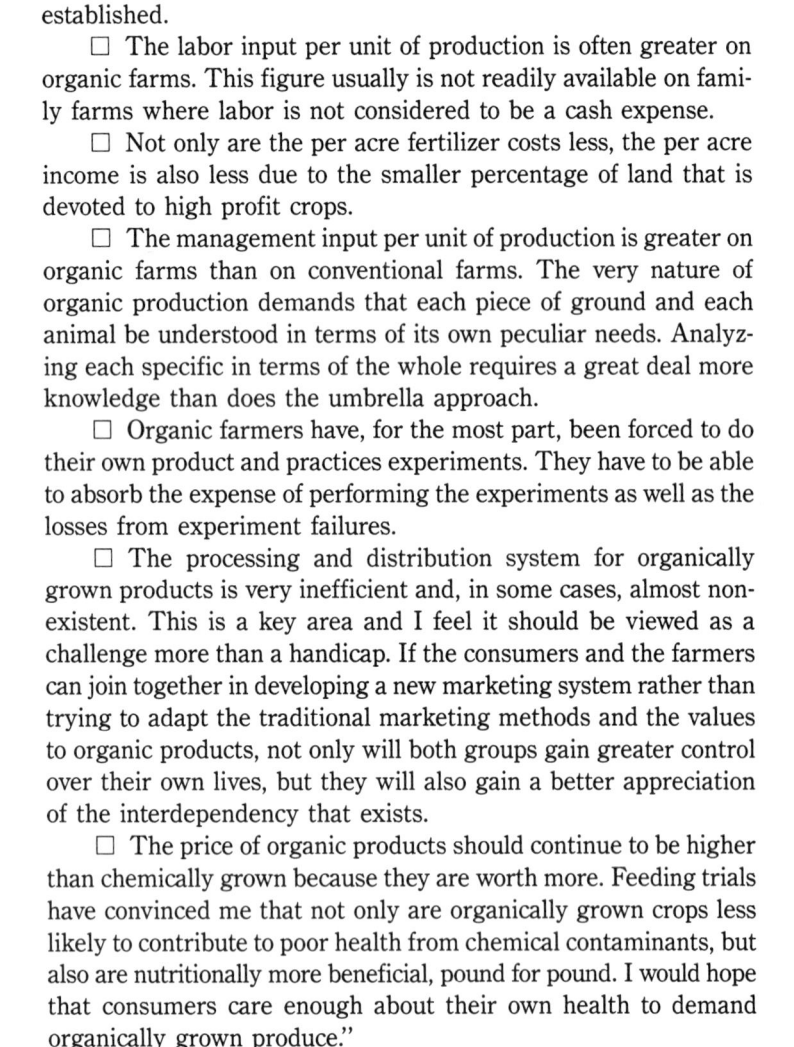

nutrition levels in the soil are usually as great and sometimes greater than the cost of chemical fertilizers. In addition, there is frequently a loss of cash crops during this period as a crop rotation is established.

☐ The labor input per unit of production is often greater on organic farms. This figure usually is not readily available on family farms where labor is not considered to be a cash expense.

☐ Not only are the per acre fertilizer costs less, the per acre income is also less due to the smaller percentage of land that is devoted to high profit crops.

☐ The management input per unit of production is greater on organic farms than on conventional farms. The very nature of organic production demands that each piece of ground and each animal be understood in terms of its own peculiar needs. Analyzing each specific in terms of the whole requires a great deal more knowledge than does the umbrella approach.

☐ Organic farmers have, for the most part, been forced to do their own product and practices experiments. They have to be able to absorb the expense of performing the experiments as well as the losses from experiment failures.

☐ The processing and distribution system for organically grown products is very inefficient and, in some cases, almost nonexistent. This is a key area and I feel it should be viewed as a challenge more than a handicap. If the consumers and the farmers can join together in developing a new marketing system rather than trying to adapt the traditional marketing methods and the values to organic products, not only will both groups gain greater control over their own lives, but they will also gain a better appreciation of the interdependency that exists.

☐ The price of organic products should continue to be higher than chemically grown because they are worth more. Feeding trials have convinced me that not only are organically grown crops less likely to contribute to poor health from chemical contaminants, but also are nutritionally more beneficial, pound for pound. I would hope that consumers care enough about their own health to demand organically grown produce."

From the Northwest Organic Food Producers Assn. in Toppenish, Wash., Pat Langan, executive director, replied to our question.

"First we must consider a new organic grower dealing with a depleted soil. He must start by adding tons of organic matter to the soil to replenish it, and we estimate that it takes three years before this slow but constant release of nutrients will bring the organic farmer up to the producing ability of the conventional grower. However, once the fertility necessary to produce a crop is present, the cost of the land is much less . . . but labor is higher, which then puts the cost close to and in some cases lower than commercial." (Note: Most Northwest Organic Food Producers Assn. members grow vegetables.)

"Most of our growers are pretty much in agreement that the freight and distribution costs on small quantities cost the consumer. Some of our growers sell produce at their stands for the same price they get from the distributor. As we are all aware, even the commercial farmer cannot understand the low price he receives and the price he sees in the stores even when he is part of the huge agribusiness marketing and distributing setup. Therefore, we as a small business, shipping small quantities to a small market, have costs from the grower to the consumer that are even greater than those of the commercial growers.

"Organic farmers cover a great deal of the cost to the consumer by finding their own markets, by packing, and also in some cases by shipping direct. The organic farmer does not receive more money for these services.

"Another cost our growers have is the cost of certification and laboratory testing for chemical residues which cost each grower a minimum of $100 a year. We believe the consumer needs to be protected from frauds and phony "organic" growers and sellers. We personally believe that a lot of food sold as "organic" is not even close to it. That is why it is important for a consumer to look for a seal of certification such as is available from Washington, Oregon and California where they do have strict standards and laboratory testing. Even backyard gardens have received drifts from tree spraying, etc. A sign or label claiming a food is "organic" isn't good enough.

"When you deal with other associations be sure they do laboratory testing for chemical residues, as there are several organic associations today that do not cover this important item. They operate on signed affadavits that the product has been grown organically. This could be true, but my wife and I feel we are good examples of why you can't depend on this.

"In June of 1973 we happened to be home when a helicopter flew over our property dispensing a find spray of Thiodan. Our by-laws allow only 10 percent or less of the FDA tolerances, and that only to allow for drift, and at no time can a grower knowingly receive a drift and not report it. In our case the test was returned with 1.46 ppm of Thiodan. The FDA tolerance was 2.00 ppm. We were decertified for 1973, filed suit, and won our case in Yakima Superior Court.

"This week we appeared before the State Supreme Court in an effort to obtain a state law on 'strict liability' against aerial drifts, but of course we do not know the decision as yet.

"Please bear in mind, however, what would have happened had we marketed our produce without testing: the consumer could have and probably would have been better off buying his produce somewhere else. I could go on and on about the need for this program, but I hope this gives some idea of what this particular association is all about.

"Back to being competitive: we wish someone could come up with a good reason for the differences in prices. For instance, I myself have approximately 20 tons of jerusalem artichokes in the ground to sell next month. My price is 25 cents a pound. At Safeway (commercially grown) they are 69 cents a pound; the paper carries ads at $2.00 a pound; and Gurney's seed catalog lists them at $3.39 for one and one-half pounds. Maybe you can come up with an answer in your research and pass it on to all of us."

We hope to do just that. But first let's listen to what some of our other respondents had to say. This comment is from Charles Walters, editor and publisher of Acres, U.S.A. and the author of several books dealing with agricultural economics.

Distribution Costs

"If the farmer gave away the grain in a box of corn flakes, the shelf price couldn't possibly be materially affected. Most of the costs of bringing farm production to the retail counter are in the distribution mechanism, not in primary production.

"An accurate breakdown of this would require a great deal of work and would vary between red meats, poultry, fresh vegetables and manufactured foodstuffs. The chain store has a refined mechanism for retailing. The so-called organic grower does not. Frequently, the organic grower is primary producer, secondary supplier (wholesaler) and sometimes even retailer. He may perform the grower function most economically and still get sandbagged in the crap game of life performing the wholesale and retail function.

"Almost all raw farm production is measured in terms of bins and bushels, not quality. This is changing, but for the moment it remains a fact of market-place economics. Some few farmers are attempting to cash in on quality, and some few consumers are willing to pay the difference. We do have eco-farmers who treat wet hay with amino acids at binding time, and this enables them to move bales of hay great distances—from Idaho to California, for instance—without nutrient destruction and with an improved economic posture in tow. Much the same can be said of quality corn, wheat, triticale, whatever. The best of the eco-farmers are commanding premium prices because their production puts more gain on an animal, results in fewer medical bills—and this means such production is worth more.

"The implication in the question may be taken to be, why should it cost more if inputs cost less? The answer has to be, it costs more because it is worth more.

"The name of the game in business enterprise should be parity—recovery of production costs plus a reasonable profit. For some 30 years running—with few exceptions—this has not been the case in farming. As a result millions have been whistled off the land. Those remaining have increased debt, not by a few percent, but by several hundred percent, as I have detailed in my book *The Case for Eco-Agriculture*. Farmers who produce corn with a better nutrient load, corn without aflatoxins, corn that delivers more to the market, should have as a goal improved farm prices, not prices either on a par with the losers or prices that mean the hard won profits are being given away.

"One other point belongs in this discussion. Without going into the matter of organic as defined, there is an implication that superior production ought to be marketed at junk food prices. The economic reality is something different. We would state it thus: cheap food means hungry people! People (farmers included), have to be income earners before they are consumers. Denial of proper price levels to the biggest industry in the nation—farming—means that the cycle of income is broken and the economy is forever at work structuring new debt and debt carrying charges in order to synthesize consumers. This is the real meaning of the thousands of federal programs, the staggering public and private debt load, and inflation. The full text of *Unforgiven* (Ed. note: another of Mr. Walter's books) could provide a suitable addendum to this 'one other point' and we are certain you would not have room to print it all."

Merle and Delmar Akerlund, of Valley, Nebraska, members of MOPA (Midwest Organic Producers Assn.), say they believe that foods sold in health food stores are priced too high for most people.

"What benefit is pure food if it cannot be obtained at a reasonable price, especially in families with several children?" They continue:

"Supermarkets buy in carload lots and dispense enormous amounts of food every day. Because they buy cheap and because of their volume, they can undersell smaller stores.

"I feel that as awareness of the benefits of properly produced foods reaches more and more people, as the demand becomes greater and stronger, and more farmers switch to decent methods of treating the soil, organically raised foods will be 'the thing,' and should come down in price to be competitive.

"As producers, however, we have no say-so or control in the retail market. We feel that what we sell direct from the farm is very reasonable. It's the processing, packaging and retailing that makes the difference. I can't see, myself, why raw sugar, for one instance, should be so high in retail price.

"However, one feature we can realize is that pure foods have much more food value. Perhaps a producer deserves a good price for his products because know-how is worth something. Also, farmers are not receiving fair and reasonable prices for their production anyway. So even if organic farmers do receive more than their neighbors, it's not more than a fair price at that.

"We all agree, I'm sure, that getting these prices down to a reasonable retail level will take time, and we constantly have that ugly monster inflation to contend with."

Frank Ford, of Arrowhead Mills in Hereford, Texas, one of the most widely known distributors of organic foods, pointed out that cost factors vary greatly by product.

"Organically produced rice, for example, requires extensive care and additional costs to handle such problems as tadpole shrimp through lowering the water level in the paddy at just the right time rather than using a poison spray. In Texas the long grain rice grower rotates rice onto ground which has been in grass for years to avoid some of the problems.

"Wheat, on the other hand, can be grown with natural soil fertility and the use of ladybugs and other beneficial insects rather easily if isolated from chemical farming. I am fortunate in that respect in that ranch country lies to the west, or upwind side, of me.

"The cost of whole foods is really less that that of highly processed foods, if real nutrition is the criteria, and this, plus the reduction of medical bills if proper nutrition is applied in the home and guidelines of good health are followed, should be the objective of every conscientious homemaker as well as those responsible for institutional feeding.

"Distribution has become more efficient in the natural foods movement over the past few years, and that continues to be our objective at Arrowhead Mills. Our purpose is to provide the best food possible at the lowest price possible. Efficient distribution is an important key."

Joe S. Francis, farm director of Natural Food Associates in Atlanta, Texas, told us that two big reasons why organic produce usually costs more are volume and distribution.

"The organic farmer must compete with modern machinery and mass production. The organic processor must compete with the same things. Also, it costs more to ship a few hundred pounds than it does to ship in truck or rail car loads.

"The commercial producer produces in volume with no regard to quality or soil fertility. Some of the land that is leased by canning companies is destroyed in four or five years, with all disregard for the soil. The big companies use one farm and move to another.

"Personally, I think organic food is worth twice as much per pound as chemically grown food. Once people are taught the value of food they will pay the price, the same as they do for an automobile tire or a new dress.

"We have a job of education. This is what Natural Food Associates is trying to do, teach the people the value of natural food grown on fertile soil"

Robert Klepper, research associate, answered for the center for the Biology of Natural Systems at Washington University in St. Louis, Mo.

"For some organic products the cost of production may be higher. The dollar outlay per acre may be less for organic production, but yields may also be lower. Therefore, the cost per unit of organic output may sometimes be higher. We have no evidence for this for field crop production but it may be true for some fruits and vegetables.

"Probably more important, the costs of marketing organic products may be higher. There are few, if any, well organized marketing channels for organic foods. The organic farmers we know in the Midwest, who sell their output as organic food, usually locate a retail outlet themselves or sell directly to consumers. In other words, they spend time and effort in locating a buyer and they quite legitimately expect to receive a price that will cover the costs of production and marketing.

Marketing Groups

"A few groups have now formed to promote the marketing of organic produce. They will undoubtedly help lower marketing costs. Organic and health food shops at the retail end of the marketing chain are generally small operations with high overhead per dollar of sales when compared with supermarkets. This would also help account for the spread between organic and conventional prices at retail.

"Finally, of course, price is influenced by the demand side as well as the cost or supply side. Many people who buy organic produce feel that it is of high quality than conventional produce and are willing to pay a higher price for it."

Don Foote, editor of the *California Organic Journal,* echoed some fo these same ideas when he said, "Libby, S & W, etc., have a marketing system which involves contracting with growers, guaranteeing them a set price range (although this is often abused), processing, packaging, and marketing . . . in other words, the whole package. Markup is small because of the closed system and the great volume. The organic farmer has no such system.

"I am not advocating that we duplicate the commercial giants, but organic farmers do need a better system than the hit-or-miss system now employed. They need real sources of technology information systems which are compatible to their system of farming which could make them competitive. When New York buyers come to California literally begging for sellers and find few, there is a real need to help educate growers in how to take advantage of the market.

"There is no doubt that there are some growers, but probably more distributors, who are guilty of price gouging. There will be as long as the public is willing to pay the prices they ask. While we know that the public would be willing to pay about 10 percent more on the average, many of the organic products on the market do not exceed the market prices of conventional producers."

Well-known organic farmer Ralph Engelken, of Greeley, Iowa, reported that during a recent trip to California he found organic products to be quite competitive and in a few places even cheaper than in the supermarkets.

"When the natural growers organizations get a better foothold they will be able to do a much better job of advertising and public relations. This will increase sales and should bring prices down. We will, no doubt, see more organic producers in the very near future, which will also help.

"Personally I feel that if we producers do our share of the work, prices should go no higher."

From Harborside, Maine, organic grower Eliot Coleman reported the following:

"The law of supply and demand (known in some circles as greed) is at work. If you can convince the average man that "organic" food is better and subsequently con him into paying more for it because it is scarce—viola, higher prices. That is the case in health food stores especially.

"The organic boys are earning the same per acre as the chemical boys on the acres they are cropping. But they are only cropping an average of three-quarters of their acreage because the remainder is in green manures or other soil improving crops that don't bring in income. So they would logically have to charge more because the customer has to pay for the soil improvement. Ergo sum demonstravit, etc.

"Henry Ford created the assembly line to keep production costs down. In other words, he set up a mechanical monoculture.

"Agricultural monoculture accomplishes the same economic goals—single-minded, large-scale, highly mechanized production of one specialized item—and it can similarly reduce costs. Good farming techniques, quality techniques, are more expensive, just as a Rolls Royce costs more than a Ford. But we don't eat cars. Cheap food is just that: cheap food.

"How about vertically integrated companies? Let's say that Amalgamated Carcinogens produces chemical fertilizers, insecticides, herbicides, sprayers, tractors, harvesters, ad infinitum. They then use all their own products on a megafarm, dump the products at sacrifice prices, and write a juicy tax loss off all the other branches. How can Ma and Pa fight that one?

"And finally there is the reality that food is ridiculously inexpensive in the U.S. at present. These low prices have been achieved by an agricultural technology that is leading to disaster in the long run. If we all want to eat 100 years from now, our chances might be improved by paying higher prices which might permit the farmer to become a soil custodian, rather than lower prices which force him into a soil-destroying, assembly line experience."

It Is Worth More

Kansas organic farmer and miller Johnny Adams says he too has wondered why organic costs more. He points out that the organic whole wheat flour he sells to some health food stores at prices equal to "regular" flour has a higher price in the store. That indicates, he said, that it's worth more and he adds, "I think it is. And if in fact it is, why shouldn't I, the grower, get more for it?" It is, after all, the grower, not the retailer, who added the value.

Adams thinks there are several good reasons why the organic grower should realize a higher price. "Generally speaking, organic farmers are smaller. Everyone is feeling the economic crunch the country is in and we organic farmers are no exception. But organic farmers usually don't have as much credit as chemical farmers. Since the colleges don't back us, the bankers aren't too anxious to either. Chemical farmers are working for the chemical companies and the banks. Organic farmers are a last link of agricultural independents. Please support us a little."

He goes on to say that when he got out of high school, before he went organic, it took about 18 pounds of feed a day for a 900 to 1,000 pound steer. "Since we have changed over completely to organic and open pollinated corn, we have found that it takes only about nine pounds under the same conditions. It is from seeing that, that we have concluded our products are worth more."

The question of prices of organic food is not confined to North America. From England, David Stickland, managing director of Organic Farmers and Growers Ltd., tells us that the growers in his organization face the same opposition. "I am afraid I approach this particular question from a very conventional and perhaps greedy point of view. Organic foods cost more because the market will pay more. If conventional farmers could get more for their produce than organic farmers, they wouldn't hesitate to do so. I do not see why organic farmers should be philosophical and see their produce for less than they can get for it."

However, he goes on to point out some additional expenses incurred by organic farmers.

"Organic farmers have done the research and taken the risks of growing organic food for people who want it, and therefore they should be entitled to every penny they can get to back and losses they might have made in the past in experimental growing. They are also carrying the weight of costs that conventional farmers get free from government advisory services and chemical companies, so again why should they not try to get these costs back?

"I have had it put to me here that we try to get far too much money for our organic produce as it is supposed to cost less to grow, and I have even had people say we should charge a lot less for it because it is a pleasure to work with and to grow!

"As far as I am concerned this is rubbish. No farmer, or anyone else, for that matter, will lose money just to make it possible for a lot of cranks to get their food cheaper.

"I would like to see all the premiums disappear in the future, as this will cut out much of the tendency to cheat. But I have no intention of trying to make it disappear until I can see our farmers' production costs substantially less than conventional farmers' and until I can see the market building up some resistance to the high costs of organic food.

"One other point, as far as this country is concerned: Political parties have always tried to give the masses cheap food at the expense of the farming community, to the extent that whenever a product looks like it's getting expensive, they have imported cheap produce from abroad and ruined the market for the home farmer. Therefore, the U.K. resident has never had to pay a proper price for food, and I think it is time they woke up to what it costs to grow. The tendency here is to make sure of your mortgage payments, your car payments and your entertainment, and if there is anything left over, buy food with it. This is coming to an end here now as people are beginning to realize what food costs, and especially so in the case of organic food which has far more built-in quality than a lot of the rubbish being produced by big companies. This, of course, is another reason why organic food should cost more, as you are buying a complete food that is nutritionally good for you and not one that has been messed about, deprived of some of its chief vitamins and so on, and in general is not giving you the nutrition you should have.

"The only way to change the situation is for much more production of genuine organic produce with government aid for organic farming equal to that of conventional farming, and for sufficient produce to be able to get continuity of supply into the big supermarkets so that we can see on the shelves next to conventionally grown food.

"It should not be forgotten that meat and milk, both very big items on organic farms, are all sold at conventional prices. It is only grains and some vegetables that are expensive, and very often it is the shop that sticks on the retail price rather than the farmer. I would very much like to bring that particular part of the business to an end, and of course the only way to do that is to get enough produce into the supermarkets to finish off a lot of these very expensive health food shops. This is one of our aims, but it does not necessarily make us very popular with the health food shops.

There are several common threads tying these responses together. One of the main ones is that a Cadillac costs more than a Chevy: you get what you pay for. Another is that producer costs and consumer costs vary from product to product. And marketing and distribution are highly significant, according to our respondents.

It's also obvious from many of the replies that the consumer of organic foods is paying not only for cheap food today, but for the assurance of a food supply tomorrow. Implicit in nearly all of these replies is the fear that continues mining of our soils will result in starvation, nutritionally or quantitatively, in the near future.

One factor that comprised a large part of our original reply, and which was lacking in all but a few of the responses we received, was that all farmers, organic or not, are subsidizing the consumer. All food is underpriced, by any reasonable standards. Consumers are willing to spend money on snowmobiles and boats and campers, on vacations and nightclubbing and household gadgetry, but think their food should appear as manna from heaven.

A point often touched upon, but perhaps not dramatized sufficiently, is the role of the middleman. In the letter which started all of this, a loaf of white bread is said to sell for 29 cents, while a loaf of organic bread costs 89 cents. What's wrong with buying wheat at $2.50 a bushel, or even $5 a bushel at retail? That comes to about eight cents a pound for the wheat, and even adding the eggs, milk, honey, etc., an industrious consumer could get a one-pound loaf of real bread for far less than the mucilage that passes for bread in the supermarket.

Organic foods should obviously not be sold for the wealthy, or the fanatics. The economics of the marketplace obviously play a role, both on the producer and consumer ends.

It seems to us that the real answer lies in a more general understanding of what food really is, and what the real cost of society of producing it is. The rise of the megafarm has been due to econocentric thinking—putting everything in terms of dollars and cents rather than in terms of true value. We can no longer afford that, and more people are coming to realize it.

All of this, of course, is at the heart of the economic problems of homesteading, or providing a portion of your own food supply. You entail real costs: how can you compete with the subsidies provided by other sectors of the economy, and by future generations?

And organic farmers, it would seem, are in the same position. They have to decide whether it's more important to be the richest farmer in the cemetery, or to leave the world a little better than they found it.

The urban consumer holds the key. And the average urban consumer doesn't know what's happening.

Chapter 3

Grain

The following section is reprinted from a 1914 circular by A.L. Stone, U. of Wis. Ag. Exp. Station.

With respect to duration of life there are three classes of plants, viz.,

Annuals,
Biennials,
Perennials.

An annual comes up from a seed, bears flowers and seeds and later dies; all within one year.

A biennial grows from a seed but produces only leaves the first year. The root and sometimes the leaves live through the winter. The second year a flower stalk comes up, seeds are produced, and the plant dies.

A perennial is one the roots of which live on year after year unless killed in some way. Depending upon conditions, the plant may or may not produce seed every year.

PLANT REPRODUCTION AND CONTROL

Plants reproduce themselves in various ways:—First, by seeds alone; Second, by roots alone; third, by seeds and roots both, and fourth by runners, suckers, etc.

Practically all annual plants reproduce themselves by seed only. Biennials, also, except for the one winter through which the roots live, reproduce themselves by seeds. Perennials may propagate by means of the roots only as does the Horse Radish which in many places is a bad weed. This plant was introduced into Wisconsin from a warmer country and while its roots live on for many years it produces no seed. Canada Thistles in many cases spread only by the roots and bear no seeds, while in other instances, where the conditions are favorable, a large amount of seed is produced.

The Wild Morning-glory when growing in cultivated ground often produces no seeds but spreads rapidly by its roots. There are other noxious weeds which reproduce and spread both by seed and root like the Ox-eye Daisy, the Snapdragon or Butter and Eggs, the Bouncing Bet, Perennial Sow Thistle, Quack Grass, and several more.

The importance of knowing the habits of any weed lies in applying this knowledge to the eradication of the plant. For instance, it would be useless to summer-fallow a field in order to kill an annual weed like the Wild Mustard which can be kept from spreading by any method that will prevent it from bearing seed. Whether the root is removed from the ground or not is of little consequence if no seeds are allowed to form.

On the other hand it would be equally unwise to attempt to destroy Quack Grass by preventing it from bearing seed when, in many cases, it really spreads more rapidly by root stocks than by seed. Hence to intelligently eradicate any weed one must know its life period and its habit of growth.

Methods for Eradicating Annual and Biennial Weeds

For purposes of eradication the annual and biennial weeds may be treated alike. Both may be kept from spreading or reproducing themselves by preventing them from bearing seed.

Means of Control

ANNUALS AND BIENNIALS:
1. Cutting or pulling
2. Thorough tillage of cultivated crops
3. Rotation of crops
4. Spraying with chemicals

PERENNIALS:
1. Summer fallowing

2. Partial summer fallowing and smother cropping
3. Thorough cultivations with crop
4. Smothering with tar paper, etc.
5. APPLICATION of salt brine, gasoline, etc.

The important thing is to decide which is the best way to prevent the plants from bearing seed, and the way chosen will depend upon whether the plants are scattered or whether they are growing closely together in large patches or fields.

Where annual or biennial plants are scattered there are two ways of killing them, either by pulling them up by the roots or by cutting them. When the plants are pulled up they may safely be dropped where pulled in the field if the seed-pods have not yet been formed. When the seed-pods are once formed, plants usually possess sufficient vitality to ripen the seeds even when they have been pulled up and thrown on the ground. In such case the plants should be carried to some place where they may be burned.

If annuals are to be cut, this should be done if possible beneath the surface of the earth. Any other method is apt to leave one or two small branches on each plant and the entire food-supply furnished by the well-developed root is sent to these branches. They thus grow very rapidly and are practically certain to ripen their seeds unless cut a second time and even then the seedpods will probably have formed and necessitate burning of the plants. A good tool for cutting scattered plants is the "spud".

Methods for Large Patches of Fields

Where annuals or biennials are growing in large patches or thickly infest whole fields, other methods than pulling and cutting must be used.

Cultivations. Careful and thorough preparation of the seedbed for every crop is a great factor in control of annual weeds. Fields which have been fall-plowed usually have a hard crust over them in the spring. The weed plantlets growing in the soil are not noticeable until cultivation breaks the crust and the white or pink stems of the young weed-plants are thrown up, sometimes by the thousand. Exposed to the sun and wind, they are practically all killed. See Figs. 3-1 through 3-6.

This same cultivation turns a new lot of seeds up to the surface to sprout, and within two or three days a new crop of weeds is growing. Another cultivation kills this crop; it would not require

Fig. 3-1. A rotary hoe, weeding corn that is several inches high.

many such operations to practically free the crop-producing portion of the soil from weeds. The disk harrow is an especially valuable tool for fitting fall-plowed land for a crop and killing the young weeds. Even after the crop is planted, the field should be harrowed whenever possible to kill whatever young weeds may have appeared.

The value of such cultivation was shown in one instance where seven acres of a certain field were not harrowed. The weather later prevented further cultivation. On portions of the field which had been harrowed a two-hundred-bushel crop of potatoes was produced. On the unharrowed portion, the weeds too complete posses-

Fig. 3-2. Several small tractors in use.

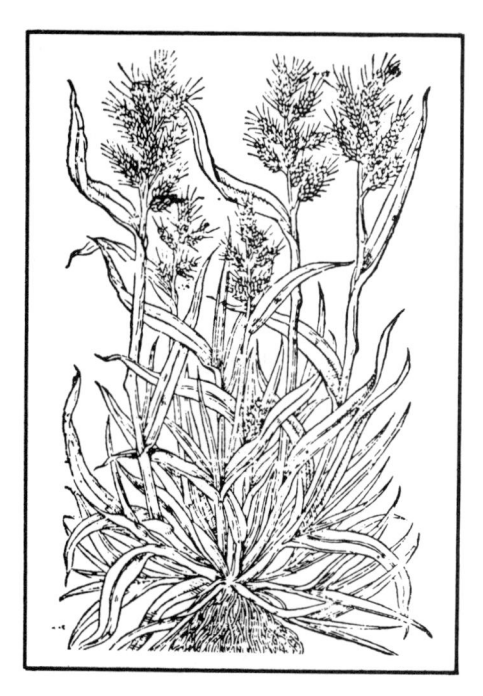

Fig. 3-3. Panick grass.

Fig. 3-4. Dandelion.

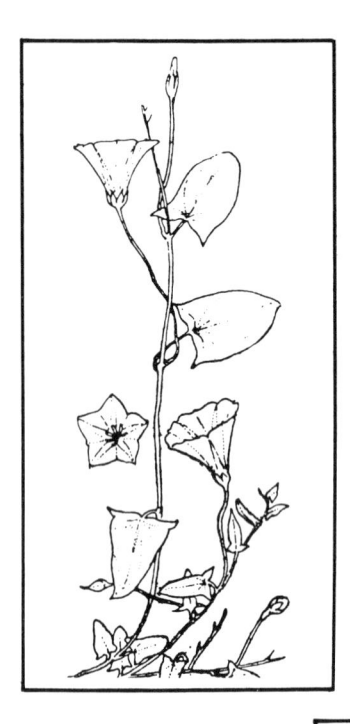

Fig. 3-5. Small bindweed.

Fig. 3-6. Musk thistle.

sion. They were so thick that the potatoes were choked out and no attempt was made to harvest a crop. Many farmers hesitate to drag corn, potatoes, or sugar beets early in the growing season, for fear of tearing out or covering up some of the young plants. If the dragging is done during the middle of the day or when the plants of corn or other crops are somewhat withered but little damage will be done. More weeds will be killed by one dragging while they are young and tender than by several cultivations when the plants have become larger and harder to kill.

Besides killing the weeds cultivation ventilates and warms the soil, supplying much better conditions for germination of the seed and giving the crop a strong, vigorous start. It also encourages chemical action and provides the nitrifying and other bacteria with better conditions in which to work, and to render available a larger amount of plant food. Every good farmer has discovered this secret and no matter what the conditions are, insists on a careful preparation of his land for crops and plenty of the right kind of cultivation afterward. In fact many farmers even insist that Quack Grass and Canada Thistles are blessing in disguise because their presence necessitates more intensive preparation of the seed bed, and better and more frequent cultivations of the crop than is often otherwise given. The importance of careful cultivation both for weed eradication and its effect upon the soil and the crop cannot be over emphasized. This fact in a measure off-sets the expense incurred in the process of eradication. Where crops like corn and sugar beet are drilled in, killing the weeds in the row, while they are small, is especially important. If allowed to grow to any height it is necessary to cover the weeds with dirt in an endeavor to kill them. This requires deep cultivation, and may cut off many of the roots of the corn, retarding its growth and lessening the yield. To offset this damage, it would be well to plant a little additional seed in the beginning.

Rotation of Crops. Perhaps one of the best means of successfully combatting weeds is by rotating the crops grown upon the infested fields.

A good rotation, especially for the dairy farmer, is one requiring four years and may include the following crops:

First year—corn with clean cultivation;

Second year—grain crop with clover (ten pounds), timothy (eight pounds);

Third year—two crops of clover-hay;

Fourth year—timothy meadow, or pasture.

For the second year of the rotation barley, oats, or spring wheat may be grown, as best suits the farmer's convenience. In the fourth year a crop of timothy hay may be cut or the field pastured, whichever plan best meets the needs on each particular farm. The sod should be manured and plowed in the fall and the field made ready for corn the succeeding spring. The degree of success obtained with this or any other rotation is largely dependent upon persistent cultivation of the corn or other cultivated crop.

Shorter rotations are not apt to be very satisfactory for weed-control, although in some cases and on some soils they serve the purpose admirably. Longer rotations, particularly those including alfalfa, would be even more satisfactory for the eradication of weeds. The establishment of a good crop rotation on a field is usually a guarantee that annual or biennial weeds will be largely destroyed and that even the perennial weeds will be partially controlled. A few weeds can produce an enormous quantity of seed. At this Station actual counts have shown that a well developed plant of Pigeon Grass will produce 142,000, Redroot or rough Pigweed 330,000, Barnyard Grass 1,290,000, and the Tumble Weed 6,000,000 seeds. These are among the common weeds infesting cornfields and none of them should be allowed to go to seed, because one crop of weed-seeds will cause untold trouble.

In this rotation if the corn is kept clean and cut close to the ground the field can be left unplowed and the ground for the oats and grass seed be prepared by disking and harrowing thoroughly the next spring. The thorough and careful cultivation of the corn should have killed all the seeds and weeds in the crop-bearing surface of the soil so that the grain-crop following should be practically free from weeds. If the ground were plowed a new crop of weed-seeds would be turned up, to grow in the grain unless killed by thorough cultivation before the grain is sown. If properly carried out, this rotation will prevent the production of weed-seeds on the field for four years, as practically no weeds grow in the hay if a good stand is secured.

"Are four years of persistent work enough to kill all weeds?" They would be, were it not for the great length of time during which weed-seeds may lie dormant in the soil only to row and reproduce their kind when turned to the surface. Instances are known of weed-seeds growing after having been buried for ten and even more than forty years! Hence the need of continued rotation.

Chemical Spray Checks. Another effective method with some weeds, notably the Wild Mustard, is to apply some sort of chemical spray. Various chemicals have been used with varying success. Iron sulphate and common salt have given good results and are comparatively cheap. The former can be bought for one dollar per hundred pounds; salt at half that price. A 20 percent solution of the iron sulphate or a 35 percent solution of the salt is effective and easily made by placing 100 pounds of the former or 125 pounds of the latter in a vinegar or kerosene barrel, filling with water and stirring until completely dissolved. It should be applied on a fair day after the dew is off, at the rate of one barrel to an acre. If rain falls within 24 hours, a second application may be needed. A sprayer throwing a fine mist that will settle gently upon the plant should be used. Success depends upon reaching all portions of the plant with the spray. The one ordinarily used for potatoes throws too coarse a spray. The proper implement should develop a pressure of 100 pounds to the square inch. By using a sprayer with a 20 foot boom, a man with a good team can spray 20 acres a day, provided he has a helper to make the solution for him.

This method is advisable only where mustard is very thick. It will kill only the plants which are in the grain at the time of spraying and will have no effect whatever on the millions of seeds buried in the soil. Its effect therefore extends only to the year's crop. The spraying would need to be continued for several years or until the mustard plants would not be thick enough to make spraying profitable, when the remainder of the work would have to be done by hand.

Probably a much greater destruction of wild mustard would result from plowing and cultivating. Successive crops of seeds would be turned to the surface, sprout, and as rapidly as the young plants appear, they would be killed by cultivation. By continued repetition of this process, the cropbearing surface of the soil could probably be freed from mustard in a single season.

Methods of Eradicating Perennial Weeds

While there are many perennial weeds which are proving troublesome on Wisconsin farms, two are pre-eminently noxious, because of their peculiar nature and habits, viz., Quack Grass and Canada Thistles. Description of these weeds and the methods whereby they may be destroyed follow.

Quack Grass

Quack Grass grows to a height of from one to five feet, depending upon the fertility of the soil and the character of the season.

Its roots are fine and fibrous, like those of other grasses. It also has underground stems or root-stocks, which give this plant its noxious character. They must be killed to eradicate it. This is difficult to do, for they possess great vitality. They resemble roots and are sometimes mistaken for them. They look like other stems, except that the color is nearly white and the joints are much closer together, usually not more than an inch and a half apart and often less than that. At each joint new roots are thrown out and at many of them new stems start. In this way the grass spreads rapidly and a piece of the rootstock with one of these joints on it will produce a new plant, although it may be not over one-half inch long.

The leaves vary from three to 12 inches in length and from one-fourth to one-half inch in width. They are rough to the touch on the upper side and smooth on the lower. The parts which clasp the stem (sheaths) are shorter than the distances between the joints (internodes).

The head is from three to 8 inches long and from one-fourth to one-half inch wide. It is slender and at first glance much resembles English Rye Grass. The divisions of the head (spikelets) in Quack Grass are turned with the flat side to the stem (rachis), while in Rye Grass the edge of the spikelet faces the stem. When the heads first appear, they are narrow but grow wider as the plant approaches maturity.

The seed of Quack Grass is about one-half inch long and one-sixteenth of an inch wide, light brown or yellowish when ripe, and resembles the oat, except that it does not close up so much on the furrow side. At the larger end of the seed and in the furrow there is a club-shaped appendage (rachilla) about one-sixteenth of an inch long.

The leaves and roots of Brome Grass are often mistakes for Quack Grass, and while the plants are young is extremely difficult to distinguish them. The roots of Kentucky Blue Grass and Red Top are also mistaken for those of Quack Grass, principally because these grasses spread by rootstocks, similar to those of Quack Grass, except that they are much smaller. It is not possible to confuse these last named grasses with the Quack Grass after they are headed out, for all of them in general outline resemble oats, instead of rye or wheat, as is the case with Quack. The heads of different plants vary greatly in appearance. In some the flower covering (glume) bears only a sharp point at the end. In others the glume bears a distinct beard (awn) one-half an inch long. Some plants are light and some are dark green in color but in the general characteristics are all alike.

How it is Spread. The whole plant grows rapidly and ripens its seed usually in July. Where growing in meadows, it may be gathered in the hay, whence it gets into the manure and so scattered broadcast over the farm.

If growing in grain it may be harvested and threshed with the rain, and if the grain is not graded with extreme care some of the Quack Grass seed will be sown on the fields the next year. If the hay or grain is sold on the market the seeds may be carried for long distances to establish patches of the grass on farms far removed from the place where the hay or grain was produced. The seeds, and, in some cases rootstocks also may be carried from farm to farm by the spring floods or the seed may be blown from place to place by the wind. While Quack Grass may have some feeding value, it is not relished by stock so much as cultivated grasses are and its presence prevents the production of crops of much greater economic value and importance.

Canada Thistle

Like Quack Grass the Canada Thistle is a perennial plant. In height it ranges from one to three feet, depending on conditions. It is said to have received its name from the fact that it was found in the French settlements in Canada, although it was later introduced by the Dutch into New York and by the English into Vermont and New Hampshire. In England it is called "corn thistle," "green thistle" or "creeping thistle."

The Canada Thistle does not have rootstocks like the Quack Grass, but has true roots, the parts of which are capable of producing plants. There are tufts of rootlets at intervals on the horizontal root. These roots are about a quarter of an inch in diameter, almost white in color and it is from these new plants are thrown up at intervals as they extend their length through the soil.

When undisturbed by cultivation the roots are apt to lie near the surface, but go deeper in cultivated soil and where it is particularly loose and porous may be found at a depth of three feet. The roots are very hardy and by means of the sharp growing points will sometimes send shoots up through two or three feet of hard packed clay soil. When the plant begins its growth in the spring,a rosette of leaves is formed close to the ground from the center of which a flower stalk is set up.

The stem is rather slender, somewhat irregular in shape, seldom more than three-quarters of an inch in diameter and bears few spines.

It separates into several branches near the top, each branch bearing a flower.

The leaves are bright green in color, smooth on the upper face and rough or hairy beneath. The lower leaves are from three to eight inches long and from one to one and one-half inches wide and the edges are curled or wavy. The edges are cut or divided and bear a large number of sharp stiff spines, which on the mature plant are yellow or almost white in color. The leaves are easily distinguished from those of the common or Bull Thistle, the leaves of which are very rough on both surfaces and bear a large number of spines of varying lengths.

The heads are purpose, about an inch long, three quarters of an inch in diameter and bear no spines but simply stiff scales or bracts. They differ from the heads of the Bull Thistle which are often two inches or more long and an inch in diameter and covered with sharp, stiff spines.

The seeds are smooth, brown, about an eighth of an inch long and larger at one end, than the other. The larger end bears a shallow depression or cup, from which projects a sharp point. Once seen and known the seed will not be forgotten. Every seed bears a tuft of downy hairs, called a "pappus," by the aid of which it may be carried a mile or more during the high winds preceeding some of our summer storms.

The seeds may be carried from place to place by water in the shape of spring floods, creeks, rivers, irrigation and drainage canals. They may also be shipped in hay or grain, but the most prolific source of introduction is through grass and clover seeds. For this reason all grass and clover seed should be carefully examined before sowing to make sure that it contains no Canada Thistle seed.

Habits. Canada Thistles seldom bear seed in cultivated fields but in clover or grass fields, in pastures, groves or fence rows where they may develop undisturbed for a time, seed is often produced abundantly. Whenever seed is produced on plants growing in cultivated fields only a few of the heads on each plant bear seed, the rest being sterile.

While Canada Thistles produce more or less seed, yet the increase of these pests is due largely to the roots which spread out rapidly in all directions and are transplanted in widely different portions of the farm by the plow, drag, and cultivator.

Methods of Eradication

Many methods have been devised and advocated for the eradication of Quack Grass and Canada Thistles. The success of any method depends very largely upon soil and weather conditions and a method which has proven entirely successful under one set of conditions has frequently failed when used under somewhat different circumstances. Quack Grass is more persistent and more difficult to eradicate than the Canada Thistle, hence any method which will eradicate Quack Grass will surely destroy Canada Thistle or any other perennial weed.

Some methods may be used effectively and economically on small patches, but will prove too costly for large areas. The method should be wisely selected and suited to the circumstances.

Methods for Large Areas

Fallowing or Cultivation Without a Crop. This method is successful except on sandy soils which leach badly, soils that are continuously wet, or are so porous that the horizontal roots are too deep to be reached with the plow. No crop can be grown while this treatment is being given. Then the field should be plowed as soon as possible after the crop has been removed, but should not be plowed while so dry that the soil turns up in large lumps, making it difficult to work. The depth of the plowing is very important as the success of the method practically depends upon it.

First ascertain the depth at which the horizontal roots or rootstocks are growing, and regulate the depth of the plowing so as to turn them to the surface. In meadows, or pastures, or any other place where the plants are not cultivated or otherwise distributed the rootstocks of Quack Grass will be found usually within 2 or 3 inches of the surface. In cultivated ground they grow deeper, in some cases below the usual plow line.

After plowing, the field should be cultivated often enough to prevent all leaf growth, for every time the leaves get above the surface they supply the root with food and thus prolong its life. Hence the cultivation must be done before the leaves appear above the ground. The plant breathes through its leaves and if its breathing appratus is destroyed, it dies for lack of air. The succeeding spring the ground should be plowed again just deep enough to turn to the surface any roots which the cultivator may have failed to reach the preceding autumn.

The object of the cultivation is to drag all the roots to the surface where the wind and sunshine will dry them out and kill them. In a damp season the roots should be removed from the field by use of a horse rake and a big fork. A spring-tooth harrow or some other good digging-tool is preferable to a disk-harrow. The latter cuts up the roots into small pieces; it requires more work to get them all to the surface where they will be killed, and a single portion of a Quack Grass rootstock bearing a joint will start a new plant even though it is only one-half inch long. It has been shown that a piece of Canada Thistle root a quarter of an inch long will often produce a new plant, so it is unwise to cut them up with a disk harrow. The field should be plowed at varying depths at least three times more during the season, to make sure that all roots are brought to the surface and killed. The cultivator should be kept going during the time between plowings to prevent all leaf growth.

In case there is any doubt about the complete eradication of the weeds, corn planted in checkrows to allow of cultivation both ways should follow the summer-fallow. Close watch should be kept of the field and if any weeds appear they can be removed by hoeing. It is not probable that any weeds will survive the preceding treatment but it is well to be certain.

This fallowing method is more certain to result in complete eradication than any other which has been tried. It gets rids of the weeds with one year's work. The thorough cultivation of the soil puts it into splendid condition, a much larger crop will be obtained the following year than possible had the weeds remained, and the field will continue to bear good crops after the weeds have been eliminated. The dead rootstocks of the Quack Grass will be converted into humus and so increase the water-holding capacity of the soil. For these reasons it is as economical a method as one which allows the production of crops but extends the treatment through several years.

Variations of the Fallow Method

Cultivating with a Crop. Where the Quack Grass or Thistles are to be removed while a crop is being raised plowing should begin the preceding summer or autumn, the earlier the better. This should be followed by careful cultivation until the ground freezes up. The next spring plowing should begin as soon as soil conditions permit and be repeated at intervals of four weeks until the first of July.

Between plowings thorough cultivation should be practiced. On the date mentioned the seed-bed should be carefully prepared and the land sown to millet or buckwheat at the rate of three pecks per acre in either case. The previous treatment will have so weakened the weeds that the millet or buckwheat will be well established before the weeds recover sufficiently to begin growth.

Hemp is another crop which has largely been introduced into Wisconsin, and which has already shown its value as a smother crop for weeds. It requires a very fertile soil for best results, but will do well on all but our more sandy soils. The preparatory treatment on an infested field should include the application of twenty loads of barnyard manure per acre followed by the partial fallow as outlined for use with the millet and buckwheat. Hemp must be sewn by May 10th in Wisconsin, hence not much spring cultivation other than a careful preparation of the seed bed can be given. Sow the hemp with a broadcast seeder or grain drill at the rate of one bushel of seed per acre. Experiments conducted by C.P. Norgord of this station show that success is practically sure on fertile soils but cannot be expected on poor soils or on badly infested fields where insufficient preparatory work has been done. All of these crops grow rapidly and provide a dense shade which smothers the weeds.

This means almost sure death to Canada Thistles, but often fails with Quack Grass and must be adopted advisely. If followed by plowing again in the fall after the crop is removed and by thorough cultivation the succeeding spring, all weeds will probably be killed. This method allows the production of a crop during the process of weed eradication, but it is not so certain of success.

Methods for Small Areas

Covering with Paper. Quack Grass and Canada Thistles in patches not over two rods square can sometimes be economically killed by cutting the weeds close to the ground just when in bloom and covering with tar or some other heavy building paper. The strips of paper must overlap sufficiently to prevent the plants from coming up between the strips and should also extend far enough beyond the edges of the patch so that no plants can reach the air and sunlight.

The paper should be weighted down with earth or stone to hold it in place. If the surface is nearly level it would be better to use planks or fence rails to hold the paper in place because the earth is apt to retain moisture and cause the paper to rot.

This method can only be used successfully on fairly level ground where the paper can be held close to the surface. In a dry season 60 days is usually sufficient to destroy the weeds, but it is best to leave the paper on until time to plow in the fall. Should any plants survive this treatment they will be so weakened as to be easily killed the succeeding season.

Close Cultivation. Where it is not possible to use the foregoing method either because of unevenness of ground or for any other reason, close cultivation may be practiced. The patch should receive the same thorough cultivation as recommended for large areas, except that much of the work may be done with a hoe.

Methods for Canada Thistles But Not for Quack Grass

Growing Alfalfa. Canada Thistles have been completely eradicated where good stands of alfalfa were secured and maintained for three years or more. To secure this result the ground should be heavily manured and plowed as early in the summer or fall as possible and cultivated as already described, continuing the cultivation until early June, when the seedbed should be carefully prepared and alfalfa sown at the rate of 25 pounds per acre.

The preceding treatment will have weakened the weeds. The manure will give the alfalfa a good start and provide a rapid growth sufficiently to prevent the thistles from growing. This method was tried by several members of the Wisconsin Experiment Association who claim that it is a complete success.

The Sod Method. The same results as above noted can sometimes be secured by manuring heavily and seeding down thickly to perennial grasses, such as Kentucky Blue Grass, Red Top, English Rye Grass, etc., but the stand must be almost perfect and the land allowed to remain in grass for a series of years.

Salting the Plant. Cut off the Canada Thistle while in bloom just beneath the surface of the earth and apply a large handful of salt, or better yet, a half pint of stiff salt brine where the thistle is cut off.

Occasionally this treatment needs to be repeated, but usually one application is sufficient. This method is especially effective when stock is pastured on the field, for in their efforts to get the salt they help to destroy the thistles.

Gasoline for Thistles. Gasoline may be substituted for salt and applied the same way. Carbolic acid may also be used, but must be handled with care. Neither of these is practicable, except for scattered plants or with very small patches, as the material is too costly.

Farmers Should Act at Once

Farmers cannot afford to ignore the danger from the encroachment of these various weeds; yet there is a lamentable lack of concerted action to get rid of these enemies of crop production. Land in this state is too high-priced for owners to permit twenty-five percent of its producing power to be destroyed by weeds. It is time that those interested in agriculture realized the situation. The legislature has named a certain number of weeds which must be kept from seeding. They are Quack Grass, Canada Thistle, Burdock, White or Oxeye Daisy, Snapdragon or Butter and Eggs, Cocklebur, Perennial Sow Thistle, Sour Dock, Yellow Dock, Wild Mustard, Wild Parsnip, and Russian Thistle.

There are laws on our statute books to compel the cutting of these weeds before seed is produced, but to prevent seeding is not sufficient. Steps must be taken to rid the soil of the roots as well as of the seed, if complete freedom is to be obtained. Cooperation between farmers in the same locality and between farmers, the Experiment Station, and the Legislature, is necessary before satisfactory results will be secured. The fact that the most noxious weeds can be eradicated should be emphasized and active efforts put forth to prevent these pests from taking possession of Wisconsin farms. Only by continuing the fight to the end with method and thoroughness can ultimate freedom from noxious weeds be attained.

BREEDING PLANTS FOR DISEASE RESISTANCE

A new concept of breeding plants for long-lasting disease resistance by returning both plants and their parasites to more "natural" states is a possibility, says a research plant pathologist at the Pennsylvania State University.

"Historically, natural populations of plants and their parasites have learned to live together over time," declared Dr. Richard B. Nelson. "Plants and parasites attained their ability to co-exist by each accumulating a number of genes for their own defense. This developed throughout a long co-evolution. Their mutual safety and survival was due to numbers of genes," he explained.

Attempts by modern man to control most plant diseases with single resistance genes have taken many cultivated plant hosts and their parasites out of balance at a catastrophic cost, he observed. As examples he listed the potato blight responsible for the Irish famine of 1840, and, in more recent years, epidemics of stem rust of wheat.

"Developing plant varieties with single gene resistance, as done widely today, is a feast or famine approach," he contended.

At the heart of the new system being advocated by Nelson and other plant pathologists is a concept sometimes called generalized resistance. With such resistance, a disease increase at a slow rate—

producing less losses than otherwise by the end of the growing season.

"This generalized resistance is what plants possess in the 'natural' states," he affirmed. "Plants evolved to that kind of resistance without man's intervention by accumulating genes for both attack and defense. Most plants can endure some level of disease without a major yield loss," he added.

Dr. Nelson and Dr. David R. MacKenzie and their associates are combining a number of resistance genes to determine if this approach can manage diseases to economically acceptable levels and remain effective over a long period of time. The research is sponsored in part by funds from the Rockefeller Foundation. The Penn State scientists believe that use of several genes together should return plants and parasites to balance and would be evident in slow build-up of disease.

STORING SEEDS

You want to save your own garden seeds from year to year but have trouble finding that "cool and dry" place.

There's a "recipe" for storage that significantly extends the life of seeds. The secret ingredient is powdered milk.

Basically, the method involves refrigerating seed packets in canning jars. Powdered milk in the bottom of the jars acts as a dehumidifier and keeps the seeds bone dry, according to extension specialists at the University of New Mexico.

The method is especially helpful for storing such short-lived seeds as lima beans, okra, onion, parsley, parsnip, and pepper. Normally germination of these seeds is decreased dramatically if they are stored for a year or two.

Here's how to store the seeds. First, unfold four facial tissues and stack them on top of each other. Place two heaping tablespoons of powdered milk on one corner and roll up the tissues to make a bundle. Secure the bundle with a rubber band.

Be sure to use powdered milk from a freshly-opened box; otherwise, the milk won't absorb the moisture as well. The facial tissue is important, too. It keeps the seed packets from touching the moist powder.

Put the bundled-up powder in a widemouthed canning jar and drop in the seed packets. Seal the jar tightly, using a rubber ring. Put the container on the lowest shelf of the refrigerator, as far as possible from the freezer.

Replace the powdered milk once or twice a year to keep the seeds at their best. When you remove the seed packets, be quick about it. Powdered milk soaks up moisture rapidly, so recap the jar without delay.

Finally, use the seeds as soon as possible. Even when they're well-preserved, seeds lose their vigor as the years go by.

IMPROVING WHEAT VARIETIES

Wheat bread and milk have been from earliest times the staple food of the world's dominant races. Fear of shortage of wheat has been voiced by economists and statisticians for many years, especially since Malthus and Crooks called attention to the greater rate of increase of wheat-using population as compared with wheat production. They overlooked, however, several important facts that must be considered in this connection:

(1) That the area that can be devoted to wheat can be greatly enlarged by the better adjustment of varieties to soils and climatic conditions:

(2) The development of breeding of varieties resistant to rust, smut, and insects and other pests:

(3) The development of higher yielding varieties:

(4) Increased production through improved cultural methods, fertilizers, and machinery:

(5) Prevention of losses in storage:

(6) The effect of better prices in increasing production.

Few if any at the time of Malthus realized the great possibilities in each of these directions of meeting the increased need for wheat.

Predicted Shortage By 1930

The time when the world wheat shortage was to come was estimated by Crooks to be about 1930. That date is near at hand, but we are apparently further away from famine danger than ever. This is due in part to contributions in all of the six fields mentioned, but especially to a discovery that was announced about the same time as the Malthus theory—viz., the theory of natural selection by Charles Darwin and Alfred Russel Wallace.

This theory is based on a most careful study of plants and animals under domestication, as well as in their wild state. It is evident to any careful student of facts that plant and animal breeders have been able to gradually modify species and genera to an extent sufficient to place them in entirely new categories. They did it through hybridizing and selection. Though they knew little or nothing of the fundamental laws involved, they laid the foundation of plant and animal breeding.

Darwin conceived the idea that limiting factors in environment might act as selective forces in nature. The plant or animal best adapted to overcome certain limiting factors would be the one to survive. He called this the "survival of the fittest." For example, if a large number of individuals were exposed to drought or cold the more tender ones would be weakened or destroyed, while others possessing greater ability to withstand drought or cold would survive. The same would be true regarding all other limiting factors of environment.

Influence of Mendel's Discovery

He found a great number of illustrations of this process, enough to set the whole biological world of work on the various aspects of the theory. As a result a great body of knowledge on the evolution of living organisms has been gained and some of the laws governing the evolutionary changes have been formulated. One in particular, discovered by an Austrian monk, Mendel, on the inheritance of unit characters, enables us to make hybrid combinations and select to pure fixed strains in a few years, whereas before his discovery was made, and understood (which latter was about a half-century after it was made), it frequently took many years to secure fixed strains.

It is sufficient for my purpose here to call attention to these facts as a foundation for the story of how they were used to lay the basis for solving some aspects of the wheat problem in America. Among the outstanding limiting factors to wheat growing in the United States are: (1) black stem rust, which is generally distributed, but which causes the greatest losses in the middle western wheat belt; (2) the effect of drought in the wheat belt west of the one hundredth meridian; and (3) the effect of winter killing in the northern part of the winter-wheat area.

In 1894 the Division of Vegetable Physiology, now a part of the Bureau of Plant Industry, began a study of the American wheat problem, especially the problem of rust resistance. This rapidly grew into a study of the basis for improvement of American wheats. A report on the rust phases of the work was published by M.A. Carleton as Bulletin No. 16, Division of Vegetable Physiology and

Pathology, United States Department of Agriculture, 1899, and in 1900 a bulletin by Carleton, on the basis for the improvement of America wheats was published, which laid the foundations of the department's program for wheat improvement.

Method of Selection

The good and bad characteristics of each of the varieties grown and tested were discussed and the lines to be followed in securing improved varieties were clearly outlined. Carleton states:

"In general, regions possessing black prairie soils and characterized by violent climate extremes, especially extremes of heat and drought, produce wheats that are hardiest, have the hardest grains, and are the best in quantity and quality of gluten content."

"Considering all qualities, the best wheats of the world are of Russian origin, coming particularly from eastern and southern Russia, the Kirghiz steppes, and Turkestan."

Among these the best known are Turkey, Crimean, and Odessa of the ordinary bread types, and Arnautka, Kubanka, and Mennonite of the durum types.

Somewhere in this general region, probably to the south, was the original home of wheat. Mr. Carleton concluded that a study of wheats in this region might yield something of value. Seed of known varieties had frequently been imported and had proved of great value. It was Mr. Carleton's idea, however, to go out into the small prairie settlements, far away from the big markets, and find wheat that had been grown for many years under extreme conditions of drought and cold, so that natural selection would have had full opportunity to get its work without the interference of mixture of varieties as would be found in the more settled areas.

Mr. Carleton's plan appealed to the department officials, and he was sent in 1899 to make a study of these areas and to secure seed of such varieties as appeared to have promise. He made a very thorough exploration, especially in remote districts, where he secured a large number of selections in accordance with his plan under conditions where he was assured that the limiting factors of environment had had unrestricted opportunity to weed out nonresistant individuals, thus resulting in building up high resistance to cold and drought and other limiting factors.

Grains Growth or Centuries

On his return from this trip Mr. Carleton told the writer that he secured selections of wheat from communities that had grown the particular strain through many hundreds of years without bringing in any seed from outside. Some years they would have very little to eat, as they must always save enough for seed. If cold or drought destroyed most of the crop, what was left was very carefully saved for seed.

Varieties of hard red spring wheat have been developed by selecting and breeding which are proving more cold, rust and drought-resistant and of better quality. Selections and hybrids of the hard red winter class, such as Kanred, Karmont, Newturk, and Miniturki, have greatly extended and improved winter wheat. It may be safely said that these new introductions of specially selected varieties have formed the basis of a constantly improving wheat culture in the Middle Western area. Improvements will continue for many years to come as the art of combining valuable characters by breeding becomes better understood.

—A.F. Woods
1927 Yearbook of Agriculture

Ordinarily alfalfa ranks among the tougher, more aggressive crops. But in 1978, set back by a series of adversities—low food reserves in the spring and insect and disease attacks during the summer—many alfalfa fields took on a bedraggled look.

But that's bygones. "It's time to survey the situation and determine the number of healthy plants that can survive the winter and fill in the empty spaces next spring," says University of Wisconsin-Extension agronomist Dwayne Rohweder. "If you have a half stand or more, nourish your field with high fertilizer rates, leave enough stubble to catch snowfall and hope for good recovery. If you have less than a half a stand, plan to reseed next spring."

"Alfalfa won't reseed nor does it spread vegetatively," says UW-Madison agronomist Mike Collins. "If properly fertilized, a healthy plant will enlarge when surrounding plants die." But too many gaps can't be filled by extra foilage, and a thin stand invites weed competition.

"A full stand should have about 25 plants a square foot at the end of the seeding year, 12 to 20 at the end of the first hay year, 8 to 12 at the end of the second hay year and 4 to 8 plants as the 3rd year passes," says Rohweder. "Divide these figures by two to determine if you have half a stand."

Then make spot checks in square foot areas scattered throughout the field. Assess whether plant losses are widespread or limited to a few scattered areas that could be reseeded.

But remember that a population figure is insignificant if some of the plants you count are infected with disease and weakened. So look for wilting or discoloration above the ground, and dig deeply to check roots for lesions on the outside or an off-color on the inside.

Phytophthora root rot is characterized by black lesions that start on the outside of the root and gradually move through the root to the core. Phytophthora was prevalent last summer, especially where young stands stood on waterlogged soils. Plants with bacterial wilt will have a yellow-brown discoloration in the cylinder of the root, and the stem and leaves wilt. Wilts and fusarium, a crown rot, are more common in older stands.

Regardless of the age of the stand and the type of infection, Rohweder says, disease symptoms are more severe in a stand grown under low fertility conditions.

"UW studies show that optimal fertilization with lime, potassium and sulfur and to some extent with phosphorus, can significantly improve winter hardiness," says UW-Extension soil scientist Keith Kelling.

A strong fertilization program ensures good root development and helps plants build up the necessary food reserves to survive the winter. Moreover, fall fertilization boosts the spring growth rate, says Kelling.

Consequently, if you've decided to amble on a strand that's been weakened by insect feeding and disease infection, Rohweder and Kelling stress applying recommended fertilizer as the best single treatment to encourage recovery and successful overwintering.

Fall is a good time to apply fertilizer to alfalfa. "Soils are usually dry, so little physical damage will occur," says Kelling. Farmers tend to have more time to have soils tested and apply recommended rates in the fall. And many can get a fall purchase discount.

THE ACRE OF FLAX

Flax culture, an ancient art, well known to the Pharoahs, but unknown to me, became my project after I read all I could find on the subject. Making linen fiber, preparing it for sprinning and finally making yarn from the fiber, fascinated me. I wanted to harvest and process flax for a long time. See Figs. 3-7 and 3-8.

I purchased a pound of flax seed and asked Jerry Balanger if I could rent a few square feet of land from him. When he heard of my plan, he said he wanted to experiment with flax too. I called him again at planting time to make final arrangements only to find

Fig. 3-7. Scutching, hackling, and flax break.

he had bought a whole bushel of flax seed. He had planted an acre. He thought it was impractical to set up his seed drill for less.

I figured he knew what he was doing and gave the matter little thought. Late June, though, when the crop blossomed into a beautiful blue field, I panicked. How was I to deal with one whole acre of flax?

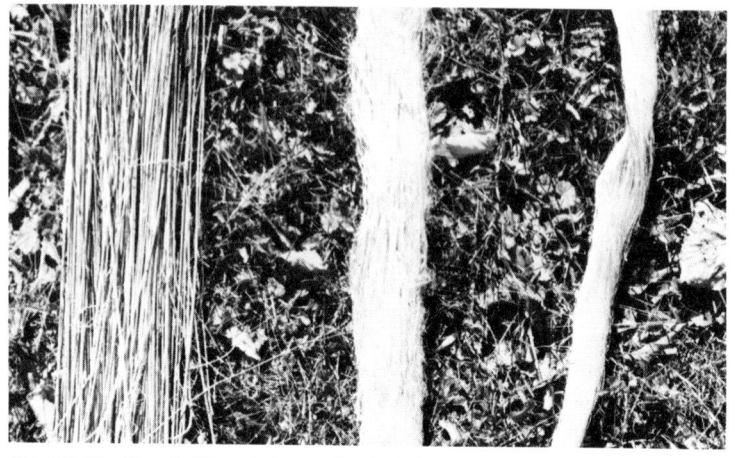

Fig. 3-8. The flax at different stages. On the left is the retted flax, then the broken flax, and finally the line flax ready for spinning.

An Acre is a Lot of Flax!

I discovered that one acre of flax produced 1-3/4 tons of dried stalks which yielded around 400 pounds of useable fiber. An acre of alfalfa, which yields four tons of hay per acre, is no cause for alarm. But flax is a tedious crop. I soon found out it required a great deal of care and preparation. Flax plants must be pulled by hand not cut, to obtain the greatest length of fiber. We kept the stems in orderly bundles, seed heads to seed heads and roots to roots, not tumbled like hay.

Hand pulling a whole acre of plants scared me, but what really worried me was the business of retting. The first book I had read said the flax for retting should be immersed in water soon after it was pulled. Sluggishly flowing waters such as those of the river Lys in Belgium were considered ideal, but I had no access to such a stream.

After reading more, I discovered that flax could be dried after harvest, stored and retted later at one's convenience. In Belgium, where the finest flax is produced, the flax is customarily stored for a year, a practice which yields better fiber.

Comforted by the knowledge that I would not have to ret the entire crop at once, I waited patiently for harvest time. When the flax stems turned yellow two-thirds of the way up, the plants were ready to be pulled. Unfortunately, by this time, the weeds had grown so tall, we could scarcely see the flax.

Bringing in the Crop

Nonetheless we worked. I pulled flax. My friends and their families pulled flax. But we couldn't harvest the whole acre. At best we pulled between 1/2 and 1/3 of the crop. I learned later that Colonial American families planted only half of an acre and that flax should be weeded when it is four inches high.

When I plant another crop, I will plant it in strips about three feet wide so I can walk between the rows to weed.

Once we finished harvesting, we tried to ret the flax. This was the most important step in processing flax. The required fibers form the outer layer of the stem. In their natural state they adhere closely to the woody inner core. By retting, we loosened the outer fibers by partially decomposing them so we could separate them from the core.

For my retting tank I used the tallest plastic garbage can available. Metal tank rust could ruin the fiber. I filled the plastic can with rain water. The water was free of any minerals which might discolor the fiber.

Before the flax could be retted, however, I removed the seeds by "rippling", I drew the seed heads through the teeth of a rippling comb which pulls off the seed capsules. A genuine rippling comb has long, sharp iron teeth and like most flax-processing implements, must be bought in antique stores. A useable comb can be improvised by driving a row of long nails one-half to one inch apart into a board.

Rippling

Once I had placed the flax upright in the plastic tank and the retting had begun, I watched carefully to insure that the decay went just so far. Just as for cakes, a "done" test indicated when the retting was completed. When the stem was bent sharply over the index finger, the woody core snapped from the outer envelope of fibers like a bone sticking out of a compound fracture. Or if I could strip the entire fiber envelope, or nearly all of it, off the core in one piece, then the flax was ready.

The length of retting depending greatly on temperature. In hot (90 degrees F.) weather, retting could take four or five days. In cold weather, it could last as long as two weeks. After retting, I laid the flax out to dry. Once dry, the flax was stored until I wished to finish the extraction process.

Breaking meant that the stems had to be beaten in a "flax break". The woody portion, which had become brittle, fell away. The fiber, being much elastic, withstood all my pounding. My flax break has three blades on the bottom and two on the top. The two top blades fit into the spaces between the bottom ones to shear the stems. I found plans for building a flax break in Worst's *How to Weave Linens.* Or you can send 25 cents and a self-addressed, stamped envelope to Berea College Appalachian Museum, Berea, Kentucky, 40403.

After the stems were broken, I beat them with a wooden "scutching" sword to remove clinging bits of inner stem. Then I drew the flax through the teeth of a "flax hackle" (or heckle, hetchel or even hatchel). By "hackling", I removed the last of the woody parts and separated the fibers, I found that a graduated series of hackles, coarse, medium, fine, worked best. But such implements are hard to find.

It's an Art

The long-combed fibers, called "line," were now ready to be spun into the best yarns. The short fibers which remained in the teeth of the hackles were called "tow". I carded and spun them into coarse yarns.

If you wish to process flax, you should be aware that there is a certain art to it. You should break a little at a time working from the end towards the middle and then switching to do the other end. Scutching and hackling are done the same way.

I learned a lot from my experiences, and some day I will plant another patch. When I grow flax again, though, I will NOT plant a whole acre.

Not all Flax is Linen

Talk about communications: it wasn't until I read Pat's story that I realized she was afraid she'd have to pull a whole acre of flax!

My interest in this crop had nothing to do with spinning and weaving. I was after the seed.

Flaxseed was once grown quite widely as a livestock feed supplement. Although the seed itself contains only about two-thirds as much protein as the linseed meal (which is made from flaxseed), it is much higher in total digestible nutrients, because of its high fat content. And since linseed meal usually runs from 32-37 percent protein, the two-thirds available in ground flaxseed is still very attractive to homesteaders.

The seed is very small, and must be difficult to combine or harvest. But, as Pat points out, ours was so weedy I didn't even bother to try. But since I know how interested homesteaders are in high protein crops such as soybeans, we'll probably attempt it again.

Incidentally, you can't have your linen and your flaxseed too. For spinning, the flax is pulled before the seeds are fully ripened.

DRY FARMING WORKS

"It's stress that makes this wheat valuable—the frosts, the wide fluctuations of temperature, and even the lack of rain give it its higher protein content," said organic farmer Steve Beck.

Steve, who dry farms 2,000 acres in the desert-like Carrisa Plain in central California, Figs. 3-9 through 3-14, thoughtfully fingered golden wheat berries and popped them into his mouth.

"This wheat is tough, and because it is, it has a high gluten content and makes an excellent milling wheat," he stated. "But it's difficult convincing people that it is possible to grow a hard red

Fig. 3-9. Stress makes the wheat valuable.

Fig. 3-10. Steve elevates one of the rod bar weeders he uses to control Russian thistles and fireweed. Tilling is a continuous process in the summer fallow system.

Fig. 3-11. The annual harvest is underway with one of three completely recycled 1958 John Deere 95-H Combines. It took a lot of passes to fill the bulk truck this year.

winter wheat in California, and organically at that."

In a normal year his yields are low—about 600 pounds per acre—because the average yearly rainfall totals only 8 inches. But this year, he'll be lucky to get his seed back because of the worst drought California's had in 131 years. He hasn't sold all of last year's crop yet because the price has not been high enough to recover costs, and yet he knows that people in the cities can't get as much organic wheat as they would like to have, he explained.

Fig. 3-12. These grain storage facilities at the Beck farm hold hundreds of tons. Steve's organic wheat is housed in the front bins.

Fig. 3-13. The templor Mountains dwarf the combine on its sweep for grain grown organically in a drought year.

He might have been summing up the problems and challenges of organic farmers as a whole who are strengthened by the stresses of weather and hardened by the great fluctuations in market prices amid an ever-growing desire by consumers who want their food to be unadulterated, and their own personal commitment to supply that food.

It seems like a bleak picture, but Steve, 27, and his wife, Deb, 25, aren't terribly daunted. "If we survive this year, we just might make it. We should be getting rain in the fall and we should be able

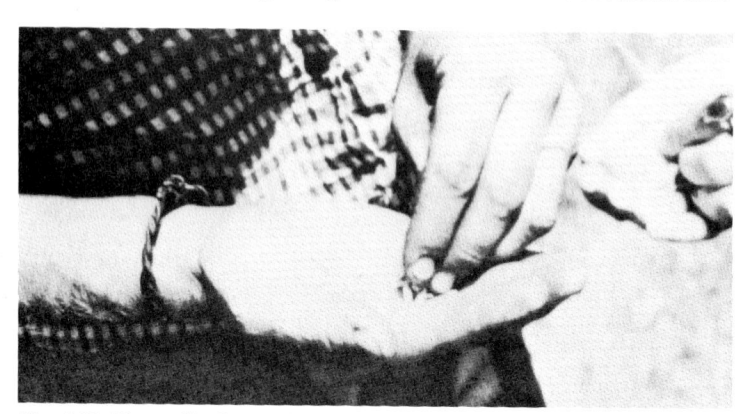

Fig. 3-14. The nutlike flavor of the golden grain proves irresistable to Deb and Steve.

to develop more customers like the fellow from Northfolk from the Sun Meadow Natural Foods Co., a distributor, who sends his truck here to pick up our bagged grain," Steve said.

Steve, who started the Carrizo Grain Co. three years ago while a history student at Sonomia State College in northern California, is a certified member of the California Organic Growers and one of the founders of that new organization. He belongs to the fifth generation of his family to farm in that isolated area. As the years went by, the family worked their way out of the mountains and into the valley, coming to their present place in 1927.

Steve is in partnership with his father, Kenneth, and his brother, Greg, who farm their part of the 10,000-acre farm with chemicals. "They've been pretty supportive both physically and morally, though," Steve said. "They're acceptive to what I'm trying to do and are willing to help me. But I must hold up my end of the operation."

The 8-×-60 mile Carrizo valley has an altitude of 2,000 feet and is ringed by low mountains punctuated by 3,622-foot Black Mountain and bordered by the Los Padres National Forest. It's nearly a two-hour drive from the nearest town of any size, San Louis Obispo, along a well-paved but twisting and diving State Highway 58. A sign out of the village of Santa Margarita warns, "Narrow, winding road. Trucks with trailers not advised. Next services 70 miles." The small city of Paso Robles lies 50 miles to the north along a similar road, and the San Joaquin valley is over the La Panza mountains to the east.

[The road is used by valley residents for weekend escapes to the cool seacoast resort towns such as Morro Bay and Cayucos and the traffic, according to Steve, "drives me nuts." His brother jokes, "Yea, all 12 cars an hour on Friday and Sunday evening."] The road pigtails through the mountains with their oak opens and coastal pine groves, past vast ranches etched with cattle trails and occasional jeep tracks, past national forest campgrounds and lookout towers, and spills onto the plain, which is richly aureoled in gold, bronze and copper dotted here and there with alkali white against the electric blue sky and the brown and black mountains. Each cluster of ranch or farm houses and outbuildings, often miles apart, is startling for its seemingly lavish setting of leaf and grass green.

The summer heat is like a wavy wall of radiance. It hovers at or above the 100° mark for days with the nights cooling to the comfortable 70s. Winter will drop the air to the teens and occasionally below zero with a "murderous wind-chill factor."

The Becks' farm is slashed by the San Andreas fault but they're not concerned because a quake in the 50s "took off the pressure." The farm—seven miles long and two to three miles wide—is "about average" in size for the valley. Steve's 2,000-acre portion makes him positively "small." Because there is so little rain and the soil's high alkalinity, yields are low and a lot of land is needed to support a family. "The asking price for a place down the road is $140 an acre, but no one could make enough on that land to pay for it," Steve asserted.

Steve left his home valley to attend California Polytechnic Institute in San Luis Obispo, an institution founded by his grandfather, Julian McPhee. He served in the Army in Germany and then attended college at Fresno State and was graduated from Sonoma State, where he met Deb. While in school he worked in nurseries and as a bricklayer, but he always felt the call of the land and wanted to have some chickens and farm animals.

"I gradually got interested in organic farming and during the '72 grain shortage reasoned that our family really had been growing organic grain for generations, until comparatively recently, and I wanted to be able to grow and sell the best, unadulterated grain I could," he said in his soft-spoken, almost shy way.

"People may snicker at what they call 'the health food nuts,' but when they're offered grain or fruit that they know wasn't sprayed, they prefer it," he maintained. "Given the choice, they'll take the pure product and they'll say that it tastes better, too."

When Steve decided to try to make a go of it organically on the family farm, he had his shoulder-length blond hair cut so his neighbors and customers could relate to him better. He and his city-raised bride moved into a 100-year-old former schoolhouse which had been moved onto the property and "just grew." They completely remodeled the place and were delighted to uncover one by 12 redwood uprights and beams.

Steve, who says he's "liberal in some respects, but conservative about the land," uses a summer fallow system, dividing his cropland in half. After the harvest in summer, the neighbors' cattle and sheep are allowed to graze "more as a service to them" than for the nominal fees the Becks charge. They eat the stubble, and of course, leave their manure. After the animals comes the tilling to replenish the soil by incorporating the manure and the crop residues. The land is tilled three, four, or as many as five times to take advantage of the organic material in every weed. As Steve says, "We try to control the weeds, not kill them." But the weeds can be a problem, especially Russian thistle and fireweed.

"It's a constant year-around battle to keep the weeds down, so we can conserve every drop of moisture that falls," Steve said. "And this year there's been no rain. The 'regular' October and November rains didn't come, but we did have a couple of snowfalls that stayed on the ground for a few days."

Steve's year is spent "getting ready to plant and planting and getting ready to harvest and harvesting." Deb recalls that he spent last Christmas Eve out on the tractor planting and finished up on Feb. 6.

Between and during the planting, tilling and harvesting, Steve helps keep the farm running including repairing leach lines and storage facilities and becoming a "self-taught blacksmith."

The Becks have a complete workshop and maintain heaps of metal to be refabricated into parts. Steve calls them "our gold mines." "Living way out here, you can't run to San Luis or Paso for repair work on every breakdown. If we can't repair a part, we'll try to make a new one. We can trust ourselves as much as any mechanic in town. If all fails, though, and we do have to go, there's another day shot. Maybe more if they don't have the part," Steve said.

He's proud of the farm's four 1958 harvesters. "Almost every part of them has been recycled or rebuilt in one way or another," he explained. "Dad bought them in 1958 for $17,000. They'd cost at least $50,000 today, and we sure couldn't afford that."

The other equipment Steve helps keep running includes three venerable Allis Chalmers 230 crawlers and their various attachments including grain planters and rod weeders and the grain loading and storage facilities. Not to mention the house. "We just can't call plumber or electrician when something goes haywire. We have to handle it ourselves," he says.

Deb thinks this is fine. "When you're out here all alone, you learn the meaning of responsibility and you discover more and more ways to be self-reliant. It's a wonderful way to grow in knowledge and maturity. I've never been happier."

A psychology graduate of Sonoma State with a minor in women's studies, Deb had prepared to be a high school guidance counselor, but is keeping that in reserve for a later date, as well as her plans for earning a master's degree.

"I love animals and I love to be outdoors. And here I can take care of my animals in this beautiful valley," she says. She remembers her New Year's Eve present, Spike, a hereford calf which was born to her wedding present, Mom, a hereford cow. "It was a terribly blustery day and chilly night out on the range, and a pesky ram wouldn't let Spike nurse, so we had to haul him in the truck and put him on the back porch. Mother and son are doing just beautifully now, though."

She has a mixed flock of 30 chickens that are "producing pretty well." Spike and Mom and a couple of steers, and her horse, Sam, which she uses to herd the cattle along with her Queensland heeler, Rose. She and Steve also raise hogs. In fact, they raise all their own meat organically.

Deb used to work in a veterinarian's office and picked up know-how that's been very useful on the farm. "When there's a problem with the animals," Steve said, "we call Deb. She keeps calm when everybody else panics."

They've planted a small orchard of apricot, apple, almond and peach trees and plan to put in rows of Monterey pines to deaden the sound from that "awful highway." Steve mutters about how "it's getting too crowded around here," (the farms are apt to be a couple of miles apart in the valley, but a real estate developer has platted and sold 25,000 acres nearby) and recalls how he had to get out of the small town of Forestville in Sonoma County because he couldn't stand so many people. Deb says she now feels uncomfortable on her infrequent trips to town because of all the traffic. Steve manages not to leave the farm for months at a time.

They were a little embarrassed when *Countryside* visited because they didn't plant a garden this year like they usually do. Instead, they took their first vacation in three years, camping with friends down the Baja Peninsula.

"When you consider the time it took getting ready and then the trip itself," Steve said, "we lost about a month and a half and missed the chance to plant the garden. It's tilled though, waiting for the rains. And we can always trade chickens and eggs for produce."

Steve has dreams of building a greenhouse and experimenting with growing vegetables hydroponically, but hasn't had time as yet to work out the plans.

Deb hopes to get outdoors more this year, driving the bulk loading truck in the fields during harvest. She bakes breads, cookies, pies and cakes and is apt to spend weeks at a time in the kitchen feeding hearty meals and a dozen pies a day to the threshing crew. Steve has built a pass-through for her to a small enclosed porch-become-dining hall, and has put in a water cooler for 10-gallon carboys of the fresh water he has to haul from a spring down the road.

The water at the farm is alkaline and disagreeable to drink or cook with. "The cooler's simply wonderful," she said. "We used a bucket and ladle for a long time." They store their food in two refrigerators and have a well-stocked freezer.

The long harvest season starts in July with the whole crew and the entire family working dawn to dusk hours. Steve's organic grain is harvested separately and stored in separate bins.

Steve is exploring the possibilities of using diatomaceous earth to prevent possible insect damage to the stored wheat and barley. "It was too expensive, last year, costing $2.45 a ton, so we just 'gutsied it' and didn't use anything. We've got a better source for the earth now, so we'll give it a try. Last year it was so dry we didn't have any problems," he said. "We were lucky on that account because although a wet year's good for crops, it's bad for storage."

Steve cleans the grain, then bags it, and labels it with his Carrizo Grain Co. tag and its certified organic imprint. His separate operation all takes extra time so he has to cut corners on other things he'd like to accomplish.

"Sometimes it's very frustrating, but we compromise and try to take each day as it comes. You learn to pace yourself and live with Nature, not against it," he says.

Steve has developed his own markets and sells a lot of his wheat to Milbrae Natural Foods in Berkeley and to Erewhon Products, an organic foods distributor and processor with main offices in Los Angeles and Boston. His wheat goes into their flour and pastas such as whole wheat egg noodles, spinach pastas, corn ribbons and whole wheat-soya-rice shell pasta.

At one time, the farm had its own flour mill which the family had imported from France. "It's nothing but a ruin now," Steve says wistfully, "but it sure would be wonderful to have our own mill and supply the local markets directly."

Steve feels that if things go in cycles, "then we've had 20 good years to be followed by 20 lean years." He doesn't know if he'll be able to make it economically. He explained that it costs $35 an acre to raise the wheat, without including interest on the land or equipment or for a crop survival loan.

In a good year he averages 1000 pounds an acre. His break-even average is 600 pounds and with the price around $6 a hundredweight, "that's marginal at best." This year's harvest averaged 500 pounds.

Then there are the cleaning, storage, and bagging costs, not to mention trucking charges. "The price of wheat may have doubled in the past few years," he says, "but the costs of producing that wheat out here have tripled."

Still, he's trying hard to open up more markets so he doesn't have to deal in small volumes. He's looking for a group of natural food stores or a large bakery which makes natural breads and cakes. He wants to see consumers get the pure food they need and he worries about the worldwide food shortages.

He believes that it is going to take a large movement to make organic farming feasible in his area. And he would like to get his neighbors to cooperate. Right now, they're tolerant, though he's concerned about dispersal of sprays and runoff from pesticides and herbicides.

But he feels organic farming will be the wave of the future and "with patience on our part and a change of attitude on the part of established agribusiness" which he sees coming "when the oil gets tighter than it is."

"Many farmers have been conditioned to use chemicals and now they're psychologically forced to because of the impact of economics. If they lose their crops, they lose their land. But this will change. Their fears will be overcome. There will be a gradual weaning away from the dependence upon petrochemicals," he maintains.

And what if Steve and Deb Beck can't swing their own financial pendulum to solid black:

"We'll never go back to the city. We'll find a place of our own with enough acres to support enough animals to self-survive. We'll homestead!"

COMFREY: THE PLANT THAT BUILDS PROTEIN

Confrey (Fig. 3-15) is reputed to be "the world's fastest protein builder." We at the Red Barn Bunny and Worm Farm started raising comfrey in July 1974. We started with 100 root cuttings purchased from the North Central Comfrey Co., located in Glidden, Wisconsin. By the fall of 1974 we knew we had a plant well worth our time and energy. In the spring of 1975 we ordered and planted another 500 cuttings.

We read all available information about comfrey and soon became reporting research members of the Henry Doubleday Research Assn. which is located in Essex, England. This association has been researching comfrey for many years and has recorded information dating back to 1790. The association has a printed booklet, *Comfrey Report, the Story of the World's Fastest Protein*

Fig. 3-15. Comfrey.

Builder. Anyone who is serious about comfrey will find this book well worth its $3 cost.

During the past year we have cut our commercial feed costs by 60 percent feeding the rabbits and chickens all of the comfrey they would eat. Besides the savings on our feed costs, we have noted that we haven't had any digestive problems with our rabbits and haven't had a single doe eat her young since the advent of the use of comfrey here in the Red Barn.

The most significant difference in the chickens has been a much richer and darker yolk and firmer whites in the eggs.

The pound per acre yield of comfrey is fantastic. When I read reports of yields from 50 to 100 tons per acre, I was skeptical; however, please note the following reported results from our test plants as reported to the Henry Doubleday Research Assn.

In our planting we followed the instructions given us by the North Central Comfrey Co. to plant with three foot spacing in the rows and the rows three feet apart.

Our test plants are in our planting which was made in Georgia red clay in April 22, 1975. The soil test we had made indicated a pH of 6.3.

We had our ground broken earlier in the spring with a large tractor and disc plow. The field was old fescue and Coastal Bermuda sod. We fertilized with cotton hulls, rabbit manure, worm castings, and lime. After the tractor and disc plow did the initial ground breaking I would guess that I went over it no less than 10 times with our rear end tiller which finally worked the soil up into a good seedbed.

We made our first cuttings from this new planting August 2, 1975, and began weighing and recording our test plant cuttings September 2, 1975.

Considering that we made 10 cuttings from our first plantings during 1975 which were planted July, 1974, it would be fair to assume that we will be able to get 10 cuttings or more from this last planting.

When planted on the recommended 3-foot spacing there are 4,880 plants per acre. Therefore, from our test plant yields, one may calculate that with 10 cuttings per year that our comfrey produced at a rate in excess of 76 tons per acre.

Inasmuch as comfrey does not reach its maximum production until the third year, I feel confident we will top the 100-tons-per-acre yield.

It isn't difficult to understand why this plant can be a real help to the small homesteader. A great amount of feed can be raised on a small plot of ground.

Another plus for comfrey is that we eat it too. *Comfrey Report* has suggestions on how to prepare comfrey for human consumption. Comfrey Soup, Comfrey Leaf Wine, Comfrey Root Wine, Candied Root, Fried Comfrey Flour, Comfrey Tea, are among the ways to use this most unusual plant.

CORN YIELDS HIGHER WITH CROP ROTATIONS

Corn yields are higher in a system of rotation than in a system of continuous corn, research workers at various universities have found.

Corn yields are especially higher when the rotation contains a legume such as soybeans or alfalfa. Even significant amounts of fertilizer don't make up for the legume.

Reasons why the yield is depressed on continuous corn are a matter of speculation. Some ideas include differences in soil moisture, microbial activity, nutrient availability, soil compaction, soil tilth, weeds, insects, and diseases.

At the Southeast South Dakota Experiment Farm from 1965 through 1978 a rotation of corn-oats-soybeans yielded 67 bushels per acre with no fertilizer, and 80 bushels an acre with fertilizer. A corn-soybeans-oats rotation yielded 56 bushels on unfertilized ground and 73 bushels on fertilized ground.

A corn-oats rotation yielded 53 bushels with no fertilizer and 72 bushels with fertilizer.

Continuous corn had the lowest annual yield with 52 bushels to the acre unfertilized and 70 bushels to the acre fertilized.

The highest yield was 80 bushels to the acre with a corn-oats-soybeans rotation and fertilizer applied.

TAILOR THE CROP TO THE SOIL

Although scientists have for the past 50 years sought ways to change the soil to meet the needs of crops, scientists of USDA's Science and Education Administration (SEA) here say that it is now often cheaper and more beneficial to tailor the crop to fit the soil.

Studies have shown that different genetic strains of the same type of plant—be it soybeans, wheat, corn, cotton, tomatoes, or chili peppers—have widely different abilities to tolerate stress conditions. For problem soils, even good soils in some cases, SEA soil scientists, Charles F. Foy and John C. Brown say that selecting and breeding plants with genes for tolerance is a sensible alternative or supplement to sometimes massive and recurring chemical treatments, such as spreading lime or phosphorus.

By using more specific plant germplasm for specific soils, farmers could use much less energy for growing crops, say the USDA scientists, because fertilizer, lime, water and fuel for machinery would be used more efficiently.

"We may be entering a new era in agriculture," Brown wrote in a recent research paper, "an era in which we finally recognize the plant for what it is. Considering the restrictions imposed (on native plants during their evolution) by extremely diverse soils and climates, it seems remarkable that so many different kinds of native plants survive and reproduce. They do so because they are genetically diverse themselves and are able to adapt to stress conditions."

Foy and Brown over the past 20 years have tested and proven their theories on many economically important species. It is now up to commercial and government plant breeders, they said, to become more aware of the idea, to incorporate stress-tolerant genes into their breeding programs, and to make information available to farmers and extension agents.

"Farmers generally know their soil, but not their plants," says Brown. "We think that soon farmers will be saying to their suppliers, "I want manganese tolerant seed, or I want seed for my alkaline soil, or seed for iron efficiency, or for tolerance to salinity, high aluminum or high boron."

Fitting plants to soils instead of the reverse also has a human nutrition angle, says Foy and Brown. "One reason different strains of the same species vary in their abilities to tolerate certain soils is that the plants vary in their nutritional requirements, they take up different amounts of mineral elements from the soil. Thus, our genetic approach to soil fertility will not only boost crop production, but will allow us to control levels of mineral elements in crops. We could raise the nutritional values of some foods or lower certain mineral contents that could cause nutritional problems in high doses."

The USDA scientists are with SEA's Plant Stress Laboratory, part of the Beltsville Agricultural Research Center in Maryland.

GLEANING THE CORNFIELDS

For several years my husband and I have gleaned cornfields after the corn has been harvested. The farmer's permission was always secured before we entered his field. After many hours of walking, tripping, stomping and picking over these fields, we would painfully drive home with our take.

Last year the job of banging on doors and picking the fields became mine. Most farmers readily granted permission to glean the fields, though a couple did so only after I assured them I would not pick any standing corn and not steal anything.

Many people think going through a cornfield in search of downed corn is more effort than the results warrant. Sure, gleaning any field is hard work. The big payoff comes not from the fact that it's free animal feed for the winter, but from the satisfaction of seeing that huge mound of corn in your own corn bin. By gleaning fields, we were able to feed our horses and 15 goats during the late fall and the winter months. The corn is a good grain ration stret-

Fig. 3-16. Corn yields are higher with crop rotations.

cher. Whole or partial ears (Fig. 3-16) may be fed as is to horses, mules, ponies and goats with no ill effects. We know some farmers who have used this method for years. The horses also enjoy munching the cobs after they have eaten the kernels.

As an experienced part-time field gleaner, I have relatively little trouble in finding the best cornfields. I organize and plan early in the corn harvesting season. While the corn stalks still stand, I drive around seeking the healthiest-looking prospective fields. Then I start knocking on doors looking for the owners of these potential gleanings. When permission is granted, I write the farmer's name and the location of each field in a book. As each field is harvested, I follow shortly to glean so that the corn does not lay on the ground and mold. I move from one field to the next saving time because of my previous footwork. All I have to do is watch for the farmer to take in his corn. Sometimes the farmer will tell you what days he intends to take in his corn.

From past trial and error practices, I found that if a farmer uses a cornpicker only, chances of finding downed corn are very good. Should he use a corn sheller in his fields, the opposite holds. I can get a general idea of which method the farmer used by the appearance of the remaining stubble. A field with evenly cut and bent stalks, one that gives the impression a mower went through cutting off or cleanly pushing over all the stalks five inches or so from the ground, usually means the field was shelled. I don't waste my time in these fields. The reapings are very little. However, a harvested field with stalks bent and twisted and of varying heights with some debris of the stalks and husks around is usually worthwhile. A corn picker was used in this field.

A good farmer picks his fields as clean as he possibly can with his machinery, but he knows he *can't* pick every ear. That's why he doesn't mind letting you go into his fields after him. The most profitable areas to search are at the ends of the rows. Downed corn can be found lying on top of the ground, partially buried or sometimes almost completely in the dirt. It can be already husked or still in its husks. It can also be hidden under the stalk debris.

After checking the ends, step into the field several yards scanning the ground for ears. In large fields, if no ears of corn are found, stoop and try to eye which way the picker traveled through. There should be several rows all tilted in the same direction. Try to find the rows leaning in the reverse. There should be three or four of these together and then the next rows will lean in the opposite direction. The three or four rows going against the grain is probably were the farmer broke into his field with his corn picker. There can be two or more such places depending on how large his field is and what method he used. When the corn picker breaks into a field, it pushes those three to four rows over and in many cases does not pick more than a few ears on the first pass. To a gleaner, such a find is lots of pure golden corn. Sometimes a farmer will take time from his work to show you where he broke into his field or to show you other possible places to find corn that he knows of.

The important thing to remember when walking a field is to always feel with your feet, whether they are bared or booted. Learn how an ear of corn feels when felt with the foot. Use your heels to scuff the fallen stalks and husks on the chance that an ear might be hidden underneath. Feeling with the feet instead of the hands saves backache and valuable time.

Courtesy in gleaning fields means keeping any and all children with you under hand. Both you and anyone with you must remember that you are on private property with permission to glean the field only. So stay away from the farmer's buildings and his equipment—a measure of safety both for you and the farmer.

Last year, it took only past remembrance of bending over to pick up the ears for me to realize I needed a definite back saving tool. With the exceptions of very large, heavy ears or buried ears, my simple tool worked remarkably well. In most fields my gleaning time was shortened.

My "corn-stabber" consists of an old broom, shovel, rake, etc., type handle; four long roofing nails; two small blocks of wood and a long screw. Assemble as follows:

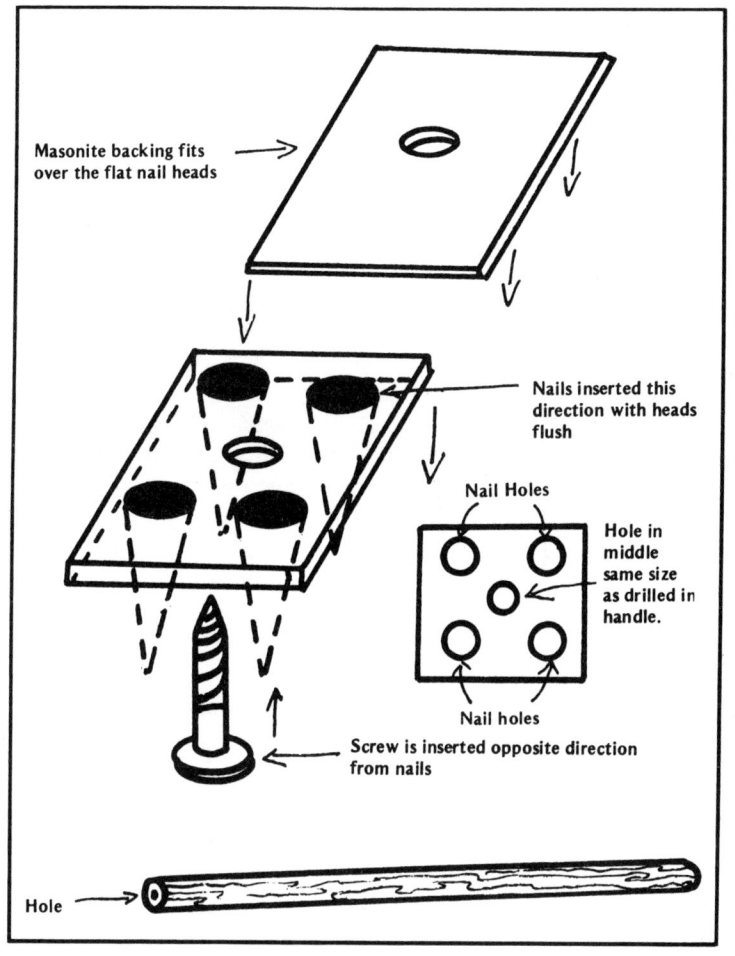

Fig. 3-17. Gleaning tool details.

A. Drill a short hole in the sawn-off end of the wooden handle. Use a smaller drill bit than the thickness of the long screw.

B. Cut a 1 1/2-×-1 1/2 square of 1/2-inch-thick wood. Drill four holes the same thickness as the roofing nails so that the nails can be pushed snugly into them. Arrange the four holes as shown in Fig. 3-17. This makes almost any ear or piece of an ear easy picked up. Note: Use roofing nails at least 1 1/4 inches long.

C. Cut a 1 1/2-×-1 1/2 inch square of thin masonite. This backing square will give strength to and help to prevent splitting of the head.

D. Into the middle of both squares drill the same size hole as was drilled into the long handle.

E. Push the four roofing nails through the holes in the first square until their heads are flush on one side.

F. Place the masonite backing against the side of the block with the flat nailheads. Screw the long screws through the middle holes of the squares. Use a long handled screwdriver (so your hand doesn't scrape against the exposed nails). The screw goes the opposite direction than the nails.

G. Next, screw the assembled head tightly to the wooden handle so the nails are sticking away from the handle.

To insure the head and handle remain together, wrap tape around the handle (to act as a bonding base) 2 inches from the head. Then, take two strips of tape and criss-cross them between the nails, reaching from one side of the tape on the handle to the other. Secure the ends of those strips to the handle by winding more tape around it.

If I'm going some distance from home, I make up extra heads and carry them along with an extra screw, tape, and my long-handled screwdriver, in the event my stabber may require a new head.

With a little practice, the corn-stabber becomes a true backache saver. Not only will it pick up the ears of corn, but it will also dislodge them if you properly catch the ear on the side of the hamper or container you are carrying.

One last tip is to take a can or two of your home canned goods to the farmer or farmers, whose fields you gleaned. A little remembrance such as this is almost a certainty that you will be welcomed in the same fields next season. These farmers may also refer you to other farmers who will let you into their fields only because of the referral.

WHY NOT GROW A BROOM?

Although brooms, like money, don't grow on trees, broom bristles do grow on corn stalks. Plus, the same plant provides food for chickens, goats and other farm animals, wild birds and the compost pile. That's a big promise from one packet of seeds, but that's what you get when you plant old-fashioned broom corn. Seeds are available from some mail order nurseries, such as Gurney's, Yankton, South Dakota, 57078.

Broom corn culture is simple. It's the same as for sweet corn or popcorn. In planning the location of your broom patch, remember to select an area well removed from any other crop to avoid cross pollination. Since we considered broom corn a novelty, we didn't find time to plant it until late May, after the rest of the garden was already up and growing. The only spot left in our garden was a corner where contractors had spread a thick layer of subsoil.

We planted the seeds 1 inch deep, every four inches. The rows were two feet apart, forming a block of several short rows to insure good pollination. We kept the soil moist until seedlings appeared and thereafter watered deeply once each week. Manure tea or fish fertilizer was applied once each month to compensate for the poor soil.

The shallow rooted broom corn, like other crop corns, is susceptible to heavy wind storms. As soon as the plants were 3 to 4 inches high, we cultivated to remove weeds and create a shallow irrigation furrow beneath each row. The dirt removed from the ditch was piled around the base of the plants covering the roots deeply. This protected against wind damage and also helped keep the roots cool and moist. As the corn got taller, we hilled the soil up higher around the plants and made the irrigation furrow deeper.

If your summers are as scorching hot as ours, you can reduce watering (and weeding) chores by applying a heavy mulch of straw, spoiled hay or other materials after the soil warms up and the irrigation furrows have been completed.

We like to hold off on thinning all our corn crops until the plants are 6 to 12 inches tall—the bigger the better—because our animals consider these thinnings a special treat. The plants which remain should be eight to 12 inches apart to allow ample room for growth.

Our garden is always full of bugs: good ones, bad ones, and some we're not sure of, but none of the pests showed any interest in the broom corn. This is truly a carefree crop, requiring little more than a watchful eye toward the end of summer, when the small seeds developed at the end of long bristles which form the top of the stalks. (Broom corn does not produce ears.)

For straight, well-formed brooms, it is important to watch and cut the stalks just as the seed heads begin to droop. This is a sign that they are fully mature. With our corn planted in May, this occurred toward the middle of August. If the seed heads are left standing for several days after they bend over, the bristles will be permanently bent and useless for brooms. See Figs. 3-18 and 3-19.

The stalks should be cut about 2 or 3 feet from the top. But, if you have livestock, don't dig up the bottom portion of the stalks yet! Continue watering. Green shoots will form where the stalks were cut. On our farm these greens are fed to sheep, goats and rabbits. If you have cows and horses, they will surely enjoy the greens as well. This second growth continues until the plants are damaged by frost.

After cutting the tops of the stalks, strip away all leaves (feed these to the animals or add to the compost) and lay the seed heads flat on a screen or table to dry thoroughly. In a few days, trim away

Fig. 3-18. Although it is considered a novelty and a curiosity, the Wisconsin State Historical Society has a plot of broom corn and a broom-making shop. Broom corn is still grown today.

Fig. 3-19. The brook corn variety raised by Davy Crockett Rose of Compton, Kentucky has a reddish color. His special variety of the corn gives shorter "sweeps" than the several ordinary kinds grown for brooms.

the ruffled edges which contain the seeds. Reserve these for chicken food or winter feed for wild birds. Also, be sure to reserve a handful of seed for next year's broom patch!

The straight bristles which remain can be stored away for a rainy day. Then when winter's storms shut you in, the material will be handy for a few cozy afternoons of handicraft by the fire.

We scavenge old broom handles and cut them into thirds (18 to 24 inches long) to form the handles of our hearth brooms. Dowels purchased from a hardware store or lumber yard could also be used or, if you have a woodlot, you might prefer to whittle your own.

First sand and wax the handles. Then gather a generous handful of bristles and wire them tightly 6 inches from one end of the handle. Take care to distribute the bristles evenly. Place another wire around the bristles about 4 inches from the end of the handle, and a third wire 2 inches from the end. I like to drill a small hole through the opposite end of the handle and insert a 6 inch length of cord or leather thong to form a loop for hanging the broom. The brooms you grow in your garden make fine gifts or sale items for flea markets and bazaars.

In times past, when the motto of the self-sufficient farmer was "If you can't make it, you can't have it," many a farmer had a patch of broom corn in an out of the way spot near the garden.

Chapter 4

Livestock

Knowledgeable cattlemen consider the cycle of boom or bust a normal part of doing business. Money lost during periods of high beef supplies and low beef prices can be made back (hopefully with interest) when supplies are low and prices are climbing.

Consumers, who don't happen to also be cattlemen, learn about the cattle cycle when prices are going up, remaining unaware that cattle producers are losing money during the periods of falling or steady beef prices.

Of course, all cattlemen don't lose money when prices are low, and all cattlemen don't make money when prices are rising, says David C. Petritz, Purdue University agricultural economist. There can be no question, however, that a lot of cattlemen lost a lot of dollars over the past two years.

The Beef Industry Council puts the loss to the total industry at $30 billion since 1976, pointing out that prior to January of 1978, there were 26 straight months during which the price paid for cattle did not top the average cost of production.

Even with prices on the upswing, cattle producers are a long way from the "parity" price that has been made a goal by many farm organizations.

The National Farmers Union, a supporter of parity prices, says that March cattle prices were $6.74 above the "breakeven" level of $41.92 per hundredweight Corn Belt cattle feeders and $5.28 above the $43.94 breakeven figure for the Great Plains. Parity, the organization suggests, would be $61 per hundred pounds.

The National Livestock and Meat Board puts the cost of producing a hundred pounds of beef on the hoof in the Midwest at $44.27.

This production cost represents a 49 percent increase over the costs incurred by beef producers since the previous round of rising beef prices five years ago, according to Petritz. Cattle prices, as of March, were up only 11 percent over the same period and for much of the time, cattle prices were lower than those of 1973.

Cattlemen understand, according to Petritz, that consumers will buy all of the beef produced, but the price per pound consumers will pay drops as beef supplies increase. The cattle cycle, which reflects this consumer behavior and producers' reaction to it, goes like this, he explains:

During one part of the cycle, cattle numbers increase as individual cattlemen react to favorable prices by expanding their herd or by getting into the cattle business. Eventually, the supply of beef becomes large enough that cattlemen begin to build up their herds, repeating the cycle.

The cattle cycle stretches out over 10 to 12 years, because producer decisions require several years before they are apparent at the meat counter. It takes two to three years to produce a market steer after the decision to do so has been made.

Does this mean that there won't be any price breaks during the next few years?

"No," Petritz predicts, "there will be ups and downs in cattle prices and ups and downs in retail prices, but the trend will be up until cattle numbers are replenished."

One result of the ebbing of the tide of liquidation has been ground beef prices which increase faster than prices of higher quality cuts. Much of the ground and processed beef comes from cows and grass-fed cattle. With the winding down of the liquidation phase of the cattle cycle, the slaughter of these cattle is declining, and thus a larger portion of ground beef supplies must come from grain-fed cattle which have a higher market value.

The increase in ground beef prices puts a particular squeeze on fast-food restaurants which use vast quantities of hamburger, Petritz notes. As a result, other specialities, such as fish sandwiches, have been getting advertising attention. Another result may be the appearance of steak sandwiches in some outlets soon.

Consumers often wonder how beef cattle, which sell for 40 or 50 cents per pound on the hoof, end up averaging more than $1.50

per pound in the supermarket—isn't someone making too much money on the transaction?

The fact is, according to the Beef Industry Council—beef is usually not a very high profit business at any stage in the processing.

A 1,000-pound steer produces a carcass of 615 pounds for the retailer. But the retailer must trim away 183 pounds of fat, bone and waste before he can make the cuts he sells to customers.

If everyone in the chain, from farm to table, were able to break even, the situation would be something like this.

Cattlemen would receive about 45 cents per pound, close to the break even figure. For a 1,000-pound steer, this would be $450. The packer would add $24 for slaughter (average 1977 cost), selling a 615-pound carcass to the retailer for $474. The retailer would trim away 183 pounds leaving 432 pounds for sale at the meat counter costing at this pint $1.10 per pound. Preparation of the meat for retail includes cost of labor for cutting, packaging and cleanup, refrigeration and display. This adds 34 cents per pound pushing the total cost to $1.44 per pound. This leaves 6 cents to cover some transportation costs. Profits throughout the system are not included.

The figures do not include potential returns from sale of hides or income from approximately 26 pounds of liver, heart, tongue, tripe, sweetbreads and brains.

A DAIRY WITH A DIFFERENCE

The Sprucetop Dairy run by Cynthia and Leonard Willis near Bantam, Connecticut, is a most unusual small dairy farm. It is licensed to produce and distribute bottled raw milk from both Jersey cows and Nubian goats.

That combination of cows and goats makes sense from a marketing viewpoint, but we don't know of another licensed dairy that has both animals.

Cynthia is the "dairyman" and handles most of the chores and bottling and distributing milk. Leonard works a full-time job. The family is milking six Jerseys and about 20 Nubians and they're selling about $1,000 worth of milk a month.

They feel they could be on their way to a nice small farm business. See Figs. 4-1 through 4-6. But it hasn't been easy. Getting licensed was costly, and there are still problems to work out.

Raw Milk Sales Legal

Connecticut is one of about a dozen states which license dairies to

Fig. 4-1. Cynthia herds her Nubian does homeward after a day of grazing at the Sprucetop Dairy.

Fig. 4-2. The purebred Nubians await their feed at the Willis dairy.

Fig. 4-3. The goats live in one end of this building and the cows in the other. The center part was remodeled for the milking parlors and milk-handling room.

Fig. 4-4. This old-fashioned cooler sprays ice-cold water over the 5-gallon tote pail and 10-gallon milk cans. The door is open only for demonstration purposes.

Fig. 4-5. Cynthia uses one of two DeLaval milking machines in her small dairy.

Fig. 4-6. The Willises paid $1,700 for this commercial refrigerator to store their bottled milk.

sell raw, unpasteurized milk. Most states require pasteurization, which means the milk must be processed in commercial equipment.

The Willises get about 20 gallons of milk a day from their Jerseys and from five to 20 gallons a day from their Nubians, depending on the season.

For about five years Cynthia Willis had a state license to sell raw milk at the farm in the customers' own containers. To get this license she had to have a proper milk-handling room with cement floors, drains, hot and cold running water, stainless steel wash sinks, etc.

She could fill bottles "by hand" for the farm sales. Actually, she used a cream separator top. It held about 20 quarts of milk at a time and she could turn a part to let the milk flow out and fill the bottle.

But selling milk only to customers who came to the farm wasn't a good way to market milk. There simply weren't enough sales to dispose of all the milk they had available.

"It was always a gamble whether 'Tom Smith' would bother to drive out today to buy milk," Cynthia explained. "If he didn't come, we had to dump surplus milk."

They decided if they wanted to make a business out of those milk sales they would have to distribute the milk to stores. They would have to get a license to sell bottled milk.

Bottle Filler Cost $2,500

That required a mechanical bottle filler. The regulations in Connecticut (and every other state that permits raw milk sales through stores) say the bottles could not be filled by hand or by the modest cream separator device, the dairy had to have a proper filling machine.

The bottle filler cost $2,500, purchased used from a Michigan dairy equipment dealer. They couldn't find anything cheaper, although they looked for two years.

"I held off getting it for along time," Cynthia said. "I felt for the amount of milk we had it was a ridiculous expense. It doesn't make our milk any cleaner than the way we were filling bottles before. We will have to sell a lot of milk to justify the cost, but we had to get it to sell milk in any volume."

She admits she's lucky. The regulations allow her to screw caps on the disposable plastic bottles by hand, if they've been soaked in a chlorine solution first. In most states she would have to buy a mechanical capping device for the bottler, and that would have cost $1,700 more.

The combination of cows and goats has nice advantages from a marketing viewpoint, Cynthia points out.

The dairy goats are Cynthia's special interest. She's proud of her herd of purebred Nubians and stresses that they have the reputation for the best-flavored goat milk. She is really trying to sell goat milk, and she just happened to have some cows also.

But Jersey milk is the "cream" of cow milk and that natural, unpasteurized Jersey milk makes a nice specialty item. The stores were glad to handle the cow milk. In fact, they were often eager to sell the Jersey milk but hesitant about goat milk. It took some serious salesmanship to get goat milk into many stores.

One health food store turned Cynthia down four times before the manager agreed to handle the milk. Now he's selling 20 gallons of cow milk and 10 gallons of goat milk a week.

It costs a lot to distribute a specialty milk that isn't sold in great volumes. Natural cow milk alone, or goat milk alone, might not sell enough to pay the effort of delivering the milk to the stores. Together the sales are decent.

Cows Paid Winter Bills

Last winter Cynthia really appreciated those cows. The goats were in late lactation and daily milk production was very low, hardly enough milk to bother bottling. The cows kept right on producing—

cows aren't seasonal breeders as goats are—and there was a nice flow of Jersey milk all winter.

"The sales of Jersey milk kept us going," Cynthia observes. "We had plenty of milk for the buyers and the income from the cow milk is what bought feed for all the animals through the winter."

A big problem has been distributing the milk. When she got the license in August, Cynthia started driving a delivery route to take milk to each of the stores two or three times a week. It turned out to be almost more work than she could handle. She was driving 100 miles and more a day, getting up at 4:30 A.M. and not getting to bed until 11 P.M. some days to get all the work done.

Then in November a health foods dealer contacted her and offered to distribute all of her milk. He was marketing a variety of food products to health food stores in the area and wanted to handle the natural cow milk and goat milk. It looked like the solution to a major problem.

But the solution lasted only two months. The man simply disappeared. His phone was disconnected, and the stores that were buying from him seemed to have no idea what became of him.

So this spring Cynthia was selling milk to two nearby stores and hoping she would not have to start doing all that driving again when the rest of the goats freshened. She had been contacted by another distributor and hoped they would handle her milk.

Cynthia sells her milk wholesale for 80 cents a half-gallon ($1.40 a gallon) for the Jersey milk and $1.40 a half-gallon ($2.70 a gallon) for the Nubian milk.

The stores mark up the milk a lot, too much in some cases Cynthia feels. Retail customers pay $1.75 or $1.80 a gallon for Jersey milk and up to $3.99 a gallon for the goat milk.

Buildings, 'Small' Expenses

Getting the buildings arranged to meet requirements and getting licensed to run the dairy was costly. Cynthia points out.

"We converted part of the barn and an old log building to make the two milking areas—one for the goats and one for the cows—and the milk handling room. We tore out floors and put in cement and drains and plumbing. There had to be washable walls and ceilings, of course.

"It cost us about $2,500 all together. I think it would have been cheaper to start from scratch with a foundation and build a new building. And it certainly would have been more efficient. We could have designed the building for our exact needs."

There were other "small" expenses. To get printed bottle caps they had to order 25,000 of them, and they had to pay $50 for the two plates to print the caps for the goat milk and cow milk. Bottle caps alone cost almost $700.

The milk handling room is in the center part of their barn. The goats are housed on one side and the cows are housed on the other. There's a small parlor for milking the goats. The cows are milked in a stanchion in their part of the barn.

The have two DeLaval milking machines—one for the cows and the other for the goats.

There has been no problem at all about handling goat milk and cow milk in the same dairy room, Cynthia says. The public health officials had no questions about this at all. When she bottles milk she bottles the goat milk first. Then she puts the cow milk in the bottler and fills the bottles of Jersey milk.

"There might be just a slight trace of goat milk in with that cow milk," Cynthia says, "since I don't wash and rinse the machine between the two milks. But I do not feel that's a problem. I make sure there's no chance of any cow milk in the goat milk—because a lot of the people who are buying goat milk get it because they have allergies to cow milk."

The milk is sold in disposable plastic half-gallon and gallon bottles. Cynthia used to sell the milk in glass bottles, but she said people brought back really dirty bottles and cleaning those bottles was a lot of work. The plastic bottles cost her seven to 10 cents each.

When they sold milk at the farm, sales were higher than $325 to $350 a month. Now milk sales are up to about $1,000 a month. Cynthia is quick to point out that's gross income—feed bills for the farm run $400 to $600 a month.

"We wish we could earn our living from the farm here and my husband wouldn't have to work nights at his job in the shop," Cynthia said. "We're certainly not ready for that yet, but maybe we have made a start in that direction."

Pediatricians Refer Customers

Some of the customers that buy goat milk from Sprucetop Dairy in Connecticut are being referred by local pediatricians who recommend the milk for sickly infants. Cynthia Willis said her family doctor is enthusiastic about the milk, and it appears there are referrals from other doctors as well.

"I had tried to tell our personal pediatrician how nice goat milk was two or three years ago," Cynthia relates, "but it didn't mean much to him. Then he was treating an infant about two weeks old and in really bad shape. The child had bloody diarrhea and vomiting and skin blemishes too, it seems.

"The doctor was about ready to hospitalize the child, but he decided to have the parents try goat milk. They did, and he was just astounded at how quickly the child got better.

"He said all together there have been about nine infants that had similar problems. They didn't do well on the artificial formulas, and they have all done just fine on the goat milk.

"He was very pleased with the results. He said he checked his modern medical textbooks to see what they had to say about goat milk, and there was just nothing. He could not find any adequate information on the use of goat milk anywhere."

The raw milk has also been prescribed for hyperactive children, Cynthia said. These youngsters can't tolerate any artificial ingredients or additives in their foods, and doctors have recommended raw milk from the Willis' dairy.

"These youngsters do equally well on either the Jersey milk or the goat milk. The problem seems to be something which is added to pasteurized milk—perhaps the vitamin D."

And the goat milk has helped some older people who have arthritis. Cynthia has seen some cases herself, and she said health food store managers occasionally mention customers who are buying the milk because of arthritis.

"There are two or three people I know of who had arthritis very badly and they went on goat milk and took themselves off the medication. One lady was so crippled she could hardly walk. She started drinking goat milk and in a couple of months you couldn't believe the difference. She was really 'doing a jig' around here. She was walking right along—she had a bit of a gimp, but was in a lot better shape than before."

THE DAIRY THAT DIDN'T

Four years ago two California dairy goat raisers, Roduska Rosales and Arlene Secondo, decided they really wanted to run a commercial goat dairy.

They found one for sale near Portland, Oregon, and bought it. They moved themselves, their dairy goats, and their total of eight children to a 7 1/2-acre Grade A goat dairy near Beaver Creek, Oregon in 1973. See Fig. 4-7.

And then they started learning what they had gotten themselves into.

Fig. 4-7. The Oregon goat dairy as seen from the air, showing the livestock buildings and the house at right.

They lost $12,000 the first year.

And two years later they sold off most of the herd and quietly shut down the commercial operation before they went totally bankrupt or worked themselves to death.

They admit it was an educational experience. They're glad to talk about it so other would-be goat dairymen can learn from what happened to them.

The dairy they bought was a licensed raw milk dairy which had been distributing milk into Portland and other cities for a number of years. The folks they bought the dairy from had operated it for 11 years. The dairy was started about 20 years ago.

The former owners were supposedly earning their living from the dairy, but Roduska and Arlyene have questions about that. Records were scanty or nonexistent.

"We knew there were problems when we bought the place," they said, "but we felt they could be overcome with good management. It was the only goat milk dairy supplying a good market. We felt it had potential.

"We were two divorced women, we had a bunch of goats, we thought certainly we could make a living from the goats. There was nothing in California for sale that we could afford. We could have gone ahead and started a Grade A or B dairy in Monterey county, except it would have cost a lot of money.

"And the market was uncertain. You could sell milk to Meyenberg in Ripon, but everyone knew it was doubtful if that plant would last much longer (it closed in the summer of 1976). And there's a lot of competition in goat milk marketing in California.

"We saw an ad in the *California Farmer* for this goat dairy in Oregon, went up and looked at the place, and decided to do it."

They paid $38,000 for the dairy portion of the farm. It consisted of six acres of land, the buildings, about 120 head of grade goats and the milk market. The home on an acre of land was purchased separately.

'Proper Management' Starts

Their efforts at "proper management" began the day they moved in.

"There were no fences on the property. He kept the animals inside the buildings all of the time. The first weekend we put up fences. It was something to watch those goats go outside for the first time.

"We took about 40 of our own purebred LaManchas, Saanens and Toggenburgs with us. They, of course, were used to some freedom outside."

"The general nutrition of the animals was poor, in our opinion. He had 60 dry animals in a barn and fed them only grass hay, no grain. These included pregnant does. The kids never got grain.

"They kept no records. They didn't know when a doe last kidded, which kid was out of which doe. He pen bred the does. We had no idea when any of them were due to freshen.

"That first year we had does freshening with dead kids, no milk in their udders. We blame it on just plain poor nutrition."

As soon as they got settled in and took a good look at the herd of dairy goats they had just purchased, they started culling.

"He was milking does once a day which were giving a pint of milk or less for that milking. They were eating feed, and weren't giving enough milk to pay for that feed.

"We had to get rid of half of the herd of milking does, for low production or nonproduction."

They made the move in late summer. The first winter was really rough as they tried to squeeze enough milk out of the herd to keep the market alive.

"We had dried off most of our does for the move up. We figured they would probably dry off anyway because of the change. The does he had weren't producing much of anything, and they weren't bred for winter freshenings.

"This man had been a 'goat dairyman' for 11 years, and he didn't even know goats are seasonal breeders! I tell you the truth."

Herd Replacements, Equipment

Then there was the problem of what to do for herd replacements for all those does they had to cull.

"The herd was all grade animals, but he had used purebred bucks. There were some nice animals in the herd, thanks to those bucks.

"The trouble was, we didn't know which kids were out of which does. And we felt poor nutrition had ruined those does as much as anything.

"We felt we had to keep most of the doe kids as potential replacements. With no records, we didn't know which doe might turn out to be a good producer after she had gone through her lactation. But this meant we had to feed all those kids—some 60 or 80 of them—and that really drained our pocketbooks."

The lack of fencing wasn't the only equipment problem on the farm.

"To feed the milkers you had to climb over a conglomeration of panels to get to some really makeshift feeders. It took two people 20 minutes just to put hay in the mangers.

"The man who put up our fencing designed some chain-link hay feeders for us which work really well. Now it takes one person five minutes to throw out the hay."

The first year, between fencing and equipment and feeding too many nonproducing animals and not having enough milk to supply the market in the winter—they lost $12,000.

Reduska points out that the loss could be looked at as less than that.

"The fencing cost can be depreciated over several years, as an investment. Other equipment we bought fits into this. But the blunt fact is that it cost us $12,000 out of our pockets to operate that place the first year. We're lucky that we had some savings."

Bottling, Distributing

Meanwhile they were learning about the wonderful world of operating a milk-distributing dairy.

"We knew the amount of time and labor involved in managing a herd. We were prepared for that.

"But this bottling and distributing thing is a whole different ball game. It is just the biggest hassle in the world. I absolutely don't know how some folks manage to run a dairy and work a full-time job too."

Their milk was bottled in quart glass bottles and delivered to health food stores, one grocery store chain, and to three home-delivery dairies in Portland. They delivered milk into Portland two days a week and Salem one day a week.

At best their sales were about 200 gallons of milk a week.

The milk was priced at 60¢ a quart at first, later raised to 75¢ per quart.

"The home-delivery dairies had been buying goat milk for years, but that came to a halt," Roduska said. They charged exorbitant prices. They paid us 60¢ a quart and charged the customers $1.20 a quart. All they had to do was take the milk out of their cooler and put it on their truck and deliver it.

"The biggest dairy got angry when I said they had to pay a bottle deposit like everyone else. I said fine, you won't handle our milk any more.

"That meant we had more milk which could be put into the stores which wanted more milk and sold at a lower price and be more available to more people. The dairies were cutting down on home deliveries anyway."

Delivering milk was taking up a lot of working time. They thought they had found a solution when a health food store owner started distributing their milk for them. It didn't work out.

"He almost lost the entire market by taking them sour milk, by offending people and being generally unpleasant. We finally figured out the only reason he did it was to be sure he had enough milk for his own store through the winter.

Refrigerated Truck

"So, we bought a refrigerated milk truck from Carnation and did our own distribution. This is the only way to do it, especially if you're marketing raw milk. That milk can't be abused. You have to take care of it. And you have to know what the store owners are thinking. Are they happy, not happy with the milk? You have to get that feedback."

The refrigerated truck was a good buy at $2,400. It was a smaller delivery truck the big dairy no longer needed. At bottling time they simply backed the truck close to their processing room, plugged it in, and loaded the cases of bottles on it as they came off the filler-capper machine.

Washing bottles was a time-consuming headache. Roduska is vocal about that chore:

"The milk room had one of those revolving-brush things to wash bottles and for six months we—one of our children, really—stood there and washed bottles for hours. How inefficient! It was really dumb.

"Besides, I never felt the bottles were really clean.

"Then the carrot juice man in Portland told us he used a regular dishwasher for his bottles and his inspector never said anything about it. We tried some bottles in the dishwasher in the kitchen and they turned out fine. So we bought a Kitchenaide dishwasher for the milkhouse and used it to wash our bottles.

"It really gets the bottles clean. We never have any trouble unless we get a really scuzzy bottle someone's had in their basement for six months. We have to put it through twice.

"Even the 48mm small-mouth bottles came out perfectly clean. We do have very good water, fairly soft, and this is probably one reason the dishwasher works well on the bottles."

"There is a huge old case bottle washer in the dairy building. It is the size of a room. We don't use it and certainly don't need it. I'm not sure if it works. I do know it would cost $11,000 to replace it!"

They admit that glass bottles are extra work and a headache. The bottle washing is one problem; bottle returns are worse. The bottles simply don't come back regularly.

"We charge a 50¢ deposit per bottle, and they still don't come back. The buyers would rather pay the extra 50¢ for their quart of milk than bring back the empty bottles regularly.

"For some reason they pack up all the empty bottles and bring them back to the store in the winter, when we can't supply as much milk as the stores want.

"In the winter you are a bottle buyer, not a milk seller. In the summer you wonder where all the bottles are and you're scrambling around trying to buy more to put your milk in."

Straightening Out

Slowly, very slowly, the two women began to straighten out the herd problems.

"We planned the breedings so we had kids arriving from late December and early January through the end of August. We did that the next two winters.

"Everyone didn't get as much milk as they wanted, but there was a decent winter milk supply.

"In the winter people stay home and think about their upset stomachs and whatever—and they require a great deal more goat milk than in the summer, when they're out drinking beer or camping.

"We made it through the winter with a minimum of problems.

We milked about 40 does through the winter, which wasn't enough, of course.

"We had the herd health in pretty good shape. The state university has been good about testing milk for us. I feel an obligation to worry about mastitis if we're selling raw milk. We want to know what's in it.

"We've never had a bad inspection, flunked a bacteria test, or anything like that. The leucocyte and bacteria tests have stayed well within limits. We managed to keep the does freshening often enough so that we weren't using mostly milk from does which were drying off, so the leucocytes were not a problem.

"We had put the herd on DHIA production test the spring after we arrived and we had records to work with.

"We had hired an accountant, and that was sort of a scene. When we went in with our records each month she would tell us how crazy we were."

'In the Black,' But

"But we finally got 'in the black' this past year. We had more income than outgo. The goats were paying their way.

"But we were not making a living, nor getting a salary for the work we did."

Then Roduska got sick, and Arlyene was operating the dairy alone.

"It was impossible for two people to handle the work, it was more impossible for one person."

That was when they decided to sell off the herd and stop running a goat dairy. They disposed of the dairy goats however possible. The best animals went to Salem, where three young men were starting a Grade A goat dairy. Others were sold as family milkers, or went to sale barns. They sold down to about 30 head and now sell milk only to customers who come to the farm.

That was not an easy decision to make. They were exhausted from the work, nearly bankrupt from the expenses, and very frightened by the recent drought and what it could do to already high feed prices. But they operated the only source of licensed goat milk in the area and there was a responsibility to the folks who bought that milk.

"When you run a goat dairy you supply milk to sickly people who really need it. There's one elderly couple and the man is in really poor health and I swear the goat milk is all that keeps him alive. The woman keeps saying she doesn't know what she would do if we ever stopped selling goat milk, her husband needs it so badly.

"You have a lot of cases like this. You are really aware of it if you sell direct to customers or through health food stores. Those stores know who is buying the goat milk. When milk was short in the winter they saved it for the customers who really needed it.

"We were the only source of goat milk for stores in Portland, and we felt this moral obligation to keep running this . . . charitable organization!"

The new dairy in Salem would supply that end of the market, and Bill Moomau of Rochester, Washington, expanded his dairy and started supplying the Portland market after they quit delivering.

Now they sell 10 to 12 gallons of milk a week at the farm. The goats are again a hobby and they really are not interested in making it a business again.

HE RAISES EYEBROWS . . . AND MILK PRODUCTION!

Roger Peters of Elkhorn, Wis., is a dairy farmer who practices natural farming. He operates a 185 acre family farm (Figs. 4-8, 4-9, and 4-10) and has a registered dairy herd of 44 milking holsteins and enjoys milking cows. The herd is producing a ton of milk.

"We use no fertilizer or chemicals on our fields," said Peters. "But we get bumper crops equal to the other farm yields in the area. We use just the cattle manure on the land and plow under the alfalfa

Fig. 4-8. Roger Peters has a dairy herd of 44 milking holsteins.

Fig. 4-9. Peters makes silage from corn, sunflowers and soybeans.

and rotate the crops on the fields."

He went on to say that the insect pests seem to be more attracted to chemically fertilized fields. He had some beautiful alfalfa fields which weren't attacked by the alfalfa weevil, but fields not far away were.

"I became interested in using natural fertilizers when I planted corn about 20 years without fertilizer," said Peters. "Over the years I've managed to raise corn that rivals fields planted with bought fertilizers. My crops were just as good, and I didn't have the large fertilzer or herbicide bills to pay either."

Peters doesn't feed ear corn to his cattle herd. He raises the

Fig. 4-10. Roger Peters and his father, Albert, look over some of the weed seeds they purchased from feed mills and seed companies.

corn to put into the silo along with sunflowers and soybeans.

"That's another thing I'm doing which is a first in this section of the state," said Peters, "I'm planting soybeans, sunflowers and corn—all in the same row. It was tricky to figure out how to set the planter so the seed could all be planted at the same time from the same setting, but I did it."

The sunflowers, corn and soybeans are all chopped, blown into the wagon and put into the silo. The cattle relish the feed.

As we went out into the alfalfa fields with Peters, he showed us how the fields were a carpet of earthworm castings. We knelt in the alfalfa field and inspected the earth around the alfalfa plants in various spots.

"These earthworm castings are the best fertilizer in the world" said Peters. "These castings have passed through the earthworm's digestive system and he deposits them on the top of the soil. They're nature's natural fertilizer."

He told that because of the numerous earthworms in his fields, the clay soil plows extremely easy. The worm holes allow water to soak into the soil and air to get to the roots.

"When you dig up some of the soil after a rain, you find numerous worms in a fork of soil," said the farmer. "When I was using herbicides and commercial fertilizers on the land, the worms were killed or retarded. We upset the balance of nature by using commercial fertilizers."

He recommends that the beginning farmer change over gradually to this system.

The farmer never cuts the alfalfa fields close to the ground, as it robs the worms of shade. He cuts the hay about the middle of the day. This is to capture plant nutrients drawn to the upper part of the plant.

While most dairymen are now keeping their cattle inside the barn and in drylot the year around, Peters is pasturing his in two 20-acre fields. These are rotated.

He feels that the cows need exercise similar to a human jogging to keep physically fit.

Peters is also doing something else which has raised his milk production and raises the eyebrows of the dairymen who hear about it. He is feeding his cattle herd weed seeds.

He has a 4,000 bushel bin and a 2,600 bushel bin filled with weed seeds he has purchased at the local mill and seed farms for about 1 1/2¢ a pound.

These weed seeds are obtained from the fanning mill used to clean seed. There are also oat hulls mixed with it. The weed seeds are rich in amino acids (protein). They are very bitter if eaten raw, but he dresses the weed seeds up and makes them tastier for the cattle with black strap molasses. He feeds them a half pound of the seeds in the morning and a half pound in the evening. They really relish them, and the purer the weed seeds, the better.

When the dairy farmer began to feed weed seeds, milk production immediately jumped over 150 pounds.

Peters went on to point out a passage in the Bible which reads: "And God said, "Let the Earth bring forth grass and the herb yielding seed and God saw that it was good."

"The herb yielding seeds are there for us to use and all we have to do is figure out how to use them to our advantage," said Peters. "My cattle relish the sunflowers and they contain different types of amino acids too."

When it's time to cultivate the fields, this farmer is very particular about how deep he sets the cultivator. It takes two men a half a day to set it to clean the weeds from the fields correctly.

"This past May, we put 75 acres of hay into the hay loft in 11 days," revealed the dairyman. "We had the Harvestor silo filled in May. We make preblossom hay, for that's where we get the necessary other protein. Others wait for it to bloom and have to make hay when they should be planting their corn."

He personally believes the farmer must get over the notion of raising so much corn. Cows, he says, are born roughage consumers.

"I have found that corn is the biggest robber of micronutrients of the soil," said Peters. "I feed my cattle a little fish worm stimulator which is actually a 'sea deposit' that contains all the micronutrients that are needed in a cow's or man's diet."

For good yields of oats, this farmer doesn't use field lime as he claims oats grow better in a slightly acid soil. This year he baled 113 of straw to the acre.

"We had only 40 acres of oats but had 4,500 bales of straw," said the organic farmer. "We had more than we could use and store so we sold some."

Peters is the 12th generation of farmers in his family and he is a descendent of the Amish people.

As a youngster he was active in 4-H and carried cattle as his project. He won the state showmanship and judging contest in the cattle class and went on to the nationals. He raised and showed cattle six years at the Illinois State Fair and took numerous awards.

As Peters looks over the benefits he derives from his organic farming methods, he astonishes neighbors with his low veterinary bill.

"For the past three years, it has been only about $350 each year," said the dairyman. "My cows keep healthy with the feed I give them."

This natural farmer has plans in the future to expand his dairy herd to 70 milking cattle. He has been producing more feed than he has cattle to consume it.

"I gross about $86,000 a year from my milk and the cattle I sell," said Peters. "Many are sold to Texas, Oklahoma, Tennessee and Wisconsin."

A cow and her daughter was sold recently to Willard Leiterity of Cleveland, Wisconsin, and scored 92 points E, and the daughter just finished in August producing 111 pounds of butterfat in 355 days.

If the dairyman has an exceptionally good cow, he sells her and raises another.

"Natural farming has paid off for me," said Peters. "I hope to keep improving my land and make my fields even more productive.

IMPRO: A REVOLUTION IN LIVESTOCK HEALTH

Mary Collins of Impro, Inc. didn't look like a revolutionary when she spoke before 600 people at the first Acres, USA conference. Yet this dark-haired diminutive farmer has devoted the greater portion of her life to the research and development of an idea that has the potential to revolutionize current thinking and practices in the field of livestock health.

And while clinging tenaciously to that idea, she has run afoul of the USDA and stood in danger of scuttling over two decades of work with her brothers Jim and Bob and brother-in-law, Phil Wieghner, on their patented Impro process for manufacturing a "whey antibody blend."

They believe, and feel they have the research to prove, that their products will radically improve the chances of a dairy or hog farmer having healthier animals and getting more milk and meat to market.

The family-controlled Impro, Inc. is headquartered in an unassuming brown storefront in Waukon, Iowa. See Figs. 4-11 through 4-14. There's a 10-speed bicycle parked against the front window. There are cardboard boxes full of clothes donated to the 22-member Laotian family Mary Collins adopted earlier this year. Every desk and surface in the place is piled high with things needing immediate attention. The atmosphere is one of enthusiasm with an almost infectious sense of well-defined purpose and an exceedingly strong commitment to seeing that purpose fulfilled.

The constant noise and activity revolve around producing the "whey antibody blend." Simply put, the whey antibody blend is a serum containing antibodies (as opposed to antibiotics) which has

Fig. 4-11. The smallness of Impro's home office is in direct contrast to the largeness of their work.

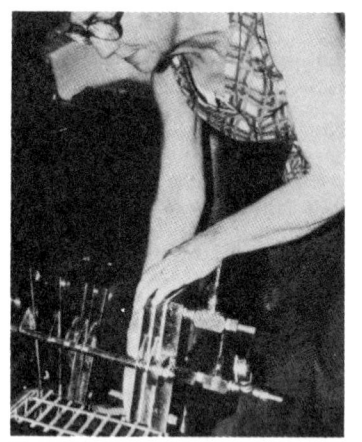

Fig. 4-12. A stack of filters is being assembled by Dorothy Brown, and Charles Byrnes demonstrates Impro's new sterilizer.

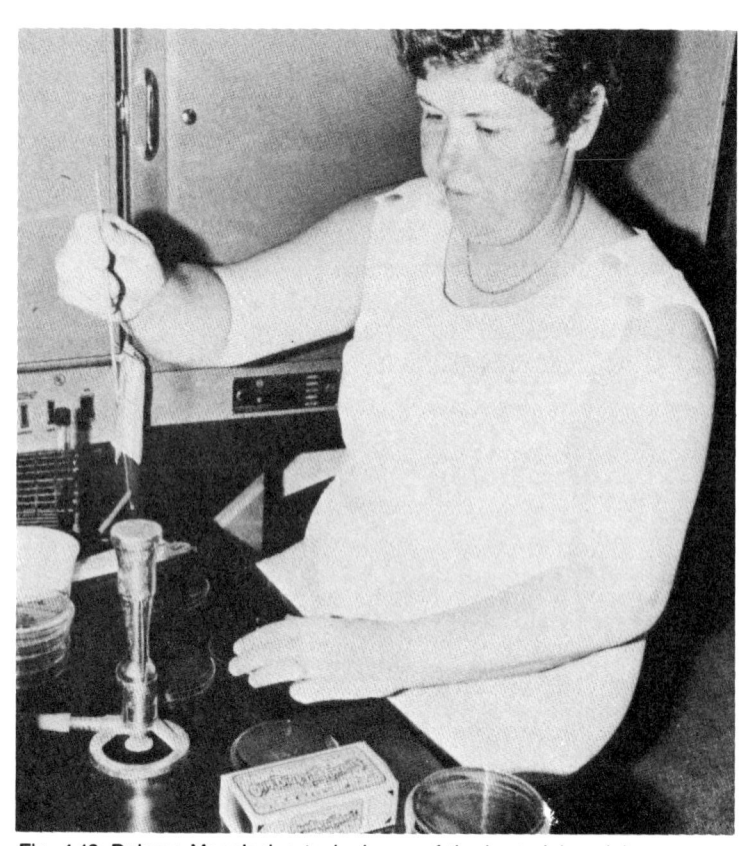

Fig. 4-13. Delores Menolasino took charge of the bacteriology lab.

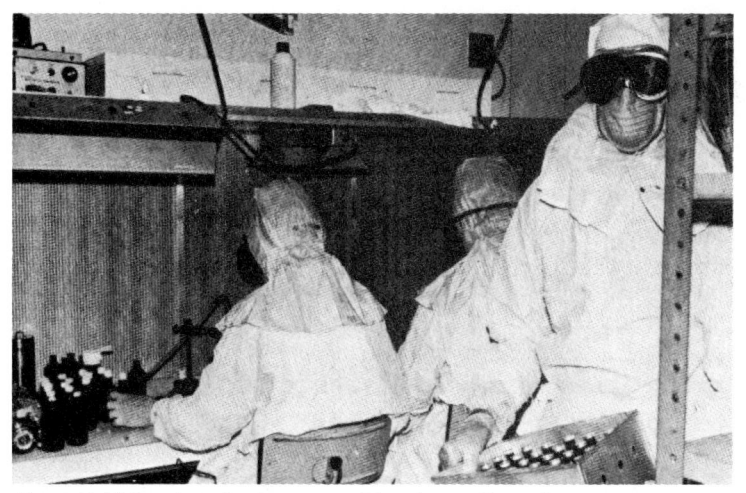

Fig. 4-14. This colset-sized room provides the sterile environment necessary for bottling Impro products.

been produced from the colostrum milk of a diary cow. Impro's complete line of antibody blends is the focal point of their entire approach to animal health, an approach that stresses sound nutrition, proper management, and preventative medicine as the keys to improved health and increased production.

For dairy farmers this means more milk, less mastitis, better conception rates, fewer birthing difficulties, etc. For hog producers it means better milking sows, more and better pigs, and fewer problems with scours.

Protection in Colostrum

Impro products have developed over the past 15 years and represent the culmination of long hours of study and observation in both the field and the laboratory. Their manufacture is based on the mechanism by which a newborn calf receives disease protection from its dam through antibodies present in colostrum milk. When nature is left to its own devices, this antibody protection is limited to only those organisms to which the cow has been exposed.

The role of antibodies in fighting disease has long been known and is the basis from which the use of vaccines such as smallpox evolved. Antibodies are proteinaceous substances produced in the body when invaded by certain types of pathogenic (disease causing) micro-organisms such as a bacteria, virus or a killed vaccine. The general term applied to any antibody-producing organism is "antigen." Each antibody is formed in direct response to only one specific organism which it attacks to neutralize or destroy.

The protective quality of colostrum milk and the role of antibodies in fighting pathogenic organisms has long held a fascination for those involved in animal science. Dr. William E. Peterson, professor of dairy science at the University of Minnesota, was just such a person. During the 1940s, he began exploring the formulation of antibodies in the udders of cows. His research established that it was possible to induce the formation of specific antibodies in colostrum milk by infusing antigens into the udder of a dairy cow shortly before freshening (approximately three weeks). To cause antibodies against a certain *E. coli* to be produced, for example, all you would have to do is to introduce the *E. coli* into the udder of a dry cow and the colostrum she produced upon freshening would automatically transfer antibody protection against that *E. coli* to here calf.

Helping Dr. Peterson at this time was a young graduate student in nutrition and genetics, Jim Collins. His contact with Dr. Peterson would not only prove to be an invaluable asset in his own farming endeavors, but it also would eventually lead to Dr. Peterson's asking the Collinses to take over his research.

Index

A
acids and bases, 30
actinomycetes, 86
alfalfa yield, 54
alfalfa, growing, 220
algae, 88
aluminum concentrations, 57

B
bacteria in soil, 38
bacteria, 40, 118, 122
bacteria, fertilizing with, 34
bacteria, soil, 36
bacteria, crop-fertilizing, 33
bases and acids, 30
blindweed, small, 210
broom, growing a, 248

C
cadmium, 72
calcium, 79
chemical and organic farming differences, 132
chemical farming, 126
chemical reactions, 31
chemical spray checks, 212
chemical versus organic debate, 39
chemistry, "organic," 31
chemistry, basic, 27
chemistry, ions and, 29
cobalt deficiency, areas of, 62
cobalt, 65

comfrey, 240
corn yields, 242
corn, organically grown, 165
cornfields, cleaning, 244
cows, 258
crop rotation, 242
crop, cultivating with a, 218
crop, fallowing or cultivation without a, 217
crops, growing selection of, 2
crops, rotation of, 211
cultivation of the land, 1
cultivation or fallowing without a crop, 217
cultivation, 207
cultivation, close, 219
cultivation, late, 14
cultivation, purpose of, 13
cultivation, early, 13

D
dairy farming, 254, 261
dairy, goat, 262
dandelion, 209
denitrification, and nitrification, 42
disease-resistant plants, breeding of, 221
disking, 11

E
environment, nitrogen use and the, 25

277

erosion, fertile soil and, 15
evaporation, preventing, 5

F
farmers, basic chemistry for, 27
farming acid soils, 52
farming, chemical, 126
farming, dairy, 254, 261
farming, dry, 2, 231
farming, organic, 91, 105
fertilization of soil, 103
fertilizer nutrient content, 78
fertilizing with bacteria, 34
fields, large, 207
flax, acre of, 227
food distribution costs, 196
food marketing groups, 200
fungi, 84
fungi, common, 85
fungus, 123

G
gardening, practical organic, 135
goat dairy, 258, 262
grain, 205
grass, panick, 209
grass, quack, 213

H
harrowing, 12
humus and tillage, 7
hygroscopic moisture, 4

I
intertillage, 13
iron deficiency, areas of, 62
iron, 63

L
land, cultivation of the, 1
lead, 69
lime, 55
lime, functions of, 59
lime, lost, 59
lime, spreading, 58
livestock health, 273
livestock, 252

M
magnesium depression, 76
manure, nutrients supplied by, 47
mercury, 73
metals, toxic heavy, 66
microflora, 121
microogranisms, mighty, 84
milk production, 268

milk, raw, 254
moisture, capillary, 5
moisture, conserving, 3, 4
moisture, free, 5
moisture, gravitational, 5
moisture, hygroscopic, 4
musk thistle, 210

N
nitrification and denitrification, 42
nitrogen use and the environment, 25
nutrient removal, 78
nutrients, "secondary," 74

O
organic and chemical farming differences, 132
organic farming works, 91, 143
organic fertilization, 104
organic food marketing, 200
organic foods, costs of, 190
organic gardening, 139
organic gardening, practical, 135
organic matter, 52, 120
organic versus chemical debate, 39
organically grown corn, 165

P
panick, grass, 209
phosphate, 48
phosphorus, 113
planking and rolling, 12
plant food, liberation, 3
plant reproduction and control, 205
plants, breeding, 221
plow, depth to, 10
plow, how to, 8
plow, when to, 9
plowing, 8
plowing, subsoil, 10
potash, 50, 117
protozoa, 89

R
rainfall, 2
rolling and planking, 12
root zones, 23
rotation and tillage, 23

S
seedbed, the, 3
seeds, storing, 222
selenium, 66, 67
soil acidity and crop yields, 54
soil animals, important, 122

soil bacteria, 36
soil fertility, 44
soil microorganisms, 37
soil organisms, 122
soil pH, 54
soil, 1, 92
soil, bacteria in, 38
soil, farming acid, 52
soil, fertilization of, 103
soil, how to improve, 17
soil, tailor crops to the, 243
subsurface packing, 11
sulphur, 82

T
thistle, Canada, 215

thistle, musk, 210
tillage and humus, 7
tillage and rotation, 23
tillage, broad, 11
tillage, forms of, 7

V
viruses, 88

W
weeds, destroying, 6
weeds, eradicating perennial, 213
weeds, methods for eradicating, 206
wheat varieties, improving, 223

OTHER POPULAR TAB BOOKS OF INTEREST

44 Terrific Woodworking Plans & Projects (No. 1762—$12.50 paper; $21.95 hard)
How to Repair Briggs & Stratton Engines—2nd Edition (No. 1687—$8.95 paper; $15.95 hard)
Security for You and Your Home . . . A Complete Handbook (No. 1680—$17.50 paper; $29.95 hard)
46 Step-by-Step Wooden Toy Projects (No. 1675—$9.95 paper; $17.95 hard)
The Kite Building & Kite Flying Handbook, with 42 Kite Plans (No. 1669—$15.50 paper)
Building Better Beds (No. 1664—$14.50 paper; $19.95 hard)
Organic Vegetable Gardening (No. 1660—$16.50 paper; $25.95 hard)
The Woodturning Handbook, with Projects (No. 1655—$14.50 paper; $21.95 hard)
Clock Making for the Woodworker (No. 1648—$11.50 paper; $16.95 hard)
Steel Homes (No. 1641—$15.50 paper; $21.95 hard)
The Homeowner's Illustrated Guide to Concrete (No. 1626—$15.50 paper; $24.95 hard)
Kerosene Heaters (No. 1598—$10.25 paper; $16.95 hard)
Clocks—Construction, Maintenance and Repair (No. 1569—$13.50 paper; $18.95 hard)
The Underground Home Answer Book (No. 1562—$11.50 paper; $16.95 hard)
Airbrushing (No. 1555—$20.50 paper)
Basic Blueprint Reading for Practical Applications (No. 1546—$13.50 paper; $18.95 hard)
Central Heating and Air Conditioning Repair Guide—2nd Edition (No. 1520—$13.50 paper; $18.95 hard)
The Complete Book of Fences (No. 1508—$12.95 paper; $19.95 hard)
How to Sharpen Anything (No. 1463—$12.95 paper; $19.95 hard)
Building a Log Home from Scratch or Kit (No. 1458—$12.50 paper; $17.95 hard)
Build It with Plywood: 88 Furniture Projects (No. 1430—$13.50 paper; $18.95 hard)
The GIANT Book of Metalworking Projects (No. 1357—$12.95 paper; $19.95 hard)
The Welder's Bible (No. 1244—$13.95 paper)

The GIANT Handbook of Food-Preserving Basics (No. 1727—$13.50 paper; $17.95 hard)
Ventilation: Your Secret Key to an Energy-Efficient Home (No. 1681—$8.95 paper; $15.95 hard)
Tuning and Repairing Your Own Piano (No. 1678—$12.50 paper)
Superinsulated, Truss-Frame House Construction (No. 1674—$15.50 paper; $21.95 hard)
Raising Animals for Fun and Profit (No. 1666—$13.50 paper; $18.95 hard)
Practical Herb Gardening . . . with Recipes (No. 1661—$11.50 paper; $15.95 hard)
Effective Lighting for Home and Business (No. 1658—$13.50 paper; $18.95 hard)
Constructing and Maintaining Your Well and Septic System (No. 1654—$12.50 paper; $17.95 hard)
Maps and Compasses: A User's Handbook (No. 1644—$9.25 paper; $15.95 hard)
Woodcarving, with Projects (No. 1639—$11.50 paper; $16.95 hard)
Sign Carving (No. 1601—$13.50 paper; $19.95 hard)
Mastering Household Electrical Wiring (No. 1587—$13.50 paper; $19.95 hard)
Cave Exploring (No. 1566—$10.25 paper; $16.95 hard)
The Radio Control Hobbyist's Handbook (No. 1561—$19.50 paper)
Be Your Own Contractor: The Affordable Way to Home Ownership (No. 1554—$12.50 paper; $17.95 hard)
Beekeeping—An Illustrated Handbook (No. 1524—$10.95 paper; $15.95 hard)
101 Model Railroad Layouts (No. 1514—$11.50 paper; $17.95 hard)
53 Space-Saving, Built-In Furniture Projects (No. 1504—$17.50 paper)
The Home Brewer's Handbook (No. 1461—$10.25 paper; $16.95 hard)
Constructing Outdoor Furniture, with 99 Projects (No. 1454—$15.95 paper)
Draw Your Own House Plans (No. 1381—$14.50 paper)
The Fiberglass Repair & Construction Handbook (No. 1297—$11.50 paper; $17.95 hard)

TAB TAB BOOKS Inc.
Blue Ridge Summit, Pa. 17214

Send for FREE TAB Catalog describing over 750 current titles in print.